Historical Problems
Studies and Documents

Edited by
PROFESSOR G. R. ELTON
University of Cambridge

21

TUDOR DYNASTIC PROBLEMS, 1460-1571

John Colet

ST. PAUL'S SCHOOL
LIBRARY

In the same series

TUDOR DYNASTIC PROBLEMS 1460-1571

Mortimer Levine
West Virginia University

LONDON: GEORGE ALLEN & UNWIN LTD

NEW YORK: BARNES AND NOBLE BOOKS
(a division of Harper & Row Publishers, Inc.)

FIRST PUBLISHED 1973

© George Allen & Unwin Ltd 1973

BRITISH ISBN 0 04 942110 7 hardback
0 04 942111 5 paperback

Published in the USA 1973 by
HARPER & ROW, PUBLISHERS, INC.
BARNES & NOBLE IMPORT DIVISION
ISBN 06-4944250-3

PRINTED IN GREAT BRITAIN
in 10 on 11 point Plantin type by
THE ALDINE PRESS
LETCHWORTH, HERTS

FOR JACOB AND ANNA LEVINE
LOVING AND UNDERSTANDING PARENTS

CONTENTS

ABBREVIATIONS

BIHR	*Bulletin of the Institute of Historical Research.*
BM	British Museum.
*For. Cal., Eliz.	*Calendar of State Papers, Foreign, Elizabeth,* ed. Joseph Stevenson *et al.,* London 1863–1950.
Hist. J.	*Historical Journal.*
*L.P.	*Letters and Papers, Foreign and Domestic, of the Reign of Henry VIII,* ed. J. S. Brewer *et al.,* London 1862–1932.
PRO	Public Record Office.
Rot. Parl.	*Rotuli Parliamentorum ut et Petitiones et Placita in Parliamento,* London 1832.
*Scot. Cal.	*Calendar of State Papers Relating to Scotland and Mary Queen of Scots,* ed. Joseph Bain *et al.,* Edinburgh and Glasgow 1898– .
*Span. Cal.	*Calendar of State Papers, Spanish,* ed. G. A. Bergenroth *et al.,* London 1862–1954.
*Span. Cal., Eliz.	*Calendar of State Papers, Spanish, Elizabeth,* ed. M. A. S. Hume, London 1892–9.
Stat. Realm	*The Statutes of the Realm,* Record Commission, London 1910–28.
St. P.	*State Papers of the Reign of King Henry the Eighth,* Record Commission, London 1830–52.
*Ven. Cal.	*Calendar of State Papers, Venetian,* ed. Rawdon Brown *et al.,* London 1864– .

*Unless otherwise stated, all references to works marked with an asterisk relate to item numbers, not pages.

INTRODUCTION

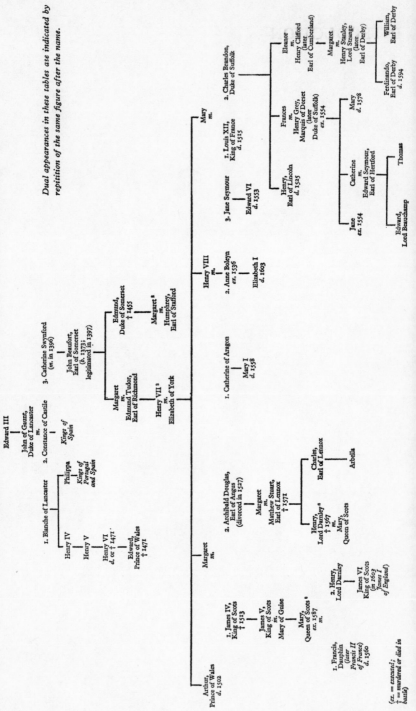

Figure 1. Some descendants of Edward III to 1603; the Lancaster and Tudor lines

Dual appearances in these tables are indicated by repitition of the same figure after the name.

Figure 2. Some descendants of Edward III; the York and Stafford lines

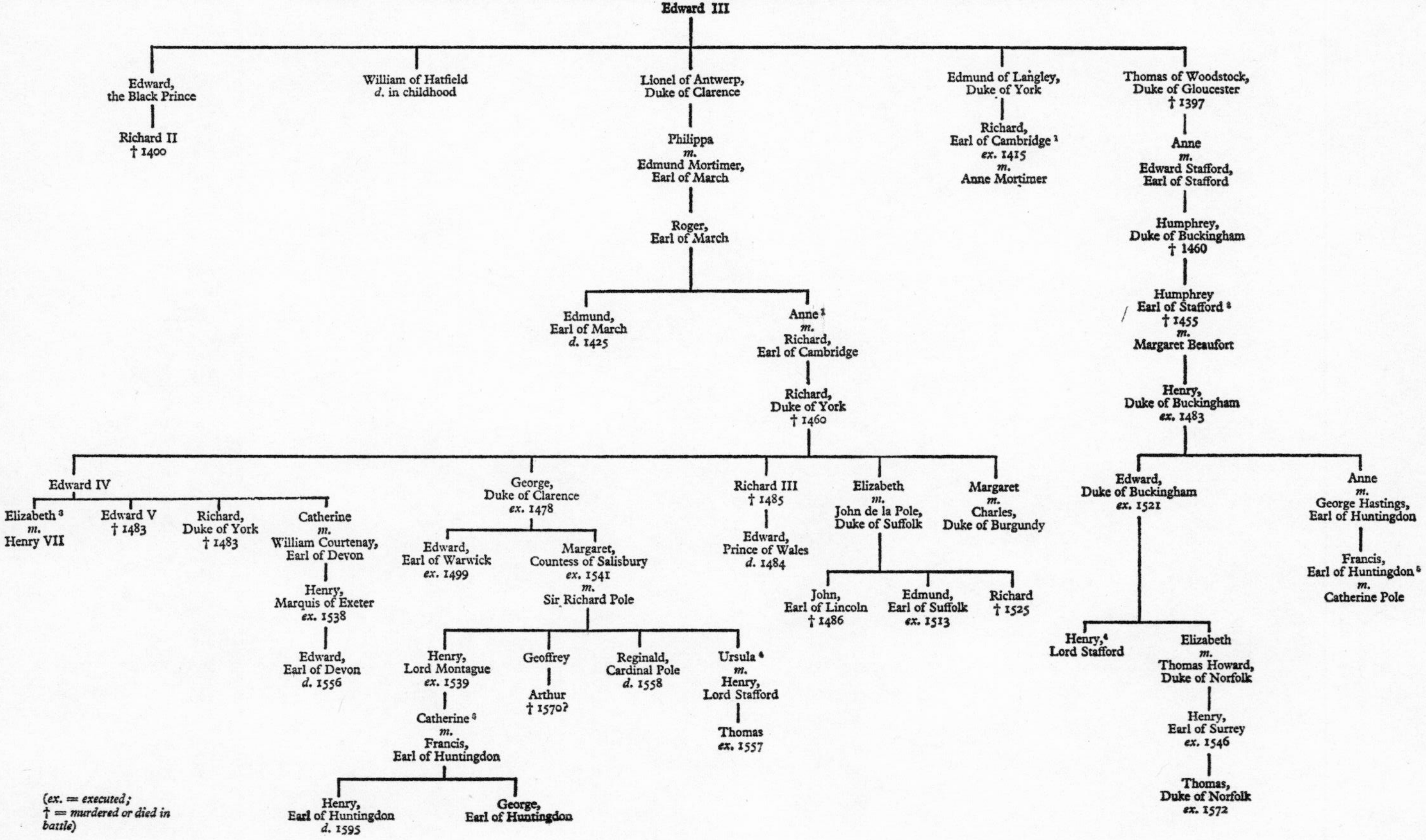

Edward III

Edward, the Black Prince
Richard II †1400

William of Hatfield
d. in childhood

Lionel of Antwerp, Duke of Clarence

Philippa
m.
Edmund Mortimer, Earl of March

Roger, Earl of March

Edmund, Earl of March
d. 1425

Anne [3]
m.
Richard, Earl of Cambridge

Edmund of Langley, Duke of York

Richard, Earl of Cambridge [1]
ex. 1415
m.
Anne Mortimer

Richard, Duke of York
†1460

Thomas of Woodstock, Duke of Gloucester
†1397

Anne
m.
Edward Stafford, Earl of Stafford

Humphrey, Duke of Buckingham
†1460

Humphrey, Earl of Stafford [3]
†1455
m.
Margaret Beaufort

Henry, Duke of Buckingham
ex. 1483

Anne
m.
George Hastings, Earl of Huntingdon

Francis, Earl of Huntingdon [4]
m.
Catherine Pole

Edward, Duke of Buckingham
ex. 1521

Henry, [4] Lord Stafford

Elizabeth
m.
Thomas Howard, Duke of Norfolk

Henry, Earl of Surrey
ex. 1546

Thomas, Duke of Norfolk
ex. 1572

Edward IV

Elizabeth [3]
m.
Henry VII

Edward V †1483

Richard, Duke of York †1483

Catherine
m.
William Courtenay, Earl of Devon

Henry, Marquis of Exeter
ex. 1538

Edward, Earl of Devon
d. 1556

George, Duke of Clarence
ex. 1478

Edward, Earl of Warwick
ex. 1499

Margaret, Countess of Salisbury
ex. 1541
m.
Sir Richard Pole

Henry, Lord Montague
ex. 1539

Geoffrey

Arthur †1570?

Reginald, Cardinal Pole
d. 1558

Ursula [4]
m.
Henry, Lord Stafford

Thomas
ex. 1557

Catherine [4]
m.
Francis, Earl of Huntingdon

Henry, Earl of Huntingdon
d. 1595

George, Earl of Huntingdon

Richard III †1485

Edward, Prince of Wales
d. 1484

Elizabeth
m.
John de la Pole, Duke of Suffolk

John, Earl of Lincoln †1486

Edmund, Earl of Suffolk
ex. 1513

Richard †1525

Margaret
m.
Charles, Duke of Burgundy

{ *ex. = executed;*
† = *murdered or died in battle* }

The Dynastic Rivalry of Lancaster and York

The Wars of the Roses [1] did not originate out of any dynastic rivalry. Doubtless the basic cause of those wars was the incompetence of Henry VI. The king's inability to rule permitted the development of a struggle for power at the centre between the Beaufort faction and the Gloucester faction, the headship of which passed after the death of Humphrey, duke of Gloucester, in 1447 to Richard, duke of York. Henry's inability to maintain law and order permitted the development of baronial feuds and gentry quarrels in various parts of the realm which often erupted into violence. Ultimately the Beaufort and Gloucester factions and many of the local contestants chose sides in a great feud between the Percies and the Nevilles which led to the initiation of the Wars of the Roses at St Albans on 22 May 1455. Whatever the secret ambition of Richard of York, who was allied with the Nevilles, no dynastic issue was involved at St Albans. [2]

Earlier, however, there was a dynastic issue of sorts. From the death of Humphrey of Gloucester, next in line according to an act of Henry IV (Doc. 2), to the birth of Prince Edward in October 1453, there was no established successor to Henry VI. Richard of York no doubt aspired to be designated heir presumptive. In the Parliament of November 1450, Thomas Young, a burgess for Bristol who had been in Richard's service for some time and must have been acting at his instigation, moved that he be so designated and was committed to the Tower for his

[1] The term 'Wars of the Roses' has been attacked as unhistorical and misleading (S. B. Chrimes, *Lancastrians, Yorkists, and Henry VII* (London 1964), pp. xii–xiv; R. L. Storey, *The End of the House of Lancaster* (London 1966), pp. 6–7; idem, *The Reign of Henry VII* (London 1988), pp. 31–2). I agree that the civil wars of the second half of the fifteenth century were not fought over roses and were not merely dynastic. Nevertheless, I shall use the customary name because it has implications that reflect the meaning given to the wars by Tudor England.

[2] The best detailed account of the origins of the Wars of the Roses is now Storey, *End of Lancaster*.

presumption.[3] Though this motion may have been doomed to failure because it was ill-timed,[4] there was also some justification for its fate.

Richard's claim to be heir presumptive to, but not king instead of, Henry VI derived from his paternal grandfather, Edmund of Langley, duke of York and fifth son of Edward III. Hereditarily this claim was inferior to that of his potential rivals, Lady Margaret Beaufort or, if, as was probable, a male were to be preferred, Edmund Beaufort, duke of Somerset, that is, if a bar sinister in their descent did not stand in their way. The Beauforts, like Henry VI, descended from John of Gaunt, duke of Lancaster and fourth son of Edward III. Gaunt had four children by Catherine Swynford before he made the lady his third wife. These children were given the surname Beaufort rather than the royal name of Plantagenet. Subsequently they were legitimated by the pope, and in 1397 Richard II issued a patent of legitimation that was ratified in Parliament.[5] When Henry IV confirmed Richard II's patent in 1407, he added a clause that barred the Beauforts from the royal succession.[6] In law this addition probably could not prevail against the original patent with its parliamentary confirmation;[7] besides, if Henry IV had authority to insert words in the patent, Henry VI, who was partial to Edmund of Somerset, equally had authority to delete the words. Richard of York's claim to be heir presumptive was shaky both legally and practically. At any rate, the claim became obsolete with the birth of an heir apparent in 1453.

Now, assuming the continued existence of Prince Edward, if Richard wanted to make a claim of any potential worth, it would have to be a greater one. Through his mother York was the heir of Lionel of Antwerp, duke of Clarence and third son of Edward III. But to assume the arms of Clarence would be tantamount to asserting an immediate claim to the crown: unless the English succession was governed by a Salic law, York's descent from Edward III's third son, which included two females, had priority over Henry VI's direct male descent from Edward's fourth son. Richard was not prepared to assert the Clarence claim in 1453; he was not prepared to do so after the St Albans victory of 1455 or at any time before October 1460.

The first battle of St Albans was more a murder than a battle. Some sixty men were slain, among them Henry Percy, second earl of Nor-

[3] *Letters and Papers Illustrative of the Wars of the English in France during the Reign of Henry VI*, ed. Joseph Stevenson (Rolls Series, London 1861–4), ii. Pt ii. 770.

[4] J. R. Lander, *The Wars of the Roses* (London 1965), p. 66.

[5] *Rot. Parl.* iii. 343.

[6] *The Reign of Henry VII from Contemporary Sources*, ed. A. F. Pollard (London 1913–14), ii. 8–9.

[7] *Select Documents of English Constitutional History*, 1306–1485, ed. S. B. Chrimes and A. L. Brown (London 1961), p. 166.

thumberland, and Edmund of Somerset. The Nevilles, Richard, earl of Salisbury, and his son Richard, earl of Warwick, had settled scores against Percy and his allies.[8] St Albans had the effect of turning a feud into a definite blood-feud that was to produce future battles. It certainly did not place Richard of York in a position to claim the crown, even if, as is more than doubtful, the Nevilles would have supported such a claim. In 1455 the York–Neville party – it is meaningless to speak of a Yorkist party before 1460 or 1461 – contained a very small minority of the peerage, and the killings at St Albans could not have added to its backing or to the popularity of its titular leader.

The party scarcely grew at all until after the disaster at Ludford on 12 October 1459, which resulted in a flight of the York–Neville leadership overseas – York to Ireland, and Salisbury, Warwick and York's son and heir, Edward, earl of March, to Calais. This was followed by the Parliament of Devils of November–December 1459, which attainted York and his chief allies.[9] Then, perhaps due to a reaction against the attainders involving forfeitures of inheritances – the right of inheritance was regarded as sacrosanct by contemporaries [10] – and to fear of the intentions of the court party, now led by Henry VI's indomitable queen Margaret of Anjou, more peers began to side with York and the Nevilles. Their party grew in numbers though it remained a minority: even in early 1461, just before the accession of the first Yorkist king, its fighting strength was some seventeen out of a lay peerage of about sixty.[11] York's support remained small and that support most probably would have disintegrated if there had been any suspicion that he intended to claim the throne.

At the end of June 1460, March, Salisbury and Warwick deemed the situation sufficiently favourable to permit their return to England. In London, about 2 July, Warwick stated publicly that they had 'ever bore true faith and ligeance to the King's person' and indicated that the main purpose of their return was to seek reform.[12] Then, after their victory over the royal forces at Northampton on 10 July, March and Warwick stated to Henry VI their desire 'to be your true liegemen, while our lives shall endure'.[13] Their subsequent respectful treatment of the king

[8] Even Somerset's death may have been the work of Warwick rather than York. See Storey, *End of Lancaster*, p. 162.

[9] *Rot. Parl.* v. 349–50.

[10] J. R. Lander, 'Attainder and Forfeiture, 1453 to 1509', *Hist. J.* (1961), iv, pp. 145–6.

[11] The best estimates of the strength of the York–Neville party between 1455 and 1461 are in J. R. Lander, 'Marriage and Politics in the Fifteenth Century: The Nevilles and the Wydevilles', *BIHR* (1963), xxxvi, pp. 124–9.

[12] *An English Chronicle of the Reigns of Richard II, Henry IV, Henry V, and Henry VI*, ed. J. S. Davies (Camden Society, London 1856), p. 95.

[13] Davies, *English Chronicle*, pp. 97–8.

gives no reason to doubt the sincerity of the earls.[14] Significantly March,
the future Edward IV, was a party to both pledges of loyalty. Neither he
nor the Nevilles, so it seems, had the slightest inkling of what his father
had in mind.

Richard of York dallied in Ireland for two months after his allies had
won the battle of Northampton. Then another month passed between
his landing at Chester and his arrival in London. The obvious explanation of York's delay is that he wanted to avoid meeting his allies, who so
recently had pledged their loyalty to Henry VI, until the Parliament
scheduled for early October was under way. He first revealed his
purpose at Abington where he 'sent for trumpeters and clarioners to
bring him to London, and . . . gave them banners with the whole arms
of England without any diversity, and commanded his sword to be
borne upright before him',[15] as if he were king. Reaching London, York
went to the Parliament Chamber at Westminster where the Lords were
in session and laid his hand upon the vacant throne. The only reaction of
the Lords was silence. When the archbishop of Canterbury broke the
silence by asking him if he would come and see the king, York made his
much-quoted utterance: 'I do not recall that I know anyone within the
kingdom whom it would not befit to come sooner to me and see me
rather than I should go and visit him.' [16]

These words ring of the bravado of a man who knew he had mis-
calculated. York must have expected a not-unfriendly assembly of
Lords – his enemies were absent from Parliament – to acclaim him king
on the spot. He did not anticipate the reluctance of peers to perjure
themselves by thus violating the solemn oaths of allegiance they had
taken to Henry VI and his son at Coventry but a year before.[17] Nor did
he anticipate public reaction. After his throne-touching performance,
according to the pro-Yorkist Abbot Whethamstede, 'every state and
grade, of whatever age or sex, order or condition, began to murmur
against him'.[18] Then, if we may believe the Burgundian Waurin, his
allies, March included, tried to persuade him to turn back.[19] But he
evidently felt he had committed himself too far. Richard of York
decided to press his claim in Parliament.

The ensuing deliberations took over two weeks (Doc. 3). On 16
October York's claim to the throne, based on the priority of his descent

[14] Lander, *BIHR* (1963), xxxvi. p. 126; Storey, *End of Lancaster*, p. 188.
[15] *The Historical Collections of a Citizen of London in the Fifteenth Century*, ed.
James Gairdner (Camden Society, London 1876), p. 208.
[16] Lander, *BIHR* (1963), xxxvi. p. 127; idem, *Wars of Roses*, p. 108.
[17] *Rot. Parl.* v. 351.
[18] Quoted in *The Chronicles of the White Rose of York*, ed. J. A. Giles, 2nd
edn. (London 1845), p. lxxx.
[19] Cited by Lander, *BIHR* (1963), xxxvi. p. 127.

from Edward III via Lionel of Clarence over Henry VI's via John of Gaunt, was formally presented to the Lords. On the 17th Henry ordered the Lords to find and raise all the objections they could against York's title. They spent several days attempting to get first the king's justices and then the king's sergeants and attorney to assume this unwelcome task. Both groups of law officers were unwilling to get involved: the matter was above the law and passed their learning; only the royal family and the peerage were high enough to meddle therein. The Lords were left reluctantly to obey the king's command by themselves.

The 'objections' raised by the Lords were too flimsy to stand. Two of them may be disposed of swiftly. The 'great oaths' made to Henry VI may have troubled the consciences of many peers, but this could not affect York's title if valid. Nor could his bearing the arms of York instead of Clarence. Of more interest is the Lords' setting against York's claim (1) 'great and notable Acts of Parliament' which were 'of more authority than any chronicle, and also of authority to defeat any manner title made to any person', and (2) 'divers entails made to heirs males as for the crown of England'. While (2) implies a title for Henries IV–VI through a rule of male primogeniture, it would be anachronistic to see (1) as implying a parliamentary title for the Lancastrian line. The conception that Parliament was competent to determine the succession was to be essentially a Tudor development. Rather the Lords merely signified that a parliamentary declaration of the succession was a more authoritative record than what was said in a chronicle and carried greater weight than a title affirmed in any other way. The acts and entails that the Lords had in mind must have been some legislation of Henry IV.

Henry IV 'settled' the succession four times. In 1399 the king with the assent of Parliament declared the Prince of Wales his heir apparent.[20] In 1404 Parliament 'recognized' that the succession was entailed in order of seniority upon Henry's four sons and their issue, which would include females as well as males.[21] In June 1406 Henry issued a charter, sealed with the great seal, the seals of all of the Lords, and the Seal of the Speaker of the Commons, which entailed the succession on his sons and their heirs male.[22] This procedure by sealed charter seems to indicate that a regular parliamentary enactment was deemed insufficient to establish for the first time what amounted to a Salic law. The Lancastrian title could now be based on direct male descent from Edward III, which would have made a good case for Henry VI's priority over Richard of York. In December 1406, however, the June settlement was repealed and the 1404 entail to Henry IV's sons and their issue generally

[20] Rot. Parl. iii. 434.
[21] Rot. Parl. iii. 525.
[22] Rot. Parl. iii. 575–6.

was restored.[23] This was accomplished by a new sealed charter,[24] the effect of which was put on the statute roll (Doc. 2) 'the first appearance of succession matters in the form of a statute'.[25] Apparently neither Henry VI's Lords nor York knew the whole of the above history; certainly the latter would have used it to demolish the Salic law case if he had known of it.

But York really had to know little more than the priority of his own descent from Edward III, for the Lords virtually destroyed any case for Henry VI with their final 'objection' that Henry IV assumed the crown as 'right inheritor' to Henry III. Henry IV's claim to be the heir of Henry III [26] was based on the allegation that his great-great grandfather, Edmund, earl of Lancaster, was actually the firstborn son of Henry III, but his 'younger' brother was made King Edward I. This claim was, as York indicated, manifestly fraudulent.[27] By basing Henry IV's title on an untruth, the Lords, who were not ready to accept the idea of a purely parliamentary title, in effect abolished the 'authority' of his 'great and notable Acts of Parliament' entailing the succession on his line. They also made absurd a case for Henry VI on the ground of a Salic law, for Henry IV descended from Edmund of Lancaster via his mother. Moreover, the claim that Henry IV was the heir of Henry III implied that the kings of England from Edward I through Richard II were all usurpers despite their reigning for a century and a quarter. This made ridiculous a case for Henry VI, whose line had reigned but six decades, on the basis of a prescriptive right. Well could York say of his own title, 'though right for a time rest and be put to silence, yet it rotteth not nor shall not perish'. Indeed, the Lords, after grounding the Lancastrian title on a counterfeit legitimism, could not very well reject the true legitimist claim of York even though legitimism beyond eldest sons inheriting from fathers was no more an established rule of the English succession than a Salic law. They almost had to conclude that York's title 'cannot be defeated'.

Nevertheless, the Lords were not prepared to depose Henry VI, who had reigned for thirty-eight years and whose only crime was incompetence, merely because York had impetuously put forward an undeniable but unpopular claim. On 31 October a compromise was reached

[23] Perhaps the main reason for this reversal was that a Salic law in England made absurd the pretensions of the English kings to the French crown. In their petition the Commons requested that letters patent announcing the repeal be sent to the French court (*Rot. Parl.* iii. 581).

[24] *Rot. Parl.* iii. 581–3.

[25] T. P. Taswell-Langmead, *English Constitutional History*, 11th edn by T. F. T. Plucknett (Boston 1960), p. 495.

[26] *Rot. Parl.* iii. 422–3; Davies, *English Chronicle*, p. 18.

[27] See Davies, *English Chronicle*, pp. 7, 152–3; Taswell-Langmead, *English History*, pp. 493–4.

and embodied in an 'act of accord'. Henry VI was to remain on the throne until his demise or abdication. York and his heirs were declared next in line and to be granted estates yielding a princely income. Henry IV's succession legislation was repealed. Prince Edward, though not mentioned, was in effect disinherited. York and his two elder sons took oaths not to violate the settlement, 'with protestation that if the King for his party duly kept and observed the same accord and act thereupon made, which the King at that time promised to do'.

Thanks to lack of resistance on the part of Henry VI,[28] Richard of York had gained as much as could be expected from a reluctant Parliament. True, Richard was ten years Henry's senior, but the ease with which the king had yielded half way must have suggested to York that an abdication might be induced before long. At any rate, if York was not to achieve the crown himself, it was now entailed upon his heirs rather than Henry's. This last, however, was to set in motion a chain of events that would be fatal to York and would alter the nature of the Wars of the Roses.

Henry VI's acquiescence in the setting aside of his son was not accepted by his queen. Margaret of Anjou, joined by the enemies of York and the Nevilles, reopened the Wars of the Roses. On 30 December 1460, her northern allies were victorious at Wakefield where Richard of York and his second son, Edmund, earl of Rutland, were slain on the field and Salisbury, the senior Neville earl, perished by mob justice. On 2 February 1461, Edward of March, York's heir, defeated Margaret's western allies at Mortimer's Cross. On the 17th Margaret routed Warwick, now the head Neville, at the second battle of St Albans and regained custody of Henry VI. Nine days later March and Warwick 'with a great puissance' entered London, which shortly before had refused to admit Margaret's turbulent northern troops. On 1 March the people of London shouted 'yea' when asked if they would have March as king. The same 'election' was repeated twice on the 4th when he assumed the throne as Edward IV.[29] This last was a foregone conclusion after a 'council' held the previous day at Baynard's Castle where Warwick and a few other magnates 'agreed and concluded that Edward . . . should then be king'.[30]

Why did Warwick and his fellows, after having disapproved of Richard of York's attempt to take the throne four months before, now agree that Richard's son should supplant Henry VI? Edward's strong position, though usually ignored by historians, was doubtless an

[28] A perusal of Doc. 3 suggests that the king could have called a halt to the proceedings in Parliament at almost any stage with the assent of the Lords.
[29] Six Town Chronicles of England, ed. Ralph Flenley (Oxford 1911), pp. 161–2.
[30] Stevenson, Wars of the English in France, ii. Pt ii. 777.

important consideration. He had entered London with the victorious troops of Mortimer's Cross; Warwick had accompanied him with the residue of those routed at St Albans. The 'great puissance', in all likelihood, was mainly Edward's, not Warwick's. It is also likely that London 'elected' Edward IV with genuine enthusiasm.[31] The desperate men who met at Baynard's Castle must have felt the pressure of Edward's strength and popularity. They also had to feel the pressure of the intransigent Queen Margaret. Her forces still had to be met. Wakefield and St Albans II had shown that defeated lords could expect no mercy from her, and Henry VI was now in her hands. 1455 and 1460 had shown that York–Neville victories only brought temporary control over Henry VI and his government. Time was on Margaret's side as long as Henry remained king. But the settlement of October 1460, which made an accommodation with Margaret impossible, provided a 'legal' way out. It could be said that Henry VI, whatever his actual responsibility for the actions of Margaret and her allies against York and his family, had violated that settlement and that the crown was thereby forfeited to the heir of York. Edward IV was a gamble for Warwick and company: if Margaret defeated him, they would face almost certain destruction; if he defeated her, they would have to deal with a sovereign lord who might not be easy to control. But the situation in early March 1461, which developed out of the settlement of the previous October, practically forced them to accept, not make, Edward IV.[32]

England now had two 'kings' and two royal houses; the central drama in the Wars of the Roses had at last become a dynastic conflict of Lancaster and York. This does not mean that the older struggles either disappeared or became merely secondary. The Percies and the Nevilles continued to contest for influence in the king's government and dominance in the north country. The only difference was that they now sought to further their interests by allying themselves with one or the other of the royal houses.[33] Other territorial magnates and lesser local rivals no doubt did the same. In most cases dynastic allegiance was secondary to private interest. This is made evident by the ease with which men changed sides in the dynastic conflict.[34] Though there were some steadfast adherents, most participants were little more than

[31] See Storey, *End of Lancaster*, p. 196, and the several accounts of Edward's accession quoted in Bertie Wilkinson, *Constitutional History of England in the Fifteenth Century* (London 1964), pp. 173–7.

[32] It is difficult to see why Warwick should be called 'the kingmaker' in connexion with Edward's accession.

[33] See Storey, *End of Lancaster*, pp. 193–5.

[34] See esp. K. B. McFarlane, 'The Wars of the Roses', *Proceedings of the British Academy* (1965), i, pp. 103–7.

'Lancastrians' or 'Yorkists' for the time being. Such fleeting loyalties were an unsafe base upon which to build a dynasty.

Edward IV, who from the start no doubt was determined to be his own master, apparently realized that it would be dangerous for him to rely too much on the backing of a magnate group. It is highly unlikely that the king in 1461 or even 1464 saw an eventual break with Warwick as inevitable, but the history of his early years on the throne suggests that he deliberately sought other bases of support than the Neville party. Following the Lancastrian example, Edward evidently tried to create a court party as a counterweight to the Nevilles. The established families offered very few prospects for such a party. Edward could count on the Bourchiers, notably Henry, earl of Essex and treasurer of England, and Thomas, archbishop of Canterbury,[35] and that was about it. A greater opportunity opened up through Edward's marriage in 1464 to the parvenue Elizabeth Woodville. The king bestowed titles and offices on the new queen's numerous relatives and secured them marriage alliances with important families.[36] Edward, who was hardly a loving husband, could not have so promoted the Woodvilles merely because his wife wanted him to; the only satisfactory explanation is that his purpose was to make a new great family which with its matrimonial connexions might rival the Nevilles and would almost have to be committed to its maker.[37]

Edward IV did not confine his search for support to the aristocracy. The king, whose accession owed so much to the people of London, obviously attempted to win wide approval of his kingship through popular fiscal and commercial policies and good relations with the House of Commons.[38] After his victory at Towton on 29 March 1461, which resulted in the flight to Scotland of Henry VI, Queen Margaret and their Prince Edward, Edward IV indeed stressed his legitimist claim and forgot his 'election', but he used legitimism to make a case for loyalty to his line. In November the king had his title to the crown by descent declared in Parliament (Doc. 4). This declaration was more than a rehearsal of an hereditary title; it stated for the first time what was to become with slight change the Tudor interpretation of fifteenth-century history. It saw all of England's troubles since 1399 as deriving from the deposition and murder of Richard II and the accession of the usurping line of Lancaster instead of the rightful line of Clarence. The consequence for England was first 'intolerable persecution, punition, and tribulation', and then under Henry VI 'unrest, inward war and trouble,

---

[35] Chrimes, *Lancastrians*, pp. 84–5, 91.
[36] P. M. Kendall, *Richard the Third* (London, New York, 1955), p. 61.
[37] See Chrimes, *Lancastrians*, p. 91; Wilkinson, *Constitutional History*, pp. 147–8. Cf. Lander, *BIHR* (1963), xxxvi. p. 137–42.
[38] Wilkinson, *Constitutional History*, pp. 141–5.

unrightwiseness, shedding and effusion of innocent blood', etc. This was distorted history – the dynastic issue did not pre-date the Wars of the Roses [39] but arose some five years after their commencement; those wars very probably would not have occurred if Henry VI, 'unrightwise usurper' though he may have been, had been half-way competent. None the less, the intended message for England was clear: maintain the legitimate line of Edward IV, the heir of Richard II, or suffer an inevitable renewal of the troubles. Dynastic loyalty was to be won by fear propaganda as well as popular governance.

Edward's efforts to find other bases of support than the Neville party proved of no avail when his break with Warwick came. That break began to develop with Edward's marriage to Elizabeth Woodville and the promotions of her relatives that followed, neither of which were to Warwick's liking. Its completion was assured by the marriage in 1468 of Edward's sister Margaret to Charles the Bold, duke of Burgundy, which frustrated the pro-French policy that Edward had allowed Warwick to commit himself to. In 1469 Warwick found a son-in-law and co-conspirator in Edward's brother George, duke of Clarence, and captured the king but, he was unable to control Edward or replace him with Clarence. In 1470 Warwick and Clarence fled to France, made their peace with Margaret of Anjou, and set sail for England to restore Henry VI. This venture in kingmaking succeeded thanks to the unexpected treachery of John Neville, marquis of Montague, who a year before had fought against his family.[40] In the end Edward had to depend on a Neville and that Neville betrayed him. Edward IV was lucky to escape to Holland.

Henry VI's 'readeption', as it was called, only lasted from October 1470 to April 1471, but this was long enough for the last Lancastrian Parliament to be held. Since no roll of the Readeption Parliament is extant, we cannot be sure of its dynastic acts. There is no reason to doubt the word of a London chronicler that it attainted Edward IV and his youngest brother, Richard, duke of Gloucester.[41] It also seems likely that Parliament acted to enable Clarence, despite Edward's attainder, to inherit his father's duchy of York,[42] in accord with an agreement made between Margaret and Warwick at Angers in July, 1470: [43] ordinarily, if an elder son was attainted, a younger son was

[39] The espousals of the Clarence claim by the Percies in their revolt of 1403 and by the three noblemen who plotted to assassinate Henry V in 1415 certainly had no connexion with the later dynastic conflict of Lancaster and York.

[40] Chrimes, Lancastrians, pp. 100, 104.

[41] The Great Chronicle of London, ed. A. H. Thomas and I. D. Thornley (London 1938), p. 213. That Edward was attainted receives confirmation from his repealing act of 1477 (Rot. Parl. vi. 191).

[42] Edward Hall, Chronicle, ed. Henry Ellis (London 1809), p. 286.

[43] A contemporary account quoted in Lander, Wars of Roses, p. 172.

unable to inherit from the father because he was unworthy in blood.[44] But did Parliament entail the crown after Henry VI and his heirs male on Clarence and his heirs male [45] in accord with an alleged pre-readeption agreement? [46] The generally accepted view that Clarence was made the heir of Lancaster, as will be seen when we consider Clarence's attainder under the restored Edward IV, is now doubtful.

On 14 March 1471 Edward IV landed with a small force at Ravenspur, the port where Henry Bolingbroke had landed in 1399 on his way to becoming Henry IV. Edward there learned that the people of southwestern England would not have him as king, proof of the failure of his earlier efforts to build a widespread loyalty to himself and his line. Edward had to follow Bolingbroke's formula further and pretend that he had only returned to claim the dukedom of York, a pretension he would maintain until he reached friendly territory.[47] He reached such territory because Henry Percy, fifth earl of Northumberland, was unwilling to stop him. Northumberland, whose grandfather and father had both died fighting under Henry VI's standard, was supposed to be a Lancastrian, but it was against Percy interests to save a Henry VI who was being used by the Nevilles to enhance their power in northern England.[48] After passing through Percy country to the Midlands, Edward re-proclaimed himself king and was joined by substantial forces raised by Clarence who, dissatisfied with the rewards of betraying his brother, now decided to betray his father-in-law. On 14 April Edward IV was victorious at Barnet where Warwick and Montague, the two great Nevilles, were slain. On 4 May Edward defeated Margaret of Anjou at Tewkesbury where Edmund second duke of Somerset and his brother John, the last male Beauforts, died and the Lancastrian Prince Edward was murdered. A little over two weeks later Henry VI either died a natural death or was murdered, completing the extinction of the royal line of Lancaster.

Edward IV now sat firmly on his throne. With the great duchies of Lancaster and York vested in the crown and the confiscation of the lands of Warwick and other rebels, the king was so much the greatest magnate that no prudent noble would dare to challenge him. Nor was there really any rival line to threaten Edward's possession of the crown or the succession of his Prince Edward, the son Elizabeth Woodville gave birth to during Henry VI's readeption. Lady Margaret Beaufort

[44] So Edmund Plowden, BM, Harleian MS. 849, fo. 207.
[45] Hall, *Chronicle*, p. 286.
[46] John Warkworth, *A Chronicle of the First Thirteen Years of the Reign of King Edward the Fourth*, ed. J. O. Halliwell (Camden Society, London 1839), pp. 9–10.
[47] *Historie of the Arrivall of Edward IV in England*, ed. John Bruce (Camden Society, London 1838), pp. 2–4.
[48] Storey, *Henry VII*, pp. 44–5.

and her son, Henry Tudor, earl of Richmond, might be called 'Lancastrians', but there was no apparent reason for regarding them as serious claimants. Indeed, the only dynastic 'crisis' that Edward IV had to deal with during the remainder of his reign came from within the house of York.

Clarence's third treason hardly constituted a real menace to Edward, but it had dynastic aspects that would not disappear with Clarence's execution. After Edward's demise Clarence's attainder would provide an excuse to debar his son Edward, earl of Warwick, and thus make 'legally' possible the usurpation of Richard III. According to his attainder of early 1478 (Doc. 5), Clarence spread the charge that Edward IV was a bastard, a charge which, if true, would make Clarence the legitimate heir of York and a charge that was to be raised again after the king's death. The story of Edward's bastardy was not new in 1478; [49] doubtless Clarence, who was specifically accused of voicing it, made use of it. But also, according to his attainder, Clarence obtained and kept secret – presumably for revelation at an opportune moment – an exemplification under the great seal of Henry VI which indicated that Clarence and his heirs were now the heirs of Lancaster.

This accusation has been taken to confirm the story in Warkworth's *Chronicle* of a pre-readeption agreement to turn the succession after Henry VI and his heirs male to Clarence [50] and/or the story in Hall's *Chronicle* of an entail to the same effect made in the Readeption Parliament. [51] Both stories and the accusation have lately been questioned by J. R. Lander. He maintains that Clarence's political position in 1470 and 1471 was not such as to call for his being named to the succession. He points out that Warkworth wrote his story sometime during the four years following Clarence's death, that Hall's first appeared in 1548, that no reference to a designation of the succession to Clarence predates that in his attainder of 1478, and that the Croyland Continuator, Dominic Mancini, Polydore Vergil, and Sir Thomas More, each of whom had opportunity to learn of it, all ignored the attainder account, presumably because they doubted its veracity. Lander suggests in conclusion that either the attainder account was a fabrication or if an exemplification under Henry VI's great seal did exist it was forged, either by Clarence to strengthen his claim to the throne or by Edward IV to clinch his brother's guilt. [52]

[49] On the previous history of this story, which probably was no more than a political smear, see Mortimer Levine, 'Richard III—Usurper or Lawful King?', *Speculum* (1959), xxxiv, p. 395; J. R. Lander, 'The Treason and Death of the Duke of Clarence: A Reinterpretation', *Canadian Journal of History* (1967), ii, no. 2, p. 26.

[50] Above, n. 46.

[51] Above, n. 45.

[52] Lander, *Canadian Journal of History* (1967), pp. 1–28.

Where does all this leave the notion of Clarence as the heir of Lancaster? Hall's story of a parliamentary entail no doubt should be dismissed as a Tudor chronicler's invention. Warkworth's story of a pre-readeption agreement may well have been derived from the attainder account's description of the exemplification as containing 'all such appointments as late was made' between Clarence and Margaret of Anjou (Doc. 5). This reference to Margaret suggests at least a possibility that the attainder was true. In 1478 the lady was living in France from whence she could safely have given it the lie. Still the weight of probability belongs to Lander's suggestion of either a fabricated account or a forged exemplification. Nevertheless, it was recorded in the Parliament rolls that there was an exemplification under the great seal of the last Lancastrian king which indicated that the Lancastrian title had passed to the line of Clarence, and this probably helped to make the existence of Clarence's son a dynastic problem for the first Tudor.

Whatever its meaning for the future, Clarence's treason had no significant effect on the rule of the restored Edward IV. Once secure on his throne, the king proceeded to build the type of strong monarchy that was to serve England best until the 1530s. Having the means to 'live of his own', he had little need for Parliament. Not being dependent on magnates, he was able to govern through a council of his own choosing. Edward may have been moving in the direction of despotism,[53] but England was getting what it wanted most, law and order. If he had lived long enough to be succeeded by a mature son, a genuine loyalty to the house of York might well have developed and there would have been no Tudor monarchs to have dynastic problems.

On 9 April 1483, however, Edward IV died in his fortieth year. Two days later his elder son, but twelve years of age, was proclaimed Edward V. With the young king reputedly not robust and his brother Richard, duke of York, only nine years old, England faced the prospect of a long minority or perhaps even two successive minorities. The Queen Mother and Richard of Gloucester, Edward V's surviving uncle, both desired to fill the power vacuum. The contest between them was quickly won by Gloucester with the help of two potentially dangerous allies, namely Henry Stafford, duke of Buckingham, a western magnate of royal descent, and William, Lord Hastings, a loyal servant and close friend of the late king who had at his call a formidable force of indentured retainers and their men.[54] By early May Elizabeth Woodville was in sanctuary, and Richard of Gloucester had custody of Edward V and was recognized as protector and defender of the

[53] See Wilkinson, *Constitutional History*, p. 159.
[54] On Hastings see W. H. Dunham, Jr, *Lord Hastings' Indentured Retainers, 1461-1438* (New Haven 1955).

realm 'with power to order and forbid in every matter, just like another king'.[55]

With kingly power so easily obtained but precariously held, the obvious next step for an ambitious uncle would be to take his nephew's place on the throne. Gloucester's first move in this direction came on 13 June when he procured the arrest and death of Hastings, who probably took seriously his obligation of loyalty to Edward IV's son [56] and who might have been able to raise sufficient forces to prevent a usurpation. Then on 16 June Gloucester, through the innocent intercession of Archbishop Bourchier with the Queen Mother, gained custody of little Richard of York, who could not safely be left in Woodville hands, even in sanctuary. Things could now proceed openly. On the 22nd London preachers in their sermons raised the old charge that Edward IV was illegitimate,[57] and one of them, Friar Ralph Shaa, added a new charge that Edward's children were bastards.[58] Two days later Buckingham exhorted a 'fair multitude' of Londoners to accept Gloucester as king; a 'small number' of them cried 'yea'.[59] By 26 June an assembly of Lords and Commons had been induced to petition Gloucester to assume the crown 'as to you of right belonging, as well by inheritance as by lawful election' (Doc. 6), which he did as Richard III.

This petition is a curious document, a desperate attempt to justify a usurpation. It cannot even be considered valid as a parliamentary petition. The Lords and Commons from whom it emanated had been summoned to Parliament by Edward V. If, as their petition indicated, he was no king, they were no Parliament: Richard III's 'lawful election' came from a group of men called by a usurper. Only in early 1484 did Richard find it expedient to give the petition an *ex post facto* legality by having it rehearsed in a regular parliamentary enactment: [60] since the 'three estates' that petitioned him to assume the kingship were not 'assembled in form of Parliament', 'diverse doubts, questions, and ambiguities' have 'been moved and engendered in the minds of diverse persons' – something of an understatement after Buckingham's rebellion!

The petition begins its case for Richard with a lengthy condemnation

---

[55] *Ingulph's Chronicle of the Abbey of Croyland*, trans. H. T. Riley (London 1854), p. 487.

[56] Dunham, *Hastings' Retainers*, pp. 14–19.

[57] Dominic Mancini, *The Usurpation of Richard III*, ed. C. A. J. Armstrong (Oxford 1963), p. 109.

[58] Thomas and Thornley, *Great Chronicle*, p. 231.

[59] Ibid. p. 232.

[60] Wilkinson, *Constitutional History*, p. 190, labels this act as 'Richard's Parliamentary Title'. This imputes too much to an act, probably resulting from the scare created by Buckingham's rebellion, which retroactively confirms a petition made by men not 'assembled in form of Parliament'.

of Edward IV's rule after his marriage to Elizabeth Woodville, that is, during the most part of his reign. Edward's was a selfish and lawless despotism. The poor and weak suffered 'murders, extortions, and oppressions'. No man was sure of his life, land, livelihood, family or servant. Every woman lived in fear of being ravished. Peace gave way to 'discords, inward battles, effusion of Christian men's blood', and destruction of the nobility. The similarity to Edward's picture of Lancastrian England (Doc. 4) is striking. No stronger indictment of the Yorkist monarchy has ever been made than in this 'Yorkist' petition, but a case for Richard could only be made by defaming his own house.

Next the petition seeks to bastardize Edward IV's children by raising four objections to his marriage with Elizabeth Woodville, the first three of which were trivial. Edward married 'without the knowing and assent' of the peerage – no requirement for a monarch who was of age. The union was made through the 'sorcery and witchcraft' of the bride and her mother – a charge usually made by a husband rather than an assembly of busybodies. The marriage was made clandestinely – it was solemnized by a priest in the presence of four witnesses [61] and not long after 'solemnly sanctioned and approved of . . . by . . . all the prelates and great lords of the kingdom'.[62] Modern defenders of Richard base his case on the objection that the petition places last, that Edward had a prior contract to marry Lady Eleanor Butler when he wedded Elizabeth Woodville.[63]

The defenders do not consider that the precontract story, even if true, hardly justified Richard's claim. Lady Eleanor Butler died in 1468. This might bastardize Edward IV's eldest daughter Elizabeth, born in 1465, but Edward V and his brother were born in 1470 and 1472 respectively. A precontract would not affect the status of sons born after it had been terminated by Lady Eleanor's death; their parents lived together openly and accepted by the Church and the nation as man and wife. An ecclesiastical court, in whose jurisdiction such matrimonial causes properly belonged,[64] could not well have denied the legitimacy of Edward V and little York, but there is no evidence that the question was ever raised in such a court. Their bastardy was pronounced in 1483 in a petition of an assembly of doubtful status. Though the Parliament of 1484 confirmed the petition, it evidently had doubts of its competence regarding the matrimonial cause: 'that Lay Court' was at first 'unable to

[61] Robert Fabyan, *The New Chronicles of England and France*, ed. Henry Ellis (London 1811), p. 654.
[62] Riley, *Croyland Chronicle*, p. 440.
[63] For a full presentation of the case for the precontract story see Kendall, *Richard the Third*, pp. 257–61, 552–6; for a detailed refutation see Levine, *Speculum* (1959), xxxiv. pp. 391–401.
[64] Frederick Pollock and F. W. Maitland, *History of English Law*, 2nd edn (Cambridge 1899), ii. pp. 367–8.

give a definition' of Richard's rights 'when the question of the marriage was discussed', but, moved by fear of his adversaries, 'it presumed to do so'.[65]

Moreover, the precontract story is most doubtful. It cannot be documented. The story was first made public after both of the parties to the alleged precontract were dead. Edward IV's marriage had not been challenged during its whole nineteen years, not even by Margaret of Anjou, Warwick or Clarence.[66] The revelation of a precontract in June 1483, when an ambitious uncle was in a position to displace his nephew on the throne, and the failure to have its authenticity ruled on by an appropriate court, more than suggest that it was a mere invention: 'colour' for an 'act of usurpation' was the judgment of a contemporary and Yorkist chronicler.[67]

Perhaps indicative of uncertainty that the precontract story was sufficient to debar the children of Edward IV, the petition seems to allude to the charge that the king himself was a bastard. The petition says that Richard was the 'undoubted son and heir of Richard, late duke of York'; he was born in England (Edward was born at Rouen), which gave 'more certain knowledge' of his 'birth and filiation'. This is no direct accusation, but, considering that the charge against Edward's legitimacy had been voiced in the sermons of 22 June, the insinuation seems clear. If the new precontract story was insufficient, recourse could be had to the old slander.

The bastardization of Edward or his children was not enough to give Richard the crown. Still before him in the hereditary order were the children of his elder brother Clarence, 8-year-old Edward of Warwick and 10-year-old Margaret. The petition handles this matter by claiming that Clarence's attainder disqualified his issue. This was debatable. The only title that Clarence's attainder specifically deprived him and his heirs of was that of duke (Doc. 5). What precedents there were indicated that the common-law rule against inheritance by persons of attainted blood did not apply to the royal succession: Henry VI's restoration despite his attainder under Edward IV [68] and Edward's restoration notwithstanding his attainder during Henry's readeption.[69] Nevertheless, the applicability of the common-law rule had never been tested judicially, and, with Edward V set aside no one was likely to make an issue of the claim of a helpless lad like Warwick.

[65] Riley, *Croyland Chronicle*, pp. 495–6.
[66] Kendall, *Richard the Third*, pp. 259–60, conjectures that Clarence knew the precontract story at the time of his third treason but did not dare to use it. Why such caution when the charge that Edward IV was illegitimate (above, p. 26) was equally dangerous?
[67] Riley, *Croyland Chronicle*, p. 489.
[68] *Rot. Parl.* v. 478.
[69] Above, p. 24.

Whatever the defects of the petition, it afforded a semblance of legality for Richard III's usurpation. Englishmen could acquiesce on the ground that the kingship was a job for a man, not a boy. But the boy and his brother constituted an inevitable problem. Their continued existence, even in the Tower, would always be a threat to Richard. Another problem, though Richard did not know it, was Henry of Buckingham. On his way to the throne Richard had eliminated a dangerous ally in Hastings, but the even more dangerous Buckingham received offices and powers which made him a virtual viceroy in Wales and the west country.[70] Richard had created a new overmighty subject whose background was Lancastrian and who through his mother represented the junior Beaufort line and through his father descended from Thomas of Woodstock, duke of Gloucester and youngest son of Edward III. Not many months after Richard's accession the two problems coalesced.

We need not consider how and at whose hands Edward V and little York met their end, probably in the summer or fall of 1483.[71] It suffices to say that by October the circulation of a rumour of their death had turned discontent in the southern and south-western shires into open rebellion. The leadership of the rebellion was assumed by Buckingham, who may at first have seen himself as the replacement for Richard III. It soon became apparent that the most acceptable candidate was Henry Tudor, earl of Richmond, who came of the senior Beaufort line, provided that he would marry Edward IV's daughter Elizabeth.[72] Buckingham's rebellion turned out to be a fiasco which brought its leader to the block. Its failure may well have been fortunate for Henry Tudor. It was not safe to owe one's throne to Buckingham. But the rebellion did at least suggest the formula that might unite the various discontented elements behind Henry when he was ready to try on his own. Late in 1483 in Brittany Henry solemnly promised to marry Elizabeth of York.

On 7 August 1485, Henry Tudor landed in Wales, and on the 22nd the Wars of the Roses came to their traditional end at Bosworth where Richard III died fighting. Richard doubtless would have won at Bosworth but for the timely intervention of the Stanleys on the Tudor side and the failure of Henry Percy, earl of Northumberland, to stop them. Northumberland came to Bosworth presumably to fight for Richard but did no more than watch the battle. Northumberland's inaction has never been satisfactorily explained. Perhaps it derived from the fact that Richard as duke of Gloucester had married a Neville, protected the remaining Nevilles,[73] and in effect had become the new great Neville. Richard III so far had left north-western England to Nor-

[70] E. F. Jacob, *The Fifteenth Century* (Oxford 1961), pp. 615, 617, 622.
[71] See Jacob, *Fifteenth Century*, pp. 623–5.
[72] Riley, *Croyland Chronicle*, pp. 490–1.
[73] See Kendall, *Richard the Third*, pp. 129–30.

thumberland, but the establishment of the Council of the North in
1484 could have been seen by a Percy as threatening dominance of the
entire north country by a 'Neville' king. This suggests that the Neville–
Percy feud, which initiated the Wars of the Roses at St Albans I, may
have played a decisive role in their 'termination' at Bosworth. Be that as
it may, Henry Tudor was now Henry VII; the house of Tudor had
begun its rule.

2

The Reign of Henry VII

Though the uncertainty of the law of succession in 1485 left much room for manœuvre, it would have been difficult to find justification for Henry VII's claim to the crown placed upon his head at Bosworth. If, as Edward IV and Richard III tried to maintain, legitimism was the determinant of the succession, the crown belonged to the house of York. Elizabeth of York would come first if her sex or bastardization did not debar her. Next would be Edward of Warwick if his father's attainder did not exclude him. Then there was a third Yorkist claimant who could not be set aside on grounds of sex, illegitimacy or attainted blood, namely John de la Pole, earl of Lincoln, the eldest son of Edward IV's sister Elizabeth and Richard III's designated successor.

If the crown was to revert to the house of Lancaster, which had reigned nearly three times as long as York, Henry VII's Lancastrian claim was doubtful. Whatever it was, it derived from his descent from the Beauforts, the legitimated offspring of John of Gaunt and Catherine Swynford. The first Lancastrian king, in confirming Richard II's patent of legitimation, had added words barring the Beauforts from the succession. Though this addition probably could not prevail in law against the original patent which had been confirmed by Parliament,[1] Henry VII and his contemporaries, his cousins of Buckingham excepted, probably did not know that the exclusion of the Beauforts was solely the work of Henry IV and of dubious validity.[2] Moreover, if the Beauforts were not precluded from the succession, priority in their line did not belong to Henry VII but to his mother, who was to outlive him. Furthermore, if Lady Margaret Beaufort was willing to surrender her place to her son, it was questionable whether the Beauforts had the first Lancastrian claim. If primogeniture was the determinant and an alien was eligible,

---

[1] See above, p. 16.
[2] Testimony at the trial of Edward, duke of Buckingham, in 1521 indicates that Buckingham had a record of Parliament's confirmation of Richard's patent and deliberately concealed it from Henry VII. *L.P.* iii. 1284.

that claim belonged to John II of Portugal, a descendant of John of Gaunt and his first wife, Blanche of Lancaster. Indeed if, as Henry VI's Lords maintained, the Lancastrian title was based on Henry IV's descent from Henry III via the same Blanche,[3] Henry VII was not a Lancastrian at all. Nor could Henry, who descended from Gaunt via his mother, use the former alternative of a Lancastrian title based on a Salic law; in fact, the only remaining direct male descent from Edward III was Edward of Warwick's via Edmund of Langley. And Warwick, according to Edward IV's Parliament roll, was now the heir of Lancaster on the authority of an exemplification under the great seal of the last Lancastrian king (Doc. 4). This would supplement a genuine Yorkist claim with a possible Lancastrian claim, and Henry, who was himself attainted,[4] could not assert that Warwick was debarred by Clarence's attainder.

Clearly it would not do to say much about Henry VII's title according to the law of succession. That might invite consideration of matters that it would be better to pass over, such as the rights of the Yorkists, especially Warwick,[5] the legitimation of the Beauforts, and perhaps Henry VI's alleged limitation in favour of Clarence's line. Henry VII's effective title to the throne came not from law but from his victory at Bosworth. Bosworth settled the matter for all practical purposes. It also was regarded by contemporaries as an expression of God's will; it was, as Henry would tell Parliament, 'the true judgment of God in granting him victory over his enemy in the field'.[6] Bosworth gave Henry a title by a 'Tudor kind of divine right'.[7] Henry, however, may have seen Bosworth as merely confirming a title already in existence. Richard III, in a proclamation issued two months before Bosworth, had accused Henry of having 'usurped upon him the name and title of the royal estate of this realm of England'.[8] And Henry would date his reign from the day before Bosworth. His obvious purpose was to make traitors of those who fought against him,[9] but he also may have intended to imply his own view of his title—'if Henry was king one day before Bosworth, why not ten days, or a hundred, or a thousand?'[10] This would amount to little more than maintaining that Henry Tudor was king because he said he was king, but, given the situation in 1485, it was not too far from the truth.

[3] Blanche was the great-granddaughter of Edmund of Lancaster. See above, p. 20.

[4] *Rot. Parl.* vi. 246–7.

[5] All things considered, Warwick probably had the best legal claim to the throne in 1485.

[6] *Rot. Parl.* vi. 268.

[7] G. R. Elton, *England under the Tudors* (London 1955), p. 19.

[8] *The Paston Letters*, ed. James Gairdner (London 1910), iii. p. 317.

[9] See *Rot. Parl.* vi. 276.

[10] Kenneth Pickthorn, *Early Tudor Government* (Cambridge 1934), i. p. 14.

On 15 September 1485 Henry VII called a Parliament for 7 November. There was a legal problem involved in that some of those returned to the Parliament were attainted, as was the king who summoned it. It was decided that the members would have to have their attainders reversed by Parliament before taking their seats, but Henry's attainder needed no reversal. The king, the judges ruled, was discharged of any attaint by the very fact of his assumption of the crown (Doc. 7). This terse opinion settled the matter and it made some hard sense. High treason, as an Elizabethan writer would indicate, was an offence against the sovereign; when Henry ascended the throne, the judgment against him ceased, for his offence was then committed against himself, an absurdity.[11] At any rate, a possible defect in Henry's title was removed.

The Parliament of 1485 made a declaration about Henry's title and the succession. This declaration, a special petition of the Commons assented to by the king and the Lords, was not, strictly speaking, an act of Parliament.[12] Nor did it attempt to justify the Tudor title. It simply stated that the inheritance of the crown resided in 'our now sovereign lord King Harry VII and in the heirs of his body lawfully come . . . and in none other' (Doc. 8). As far as the king's title was concerned, this was merely a formal acknowledgment of a fact; Parliament's existence testified to Henry's kingship. Doubtless more important to Henry, who wanted to make clear that his title was good of itself, was the entail of the succession on *his* heirs—his heirs by any wife, not a specified wife.

On 10 December, the day of its prorogation, Parliament expressed its desire that the king take to wife Elizabeth of York, and he indicated his intention to do so.[13] Henry almost had to marry Elizabeth. He could not lightly repudiate his widely known pre-Bosworth pledge and expect his subjects to respect the kingly word of their new and untried sovereign. The union with Elizabeth would help to retain the loyalty of those former servants and adherents of Edward IV whose services and support Henry needed. Above all, if Henry did not marry Elizabeth, someone else might. The dangers involved in anyone but the king gaining possession of Edward IV's eldest daughter must have been only too obvious.

It was not until mid-January 1486 that Henry felt that he no longer had cause to delay his marriage with Elizabeth. Parliament had removed one reason for delay when it formally acknowledged his title to the crown and vested the succession in his heirs by any wife. Parliament had also removed an obstacle concerning Elizabeth's status, to wit, Richard III's act which bastardized the children of Edward IV (Doc. 6). No matter how false the bastardy charge, Richard's act recorded it and gave

[11] BM, Harleian MS. 4627, No. 2. p. 14.
[12] See G. R. Elton, *The Tudor Constitution* (Cambridge 1960), p. 1.
[13] *Rot. Parl.* vi. 278.

it some force in law, and it would not do for Henry to marry and have
children by a woman whose legitimacy could be impugned. Hence Parliament's unusual way of voiding Richard's act: the act repealed was not
rehearsed or summarized as was customary; the record of that act in
Richard's Parliament roll and all copies of it were to be destroyed, 'so
that all things said and remembered' therein 'may be for ever out of
remembrance and also forgot' (Doc. 9). Parliament had done what it
could, but Henry still had one more requirement before he could marry
Elizabeth. A dispensation was needed because Henry and Elizabeth
were both great-great-grandchildren of John of Gaunt.[14] On 16
January the dispensation was granted by a papal legate who had happily
arrived in England with power to grant dispensations for marriage.[15]
Two days later Henry VII married Elizabeth of York.

Two months later Innocent VIII issued a bull confirming Henry's
title and marriage, which was quickly translated in a popular form for
circulation in England (Doc. 10). One would have to be naive to believe
that this bull was, as it said, made by the Pope on his own initiative
'without procurements' of the king. Its terms are indicative of a propaganda piece composed by Innocent at Henry's suggestion. The king's
title is justified on grounds of hereditary right, victory in battle, election,
and parliamentary enactment. It is specificially stated that if Elizabeth
should die without issue, the succession to the crown would go to
Henry's issue by a subsequent wife. The most significant feature of the
bull, however, is its confirmation of Henry's marriage with Elizabeth.
That marriage is pictured as a union of the houses of Lancaster and
York whose 'grievous variances, dissensions and debates' had long
divided England. Here we have the beginning of the Tudor tradition of
the marriage as the final peace settlement of wholly dynastic wars. The
growth of this tradition would not even be impeded when time would
prove that Bosworth was not the last battle of the Wars of the Roses.

By the middle of the fourteenth month of his reign Henry VII may
have felt secure on his throne. 1486 had seen two abortive risings, one
led by Lord Lovel, a close associate of Richard III, and the other by
Thomas and Humphrey Stafford. These were but minor conspiracies
and, as far as we know, no potential rival for Henry's crown was
involved. Henry had reason to feel safe about the Yorkist claimants.
John de la Pole, earl of Lincoln, though Richard's chosen successor, was
apparently loyal to Henry and had entered his service. Warwick, whose
claim Henry had to fear most, was imprisoned in the Tower. And
Elizabeth of York was the king's possession by matrimony. On 20

[14] Henry via his mother; Elizabeth via Edward IV's mother, Cecily Neville,
who was the daughter of Gaunt's daughter, Joan Beaufort, countess of West-
morland.
[15] R. L. Storey, *The Reign of Henry VII* (London, 1968), p. 60.

September 1486 she bore Henry a son, Prince Arthur, whose birth could be said to complete the union of Lancaster and York.

If Henry believed his position to be secure, he was soon to learn differently. Probably in January 1487, Lambert Simnel, the 10-year-old son of an Oxford tradesman, appeared in Ireland. This lad had been induced to pose as Edward of Warwick, who seems to have been presumed to have disappeared. The Irish, whose attachment to the house of York dated from Richard of York's lieutenancy, accepted Simnel's pretension. So apparently did Margaret, dowager duchess of Burgundy, sister of Edward IV, and intransigent enemy of Henry VII. Henry exhibited the real Warwick in London, but this did not deter John of Lincoln, who proceeded to Flanders and aunt Margaret. Lincoln, accompanied by 2,000 German mercenaries provided by Margaret, landed at Dublin on 5 May and assumed the headship of the conspiracy. He had Simnel crowned as Edward VI on 24 May and on 4 June invaded England with the purpose of unseating Henry VII. Lincoln could hardly have intended to replace Henry with Simnel; maybe he planned to enthrone the real Warwick, but more likely his scheme was to dispose of both Warwicks and take the crown for himself – an appropriate John II!

Lincoln's army of Germans, Irish and some English met Henry's numerically superior forces at Stoke on 16 June. The king's victory was not an easy one, but Lincoln was slain and Simnel taken, to assume a proper position as a turnspit in the royal kitchen. Stoke, not Bosworth, actually concluded the Wars of the Roses: never again would a genuine scion of the White Rose do battle on English soil with the crown at stake. Henry VII, however, could not have been too sanguine over the situation. His subjects had answered his call to arms with little enthusiasm. The wings of his army at Stoke had held back from the fray, perhaps to join Lincoln if the tide of battle turned his way. And Lincoln reportedly was killed by royal soldiers to prevent any chance of his revealing to the king the names of his sympathizers. Stoke may well have inspired in Henry VII a feeling of identity with Richard III.[16]

The last serious threat to Henry's crown began in the autumn of 1491 when 17-year-old Perkin Warbeck appeared in Ireland. Warbeck, according to his confession made five years later, was the son of a Flemish burgher. After suggestions that he pose as Edward of Warwick or Richard III's bastard son, both of whom were in Henry VII's custody, were rejected, it was agreed that he should pretend to be Richard, duke of York, the younger son of Edward IV. Warbeck's Irish promoters, who were not men of great consequence, assured him of the backing of the earls of Desmond and Kildare, made him learn English, and taught

[16] On Simnel, Lincoln, and Stoke see Storey, *Henry VII*, pp. 74–6; J. D. Mackie, *The Earlier Tudors* (Oxford 1952), pp. 68–75.

him what to 'do and say'. Then he embarked on his travels which led
him to France, Flanders, Ireland again, Scotland, and finally captivity
in England.[17]

Though Warbeck's confession was made under duress, there is no
reason to doubt its essential accuracy. Today it would take an incurable
romantic to believe that Warbeck was indeed Edward IV's younger
son.[18] At the time, however, even Henry VII could not be sure he was
an impostor. While it may have been commonly assumed that Edward V
and little York had been murdered during Richard III's reign, the fact
that their remains had not been found left some room for doubt.
Warbeck, in a letter to Isabella of Castile, whom he boldly addressed as
'cousin', claimed that he, York, had escaped the fate of his brother
thanks to the pity of 'a certain lord' who had been assigned the job of
killing him.[19] Isabella did not accept Warbeck's claim, but others
believed or pretended to believe his story.

Charles VIII invited Warbeck to France and treated him as a 'duke
of York' until an Anglo-French peace was concluded at Étaples in
November 1492. Warbeck then moved on to Flanders where Margaret
of Burgundy acknowledged him as little York returned from the dead.
More serious, the pretender was accepted by her son-in-law Maximilian,
king of the Romans and in 1493 emperor, and for a time by his son
Philip, duke of Burgundy. Philip's refusal to stop Margaret's activities
in behalf of her 'nephew' caused Henry VII to break off trade relations
with the Netherlands in September 1493, a disruption of England's
principal commerce that lasted for two years. Even more serious,
Warbeck's story reached England where it was 'not merely believed by
the common people, but . . . many important men . . . considered the
matter as genuine'.[20] A conspiracy in Warbeck's behalf was discovered
which reached as high as Sir William Stanley, Henry's lord chamberlain,
who, with several others, was executed in 1495.

By the summer of 1495, when Warbeck, whose presence in Flanders
was no longer desired by Philip of Burgundy, sailed for the British
Isles with a force provided by his host, the situation had changed.
Maximilian still recognized the 'duke of York', but the Emperor's main
interest had been turned southward by Charles VIII's invasion of Italy.
Henry VII's strong measures had quieted Warbeck's English supporters, and the king, with the help of Sir Edward Poynings, had established a limited royal authority in Ireland. On 3 July Warbeck attempted
a landing at Deal in south-eastern England, found formidable opposi-

---

[17] *Chronicles of London*, ed. C. L. Kingsford (Oxford 1905), pp. 219–21.
[18] See Mackie, *Earlier Tudors*, pp. 116–20
[19] *England under the Early Tudors*, ed. C. H. Williams (London 1925), p. 31.
[20] *The Anglica Historia of Polydore Vergil, A.D. 1485–1538*, ed. Denys Hay
(Camden Society, London 1950), p. 67.

tion instead of a hoped-for rising against Henry, abandoned the project, and made for Ireland. There he attracted little support of consequence, notably none from Kildare, the most powerful Anglo-Irish lord. Then he went to Scotland where James IV thought the pretender might be useful in regaining Berwick from England. Scottish invasions of the north of England, in September 1496 and August 1497, came to nil. In September 1497 Warbeck, who had dallied too long to co-ordinate his attack with that of the Scots, landed in Cornwall, attracted a few thousand followers, proclaimed himself Richard IV, got nowhere, and surrendered to Henry VII.[21]

Though Warbeck had caused him troubles, foreign and domestic, for six long years, Henry had stood the test well and was not vengeful. He lodged the confessed impostor comfortably in the royal household; only after an attempted escape in June 1498 was Warbeck's residence changed to the Tower. So far Henry had displayed remarkable leniency towards potential replacements on his throne: it is difficult to see any of his Tudor successors, excepting Elizabeth I who resembled him most of all, allowing one with a claim as strong as Edward of Warwick's to survive in custody for a decade and a half. 1499, however, saw the King temporarily abandon his policy of mercy.

Early in the year one Ralph Wilford made an unsuccessful attempt to impersonate Warwick in eastern England. This lad, who may have been deranged, was quickly brought to London, tried, and, on 12 February, hanged.[22] It is possible that this insignificant 'conspiracy' was the straw that broke Henry's patience and led to the more notable executions of November. Then another 'conspiracy', probably provoked by an agent of the king,[23] was unveiled, implicating Warbeck, who was easy to lure into any plot, and Warwick, who probably was too long out of contact with the real world to know what he was doing. Warbeck, whose crimes against Henry were many, was hanged, and Warwick, whose real crime was his being the last direct male descendant of York, was beheaded.

The judicial murder of Warwick, terrible though it was, helped to secure the Spanish marriage. Since 1488 Henry had been negotiating intermittently with Ferdinand of Aragon and Isabella of Castile for a match between Prince Arthur and the Infanta Catherine. A marriage had been celebrated by proxy six months before Warwick met his fate, but the union would not be regarded by all parties as safely made until late 1501 when Catherine of Aragon arrived in England and an in-person solemnization took place. Sometime after the events of 1499, according

[21] For a fuller account of Warbeck's adventures, 1491–7, see Mackie, *Earlier Tudors*, pp. 116–45.

[22] *The Great Chronicle of London*, ed. A. H. Thomas and I. D. Thornley (London 1938), p. 289.

[23] On this see Mackie, *Earlier Tudors*, pp. 165–6.

to Edward Hall, the view spread that Ferdinand had refused to 'make full conclusion of the matrimony' or send his daughter to England while Warwick remained alive; 'for he imagined that as long as any earl of Warwick lived, that England should never be cleansed or purged of civil war and privy sedition'.[24] Years later, if we may believe Francis Bacon, when Catherine first learned of Henry VIII's intention to obtain a divorce from her, she used words to the effect that 'she had not offended, but it was a judgment of God, for that her former marriage was made in blood; meaning that of the earl of Warwick'.[25] Whether or not Henry VII was actually pressured by Spain, a letter of early 1500 from the Spanish ambassador to his sovereigns indicates the importance of Warwick's demise to Ferdinand and Isabella: thanks to the recent executions, 'not a doubtful drop of royal blood remains in this kingdom except the true blood of the King and Queen and above all that of the lord Prince Arthur' (Doc. 11). Warwick's beheading removed a major obstacle to the completion of the marriage of Arthur and Catherine, a match which did not gain for England a reliable ally but enhanced the prestige of her new dynasty through matrimonial acceptance by an established royal house.

In January 1502 Henry arranged a marriage between his elder daughter Margaret and James IV of Scotland, the final solemnization of which took place in August 1503. This matrimonial alliance did not succeed in providing anything more than a temporary halt to Anglo-Scottish hostilities which were to continue intermittently for the rest of the century, but its end product was to be the accession of a Scot to the English throne in 1603. When the match was being negotiated, if we may believe the 1546 edition of Polydore Vergil's *English History*, the possibility of such an end product alarmed some of Henry's councillors, who feared that it might lead to the absorption of England into Scotland. The king shrewdly foresaw a different outcome: England, as the greater realm, would draw Scotland, the lesser, 'after the manner that Normandy formerly came into the dominion and power of our English ancestors' (Doc. 12). This story first occurs in the 1546 Polydore and may be a mere invention, but the comment attributed to Henry reflects the commonsense position that one would expect him to take on the matter: a position that most Tudor Englishmen, whose prejudices against Scots and Scotland were ingrained, would be unable to accept. As a result of the Scottish marriage, a Britannic question was to be a complicating element in several subsequent Tudor dynastic problems.

By February 1502 Henry VII had reason to be sanguine about the dynastic situation. Prince Arthur was finally married to a daughter of

---

[24] Edward Hall, *Chronicle*, ed. Henry Ellis (London 1809), p. 491.
[25] *Bacon's History of the Reign of King Henry VII*, ed. J. R. Lumby (Cambridge 1902), p. 179.

the great Spanish house. The Scottish marriage was arranged by treaty, its completion only awaiting Margaret's coming of age. Sometime after the executions of 1499, the role of Yorkist rival had been assumed by Edmund de la Pole, earl of Suffolk and brother of the late John of Lincoln. Suffolk was now at the court of Maximilian, who could use him for purposes of diplomacy but do little more. As yet Henry did not have to lose much sleep over Suffolk. The situation, however, was soon to be altered by a tragedy.

On 2 April 1502 Prince Arthur died in his fifteenth year. It has been suggested that this misfortune, albeit a personal disaster to Henry VII, may have been a blessing in disguise for Tudor England in that it prevented the establishment of a cadet branch of the royal family descending from Arthur's brother Henry, duke of York. This might have led to troubles similar to those of the later fifteenth century.[26] Be that as it may, Arthur's death was more than a personal tragedy to the king. His remaining son Henry, soon to be created prince of Wales, was but ten years of age. After young Henry, if he were to meet an untimely end, came his sisters Margaret and Mary, but a queen regnant was unprecedented in England. And if King Henry, who fell ill soon after Arthur's death, did not live long enough for Prince Henry to reach mature years, Edward IV's sons were a terrible but suggestive memory. The precariousness of the situation is indicated by a discussion held by some of Henry VII's trusted servants at Calais about 1503 (Doc. 13). One of them said that they must consider the future, for the king 'is but a weak man and sickly', and unlikely to be long-lived. He recalled that at the time of the king's late illness he had heard many great men speak of the succession in the event that the illness proved fatal. Some spoke of Edward, duke of Buckingham, others spoke of the traitor Suffolk, but none spoke of Prince Henry.

Suffolk, safe in the protection of Maximilian and later Philip of Burgundy, was to be Henry VII's main concern until 1506. Diplomatic efforts to secure custody of Suffolk proved vain, but Henry successfully struck at the pretender's relatives and suspected adherents in May 1502. Lord William de la Pole, Suffolk's brother, and Lord William Courtenay, Suffolk's cousin by marriage, were taken into an imprisonment which would last until after Henry's death. Sir James Tyrrell, captain of Guisnes, and several others were executed as traitors. Suffolk himself finally came into the king's hands as a result of an accident. In January 1506 Philip, on his way to Spain to claim the crown of Castile for himself and his wife Joanna, Isabella's heir, was driven by storm into an English port. During Philip's stay in England he entered into a treaty of alliance with Henry and agreed to surrender Suffolk provided his life be

[26] See Storey, *Henry VII*, pp. 88–9.

spared. In March Suffolk was brought to England and confined in the Tower, which was to be his dwelling until 1513 when Henry VIII disposed of him.[27]

Arthur's death, besides leaving the Tudor future dependent on the life of a boy, left Henry VII without a matrimonial alliance with a significant continental house. During the king's remaining years matrimonial diplomacy would be a major preoccupation. The relative importance of foreign policy and dynastic policy in this diplomacy is impossible to determine. In the sixteenth century it is difficult to separate the two. Experience had certainly taught Henry that alliances of any kind tended to be transitory. Experience also indicated that dynastic rebellions in England usually succeeded or failed in too short a time for a continental ally to be of help, though he might be of use in dealing with a pretender who was manœuvring on the Continent. In any case, a matrimonial alliance was of temporary value diplomatically and did enhance the respectability of a new dynasty both at home and abroad.

Available for the marriage market were Prince Henry, his younger sister Mary, and, after Elizabeth of York's death in February 1503, the king himself. With regard to Henry VII's availability, it has been maintained that he did not seriously intend to remarry; he merely used his marriageability 'as a diplomatic pawn'.[28] This seem improbable. True, Henry did not pursue his marital prospects with great urgency, but that was the way of a normally cautious man. Also true, his suits shifted with shifts in foreign policy, but that was standard practice in the diplomatic game. Henry obviously desired more males in the line of succession and his son and daughters were all too young to be likely to produce them for years; only a remarriage of the king offered the possibility of another male heir within a reasonable period of time. And Henry, who was not prone to having mistresses, may well have wanted a new wife to share his bed. More likely than not, his failure to marry again was due to chance rather than lack of intent.

After the tragedy of April 1502, negotiations began for a match between Arthur's widow Catherine and his brother Henry. Since Ferdinand and Isabella at the time had great need for an English alliance, Henry VII held out to exact the best terms he could. Then the king, after his queen's death, spoke of substituting himself for young Henry as a mate for Catherine. Isabella rejected this idea as 'a very evil thing . . . never before seen. . ., the mere mention of which offends the ears'. She preferred to proceed to the betrothal of her daughter and Prince Henry and offered King Henry her niece Joanna, queen of Naples, as a more suitable wife.[29] On 25 June 1503 Catherine of

---

[27] For a fuller account of Suffolk, see Mackie, *Earlier Tudors*, pp. 167–71.
[28] Storey, *Henry VII*, p. 89.   [29] *Span. Cal.* i. 360.

Aragon and Prince Henry were formally betrothed. The negotiations in connexion with this match, which would not be completed until the next reign, reveal Henry VII's deep concern for a secure succession. A dispensation was required because of the Levitical prohibition of marriage to a brother's widow.[30] The Spaniards insisted that Catherine and Arthur had never consummated their marriage, but Henry would make no marriage treaty until they agreed to admit consummation and ask Rome to include such an admission in the dispensation. Henry clearly wanted this matter covered in the dispensation to preclude a possible challenge to his heir apparent's marriage and its offspring. As Ferdinand put it, 'the right of succession depends on the undoubted legitimacy of the marriage'.[31] When Julius II's dispensation finally arrived in England in March 1505, it described Catherine's first marriage only as 'perhaps consummated',[32] but by then Henry did not care if the word 'perhaps' weakened his intended meaning.

The death of Isabella of Castile in November 1504 had led to a diplomatic volte-face. Ferdinand, who was only king in Aragon, took over the rule of Castile which of right belonged to his daughter Joanna, the wife of Philip of Burgundy. Knowing that this meant conflict with Philip and Maximilian, Ferdinand allied himself with Louis XII of France. Henry's reaction was to seek Philip and Maximilian as allies. He no longer wanted his son to marry Catherine and gave up whatever intention he may have had of marrying young Joanna of Naples. On 27 June 1505, the eve of his fourteenth birthday, Prince Henry was made to make a protestation against his contract with Catherine on the ground that he was not of age when he accepted it two years before.[33] In the course of 1505 Henry VII treated for French marriages for himself, his son Henry, and his daughter Mary, perhaps futile attempts to lure the French king away from Ferdinand; he also treated 'very secretly' to marry Prince Henry to Philip's daughter Eleanor.[34] Henry VII's diplomatic and matchmaking efforts of 1505, which strike one as naive, were deservedly unproductive.

Philip's chance visit to England in early 1506 saw the beginning of what seemed to be more substantial matrimonial prospects for the Tudors. The king concluded a treaty with Philip in which he promised to marry Philip's once unsuccessfully betrothed and twice-widowed sister, Margaret of Savoy. Later in the year Henry and Maximilian began negotiations for a match between Henry's daughter Mary and

[30] Lev. 20: 21. Cf. below, p. 55, n. 35.

[31] Span. Cal. i. 370.

[32] Span. Cal. i. 389.

[33] Span. Cal. i. 435.

[34] Letters and Papers Illustrative of the Reigns of Richard III and Henry VII, ed. James Gairdner (Rolls Series, London 1861–3), i. 247, ii. 146–7.

Philip's son, Archduke Charles, the future Charles V. The Margaret of Savoy marriage, which Henry probably sincerely desired, was frustrated in 1507 by the lady's obstinate refusal to hazard a fourth marital venture—three misfortunes were sacrifice enough for dynastic interests, even for a Habsburg.[35] The marriage of Mary and Charles was arranged by treaty in 1508 and would remain a possibility until 1514 when Henry VIII broke it off on account of Charles's failure to keep his engagement —Europe's greatest matrimonial prize was not for the Tudors.

Meanwhile Philip's death in September 1506 inspired Henry VII's most bizarre matrimonial scheme. Ferdinand was informed that Henry wished to marry Philip's widow, the now mad Joanna. The match, so the English said, would be advantageous to Ferdinand in that Joanna's presence in England would assure him of the regency of Castile. Joanna's insanity was no bar. A husband such as Henry might restore her reason. Anyhow, the English were assured by the Spanish ambassador that her mental condition would not prevent her from having children.[36] It has been said that Henry's real purpose in seeking the match was to gain for himself the government of Castile.[37] If he seriously thought that he could take Castile from Ferdinand, however, he was crazier than his intended bride. Henry's proposed union with Joanna, like his other matrimonial projects following Isabella's death, came to nil. When his end came on 21 April 1509, as a result of chance, some inept diplomacy, and perhaps too high aims, he left his successor with little choice but to pursue a renewed proposal for the hand of Philip's daughter Eleanor or to revert to the betrothal of 1503. Indeed, if we may believe Henry VIII, his father's dying wish was that he complete the contract with Catherine of Aragon,[38] perhaps a better than deserved conclusion to some rather tortuous diplomacy.

Even in his last days Henry VII probably still feared for his own safety and that of his line. As late as October 1507, he had Thomas Grey, second marquis of Dorset, and Lord William Courtenay, both of kin to Elizabeth of York, transferred from the Tower to confinement at Calais and allegedly would have had them 'put to death if he had lived longer'.[39] The allegation seems unlikely. Surely Dorset and Courtenay were not so dangerous as to cause the King to return to the policy of 1499 and abandon his normal disinclination to execute potential Yorkist rivals or their relatives. It was his successor, whose position was far more secure,

[35] See *Span. Cal.* i. 560.

[36] *Span. Cal.* i. 511.

[37] See H. A. L. Fisher, *The Political History of England*, vol. v, *1485–1547* (London 1913), p. 121.

[38] *L.P.* i. 84.

[39] *The Chronicle of Calais in the Reigns of Henry VII and Henry VIII to the Year 1540*, ed. J. G. Nichols (Camden Society, London 1846), p. 6.

who did away with Yorkists on the slightest excuse. Actually Henry VII, despite the failures of his matrimonial diplomacy, was more successful than he may have realized. He weathered every storm. He made the name Tudor respected if not loved at home and abroad. He gave England sound government, law and order, and a measure of economic well-being, the best props for any royal house. He managed to live long enough to spare his subjects the perils of a minority and he left them a successor whose claim to the crown was much better than his own. In short, Henry VII securely established the Tudor dynasty.

3

The Reign of Henry VIII

'The Rose both White and Red in one Rose now doth grow,' wrote John Skelton in a poem praising his new king.[1] Henry VIII was the 'indubitate flower and very heir' of both Lancaster and York, said the title page of Hall's *Chronicle* when it appeared in 1548, the year following the second Tudor's death. These statements, which reflect the contemporary view of Henry VIII's title, are substantially correct. If the Lancastrian title of the Tudors left something to be desired, Henry VII's twenty-four years on the throne had given it some degree of prescription. Moreover, Henry VIII could, if necessary, invoke a more impressive Yorkist title. Through his mother he was Edward IV's grandson and indeed the senior male descendant of Edward III. Not since Richard II had England known a king with a better title. For this reason and thanks to his nearly eighteen years, which made a minority unnecessary, Henry VIII's accession was both popular and untroubled.

On 11 June 1509, less than seven weeks after his accession and a month after his father's funeral, Henry VIII solemnized his marriage with Catherine of Aragon. Maybe the king rushed into this union because Catherine was on hand and of an age at which she might be expected to produce an heir quickly. Obedience to his father's dying wish served as an excuse to the Habsburgs for rejecting their young Eleanor, who would not be marriageable for three or four years. Henry VIII did not want to lose the contracted marriage between his sister Mary and the Habsburg Charles. He no doubt hoped to be instrumental in having the match approved by his new father-in-law Ferdinand, who, like Maximilian, was a grandfather of Charles. It is possible that the rash young king thought in terms of a matrimonial diplomacy far more ambitious than his father's: a matrimonial diplomacy aimed at bringing about an alliance of Ferdinand, Maximilian and himself against Louis

---

[1] *The Poetical Works of John Skelton*, ed. Alexander Dyce (Boston 1864), ii. 340.

XII, not for purposes of England's security but to 'recover' for her king his realm of France.

When such an alliance did come four years later, Henry VIII was not its maker but its dupe. It was part of Julius II's Holy League, the ostensible purpose of which was to punish Louis XII for summoning the schismatic Council of Pisa. In the ensuing hostilities the Pope got the French out of Italy, Ferdinand won Navarre and defected, and Maximilian contributed next to nothing and defected. Henry was left with the glory of a dramatic but useless victory in the so-called Battle of the Spurs and a bitter but valuable lesson in the ways of Renaissance diplomacy. More relevant to this study, however, are the English dynastic aspects and consequences of Henry's brief and futile renewal of the Hundred Years' War.

In the spring of 1513 the king used his coming departure for France as an excuse to dispatch Edmund de la Pole, earl of Suffolk. Even after Philip of Burgundy's death Henry VII had kept his promise to spare Suffolk's life, but Henry VIII did not feel bound by his father's promise. He alleged that Suffolk had engaged in treasonable correspondence with his brother Richard, who had taken up arms with France against England,[2] and had him quietly executed without trial. The deed was, however, legal, for Suffolk's old attainder under Henry VII had never been rescinded. As would be Henry VIII's practice in all of his dynastic murders, Suffolk's was a lawful murder. At any rate, the de la Pole 'menace' in England was done with.[3]

While Henry was campaigning in France, England, left in the charge of Catherine, was invaded by his brother-in-law of Scotland. The result was a great English victory on 9 September 1513 at Flodden where James IV perished. Henry's sister Margaret became regent for the child James V, relieving Henry for a time of worry about his northern neighbour. Henry had reason to be pleased with Catherine for her role in achieving this one real success of 1513, yet in the summer of 1514 it was reported on the Continent that the king meant to repudiate his queen 'because he is unable to have children by her' and intended to take a French wife.[4] Henry VIII's so-called divorce project of 1514 doubtless was mere rumour: Catherine was pregnant at the time,[5] and it is incredible that a Tudor king would contemplate a divorce when an heir was in the offing. Nevertheless, the rumour was symptomatic of the

[2] *L.P.* i. 4324.

[3] Richard de la Pole took his brother's place as Yorkist pretender. Francis I once promised to make de la Pole king of England (*L.P.* ii. 1973), but the pretender never reached his native land. He died fighting for Francis at Pavia in 1525.

[4] *Ven. Cal.* ii. 479.

[5] See *L.P.* i. 5718.

diplomatic turnabout that Henry, now influenced by Thomas Wolsey, was in the process of making.

Henry VIII had not only been doublecrossed by Ferdinand and Maximilian in the French war; they had also prevented the union of his sister Mary and their grandson Charles from being completed in May 1514, as provided in the original compact.[6] In August Henry, certainly with abundant justification, betrayed his 'allies' and concluded a French alliance to be cemented by a match between Mary and Louis XII. The marriage took place on 9 October. Ordinarily this might be considered a brilliant achievement of matrimonial diplomacy: no other Tudor princess ever married so highly. The defect was that Louis, nearly three times Mary's age, was not long for this world. Mary actually was the 'French Queen', the title by which she would continue to be known, for only eleven weeks. Shortly after Louis's death on 1 January 1515, Mary, ignoring her dynastic duty, married her true love, Charles Brandon, duke of Suffolk, whom Henry had sent to France to bring her home. The king, for an exaction of money, forgave his favourite sister and his close friend and accepted their marriage, but it left him for the time being without a significant relative available for use in matrimonial diplomacy.

On 18 February 1516 Catherine of Aragon gave birth to a daughter, named Mary after her aunt. Henry would have preferred a boy, but that his queen had at last produced a child likely to survive made him confident that 'the sons will follow'.[7] Meanwhile little Mary, in that age of child matches, provided a needed diplomatic asset. In October 1518, Henry, in one of his reversions to alliance with France, made a compact with Francis I whereby Mary, aged two, was betrothed to the 7-month-old Dauphin. In the next month Catherine was delivered of a stillborn child. Henry did not know that this was to be her last pregnancy, but the situation was not conducive to continued sanguineness. Though the king regarded his daughter as his heir presumptive, England almost certainly would reject a little girl as his successor. His death by natural or other cause would present an obvious opportunity for someone else to seize the crown. Such a thought may explain Henry VIII's apparent panic in the beginning 1520s.

Probably in 1520 or early 1521 Henry, though writing was 'somewhat tedious and painful' to him, deemed it necessary to write a secret and mysterious letter to Wolsey, who had been made cardinal and Lord Chancellor in 1515. He wanted Wolsey to 'make good watch on' Charles Brandon, duke of Suffolk, Edward Stafford, duke of Buckingham, Henry Algernon Percy, earl of Northumberland, Thomas Stanley,

[6] J. S. Brewer, *The Reign of Henry VIII from His Accession to the Death of Wolsey*, ed. James Gairdner (London 1884), i. p. 37.

[7] *Ven. Cal.* ii. 691.

second earl of Derby, Henry Stafford, earl of Wiltshire, and 'others which you think suspect to see what they do with this news'.[8] We do not know what 'this news' was, but, considering the action that the king was to take in May 1521, it seems likely that he suspected some conspiracy in relation to the crown. It is a bit difficult to imagine any other reason than that Henry was in a state of panic, perhaps stirred up by Wolsey, for Suffolk's being named at all, to say nothing of his being named first. Suffolk, his dukedom notwithstanding, was as much a creature of the Tudors as Wolsey. Unthinking loyalty to Henry VIII was and would be his trademark.[9] Surely even Suffolk was not so foolish as to think that he could use his marriage to the king's sister as a route to royal power. The one man of real potential danger named by Henry was Edward of Buckingham.

Through his father Buckingham descended from two sons of Edward III.[10] He had been mentioned as a possible successor to Henry VII in 1502 (Doc. 13). In 1519 the Venetian ambassador thought that he 'might easily obtain the crown' if Henry VIII died 'without male heirs'.[11] Moreover, Buckingham was a great magnate of the fifteenth-century cast with vast lands, fortified castles, and hundreds of armed retainers.[12] He had made a network of marriage alliances with great families much in the manner of the fifteenth-century Nevilles. He himself married a Percy; he matched his son with Ursula Pole, grand-daughter of George, duke of Clarence; he married his eldest daughter to Thomas Howard, earl of Surrey and later third duke of Norfolk, and his two younger daughters to Nevilles. Furthermore, of the three named after Buckingham in Henry's letter, Northumberland was his father-in-law, Wiltshire was his brother,[13] and Derby was a fellow west-country magnate.

Whether moved by unfounded fear, a genuine conspiracy, or the machinations of Wolsey,[14] Henry VIII decided to strike at Buckingham. In April 1521, Buckingham was unexpectedly summoned to London and arrested; in May he was attainted and beheaded. The case against Buckingham rested on the testimony of his servants. He was heard to

---

[8] J. J. Scarisbrick, *Henry VIII* (London 1968), p. 120.

[9] His marriage to Mary may have been a momentary lapse but then he was the victim of an insistent woman.

[10] John of Gaunt and Thomas of Woodstock.

[11] A. F. Pollard, *Henry VIII* (London 1905), p. 146.

[12] See Lawrence Stone, *The Crisis of the Aristocracy, 1558–1641* (Oxford 1965), pp. 201, 217; A. F. Pollard, *Wolsey* (London 1929), pp. 71, 322.

[13] Not his son, as Scarisbrick, *Henry VIII*, p. 559, would have it. Cf. *The Complete Peerage* (London 1910–59), xii. Pt ii. 738.

[14] Cf. Pollard, *Henry VIII*, p. 146; Brewer, *Reign of Henry VIII*, i. pp. 379–384. While Wolsey doubtless was hostile to Buckingham, the king probably was the chief mover in his destruction.

say that he had a record of the parliamentary confirmation of Richard II's patent legitimating the Beauforts, no longer a matter of great import to the Tudors. Buckingham was said to have corresponded with a monk who prophesied that 'he should have all' and that Henry would have no male issue. Buckingham was heard to say that the king's lack of sons was God's punishment for his father's execution of Warwick and that he would await a 'convenient time' to act against Henry. And he was heard to say that, if committed to the Tower, he would stab the king.[15] The testimony, if true, may indicate little more than that Buckingham was careless in correspondence and conversation, but to Henry and the peers who sat in judgment it was enough to establish treason. Buckingham evidently was not given the opportunity to confront and cross-examine his accusers or to present evidence in his own defence,[16] which was not unusual. Even if he was innocent, however, Buckingham's execution served more purpose than merely satisfying the king. It rid England of her last authentic overmighty subject and the man best qualified to play the role of Richard III if Henry died in the 1520s.

Nevertheless, England's main dynastic problem remained: her king's heir presumptive was a little girl. It has been argued that Henry VIII's foreign policy from 1521 to 1525, which involved England in war with France, was dominated by his desire to provide for a peaceable succession by marrying his daughter Mary to his sister Mary's former fiancé, the Habsburg Charles, now King of Spain and Emperor Charles V.[17] Underlying this argument is the unverified assumption that by 1521 Henry had despaired of a son by Catherine.[18] Then he supposedly concluded that the best solution was to marry his daughter to a prince powerful enough to assure her a peaceful succession. In 1518, when Henry still hoped for a son by Catherine, he had pledged Mary to the Dauphin, but now such a match was undesirable because the English would not take to the possibility of a Frenchman as king. Hence the arrangements of August 1521 to June 1522, whereby Charles V promised to marry Mary when she came of age and to help Wolsey become pope,[19]

---

[15] Brewer, *Reign of Henry VIII*, i. pp. 389–92.   [16] Ibid. i. p. 392.

[17] R. B. Wernham, *Before the Armada: the Growth of English Foreign Policy, 1485–1558* (London 1966), pp. 98–110.

[18] The assumption would be more likely in 1525 when Catherine was in her fortieth year and Henry's ambassadors dared to let him know that they had told Charles that she was 'past that age in which women most commonly are wont to be fruitful and have children'. (*L.P.* iv. 1484.) Buckingham's case indicates that such words would have been dangerous in 1521.

[19] Pollard's view that Henry's decision for war with France was determined by Wolsey's desire to make England's policy conform with Rome's and his ambition to become pope doubtless overestimates Wolsey's influence and ambition. Cf. Pollard, *Wolsey*, pp. 124–7, 161–4; Scarisbrick, *Henry VIII*, pp. 46–8, 107–10; Wernham, *Before the Armada*, p. 98. The war policy certainly smacks of Henry's initiative rather than Wolsey's.

and Henry agreed to an Anglo-Imperial invasion of France.[20] Charles was the ideal consort for Mary: he was the greatest prince in Christendom; as the representative of England's traditional allies and as the ruler of the Netherlands, England's best market, he would be acceptable in England.[21] A French war was a small price to pay for such future security.

The course of events from 1521 to 1525, however, suggests that Henry's main concern was not to marry Mary to Charles but to 'recover' his realm of France or at least part of it. In September 1522 the king boasted to Sir Thomas More that he 'trusted in God' to be 'governor' of France soon and that Francis I would 'make a way for him as King Richard did for his father',[22] that is, that he expected another Bosworth in France. Henry sent armies to France in 1522 and 1523, but they achieved nothing more than to exhaust the royal treasury. The English received some help from Charles, duke of Bourbon, who had his own inheritance in France to recover, but Charles V concentrated his efforts on pursuing Imperial interests in Italy. Besides, when the papal throne became vacant in 1523 Charles gave Wolsey only feigned support and secured the election of his own nominee as Clement VII.[23] Henry should have remembered that Charles was Ferdinand of Aragon's grandson. In 1524, though Bourbon promised to 'spend his blood' to put the French crown upon Henry's head, the disillusioned king decided that he would not fight until he saw an easy opportunity to 'attain the said crown or some great part of his inheritance'.[24] In fact, he began secret peace talks with France.

In 1524 Henry VIII not only sought to extricate himself from the war with France; he also engaged in probably serious negotiations with the Scots for a match between Mary, who was still betrothed to Charles V, and the 12-year-old James V. Early in August Wolsey informed Queen Margaret that, if the Scots 'proceed directly lovingly and nobly' with Henry, 'it may fortune that such a marriage may be found for' James 'as never king of Scots had the like'.[25] On 31 August Margaret sent word to Henry that the Scots desired a union between James and Mary; for the marriage they expected that James be declared 'second person' of England, that he be assigned lands appropriate to an English prince, and that he be recompensed with Berwick and the lands in dispute between England and Scotland if Henry had a son.[26] On 2 November Wolsey sent

[20] *L.P.* iii. 1508, 1802, 1876, 1884, 2333.
[21] His son Philip, who had most of his qualifications, was not to prove too acceptable to the English.
[22] *St. P.* i. 111.
[23] See Pollard, *Wolsey*, p. 127.
[24] Scarisbrick, *Henry VIII*, pp. 132–3.
[25] *St. P.* iv. 94; *L.P.* iv. 551.
[26] *St. P.* iv. 113–14; *L.P.* iv. 600.

secret word to Margaret that Henry would 'find the means' to break Mary's engagement with Charles 'in brief time' and then would 'conclude the marriage' between his daughter and 'his dearest nephew, the young King of Scots . . .'.[27]

Now James was not a good replacement for Charles if the objective of Mary's marriage was to assure her a peaceful succession: a king of Scots, even if of mature years, was not a powerful prince, and a Scot, even with an English mother, would hardly be much more acceptable in England than a Frenchman. If Henry gave any thought to a safe succession for Mary, it would have to be in terms of his living long enough for James to mature and anglicize. Henry's main consideration, however, must have been the diplomatic situation in 1524: he saw no prospect of getting anything in France through alliance with Charles, but the Scottish match, thanks to a decline of the pro-French party in Scotland in the second half of the year, offered him an opportunity to tie Scotland to England. This was a sensible objective, but early in 1525 Henry was diverted from it by surprising news from Italy.

On 14 February Imperial forces inflicted an overwhelming defeat on the French at Pavia and captured their king. Pavia gave the 'deserter' Henry VIII no claim to credit or reward, but in March he sent Cuthbert Tunstal, then bishop of London, and Sir Richard Wingfield to Charles V to present a grandiose design (Doc. 14), which, if nothing else, reveals the priorities in Henry's foreign policy. Pavia, Henry argued, created a unique situation which he and Charles should take advantage of. With Francis I a prisoner, his army defeated, and his realm disorganized, it should be easy to deprive the Valois line of the French crown and to prevent any Frenchman from having it. Therefore, Henry and Charles should invade France. When they both reached Paris, Henry should receive the French crown which belonged to him 'by just title of inheritance'. Then he would, if required, hand over Mary to Charles without any guarantee 'how she should be entreated and ordered touching her marriage' when she came of age. The implication seems clear: Henry would surrender his heir presumptive without any firm commitment from Charles to marry her. But marrying her would offer him an 'irresistible' possibility. If Mary succeeded Henry, the crowns of England, France, and Ireland plus suzerainty over Scotland would be added to what Charles already had by inheritance and election: 'the whole monarchy of Christendom' would be his.

Henry did not intend to be greedy. Charles and Bourbon could have appropriate shares of Francis I's kingdom. Henry would even take less than the remainder and without the crown, thus leaving Francis as king of a reduced France. If necessary Henry would be satisfied with Nor-

[27] St. P. iv. 200; L.P. iv. 767.

mandy or Picardy plus a few towns. He apparently was desperate to gain at least one major holding of his ancestors. But he expected to get more, for the more he got the lower Francis would be and the larger Charles's possibilities through his marriage with Mary. And Mary's delivery to Charles before she came of age required a joint invasion of France and the French crown for Henry. Obviously Henry primarily regarded his daughter as bait for the satisfaction of his French ambitions, which meant less than little to England; if he gave any thought to ensuring Mary a peaceable succession, which would have meant a great deal to England, that was only a secondary consideration.

Tunstal and Wingfield did not find Charles receptive to the grandiose design. He doubtless realized that conquering even a headless France was a far greater undertaking than defeating a French army in Italy. He put forward terms for a joint invasion that were financially impossible to Henry and offered next to nothing if Henry decided to invade without him. The ambassadors concluded that Charles intended 'little or nothing' to Henry's 'commodity, profit, or benefit'. In reality, Henry's proposals, even if feasible, were of little attraction to Charles. Only for Henry was there much present commodity to be gained; Charles mainly had future possibilities through marrying Mary, and these might not materialize. In fact, Charles wanted to break his pledge to the 9-year-old Mary. His Spanish subjects were anxious that he marry to provide for the succession. They preferred that he marry the 22-year-old Isabella of Portugal: a match that might produce an heir quickly and would unite conflicting claims to the crown of Castile. Experience had taught Charles that it was more important to please Spain than to pursue chimeras with Henry. He made the unreasonable demand that Mary be sent to Spain immediately with her dowry; otherwise he asked to be released from his contract. The ambassadors advised Henry to give Charles his release lest he consider a French marriage. In early 1526 Charles secretly married Isabella of Portugal.[28]

In 1525 Henry VIII was frustrated not only by Charles V but by his own subjects. Henry most probably intended to invade France even without Charles. The invasion was to be financed by a so-called Amicable Grant which would amount to a sixth of lay and a third of clerical income. When commissions went out late in March to demand money from a nation that had already paid heavily for the expeditions of 1522 and 1523, the commissioners met with alarming resistance. Archbishop Warham reported from Kent that the people opposed the French war, regretted Francis I's captivity, and compared their king unfavourably with his predecessor.[29] The dukes of Norfolk and Suffolk found insurrection in Suffolk and Essex and suggested that Henry look

[28] *St. P.* i. 160, vi. 526; *L.P.* iv. 1378, Pollard, *Henry VIII*, pp. 133–4.
[29] *L.P.* iv. 1243.

to Lords Stafford and Abergavenny, Buckingham's son and son-in-law.[30] The implication was ominous: if the second Tudor continued to squeeze his subjects, they might remember that Plantagenet blood flowed in the veins of the Staffords. Henry prudently decided to abandon the Amicable Grant and with it any hope of invading France in 1525.

It is not inconceivable that the king's bitterness over the defeat of his French ambitions inspired his elevation in June of his illegitimate son, Henry Fitzroy, to the dukedoms of Richmond and Somerset. Richmond, Henry VII's pre-Bosworth title, and Somerset, the title of Henry VIII's short-lived brother Edmund, could imply an intended successor. Henry VIII was not beyond venting his anger with the distant Charles V through a creation that would have to hurt his aunt Catherine and his cousin Mary. At any rate, if Henry really thought of turning the succession to a bastard, he gave up the idea in due season. In the second half of 1526 Henry treated for a match between Mary and Francis I and promised to make his daughter his heir if he had no sons subsequently.[31] Francis could hardly have been more acceptable to the English than the Dauphin, but by this time Henry probably intended to divorce his wife and anticipated sons by another wife.

In early 1527 it came into the open that Henry VIII was contemplating the termination of his marriage with Catherine of Aragon by divorce.[32] In November 1528, due to public reaction over the coming of Cardinal Campeggio to try the case with Wolsey, the king found it expedient to explain his predicament to a group of notables (Doc. 16). He expressed his concern about the succession, reminding his audience of the Wars of the Roses. He claimed that when his embassy was last in France to negotiate a match between his daughter and the duke of Orleans, Francis I's second son, Mary's legitimacy had been questioned because 'he begat her on his brother's wife, which is directly against God's law and his precept'. These words troubled Henry's conscience. He had sent for Campeggio 'as a man indifferent only to know the truth and to settle my conscience . . . '. He would be happy if his marriage were adjudged valid according to God's law, for no wife could be comparable to Catherine. But if the marriage was adjudged void, he would have to depart from her to save his soul.

Shortly after Henry spoke his piece Campeggio and Wolsey went to Catherine (Doc. 16). She naturally wondered why after almost twenty years without any question being raised Henry's conscience should now be troubled about their marriage. She laid the blame on Wolsey: it was

[30] L.P. iv. 1319.
[31] L.P. iv. 2481, 2606, 2651, 2705, 2707, 2726.
[32] Though pedants like to point out that what Henry sought was an annulment, not a divorce, I shall follow contemporaries and tradition and call the matter a divorce.

his means of getting back at her for opposing him, and especially of taking vengeance on her nephew, Charles V, for failing to make him pope. Catherine was not alone in regarding Wolsey as the instigator of the divorce. Francis I spoke of Wolsey as its inventor,[33] and William Tyndale and Polydore Vergil wrote that Wolsey used John Longland, bishop of Lincoln and royal confessor, to plant in Henry's mind doubt about his marriage.[34]

In 1536, the year he was made cardinal, Reginald Pole, from his safe abode in Italy, expressed in writing what must have been from the beginning the popular explanation of the divorce (Doc. 18). Pole accused Henry of having been enslaved by his passion for Anne Boleyn. She, having learned from the experience of her sister Mary, Henry's former mistress, would not yield except at the price of matrimony. So the king, who was not 'ignorant of the law which certainly no less prohibits marriage' with a concubine's sister than with a brother's widow,[35] rejected Catherine simply to satisfy his lust for Anne.

Of the several contemporary explanations of the divorce, the claim that Henry's doubt about his marriage was inspired by French questioning of his daughter's legitimacy may safely be discarded. The story first appears in a letter of Wolsey of July 1527 which says that the question was raised by the bishop of Tarbes during an embassy from France in the spring of that year in connexion with a proposed match between Mary and Francis I.[36] When Henry told the story to the notables in November 1528, Tarbes was not named, the locale was France, and the prospective husband was the duke of Orleans. Then in 1529 Henry told the legatine court at Blackfriars that his conscience had first been pricked by words spoken about the Orleans match by Tarbes when he came to England as Francis's ambassador in 1527.[37] The discrepant versions of the story make it suspect; so does Wolsey's letter of Decem-

---

[33] Philip Hughes, *The Reformation in England*, rev. edn (New York 1963), i. p. 157.

[34] William Tyndale, *Expositions and Notes on Sundry Portions of the Holy Scriptures together with the Practice of Prelates*, ed. Henry Walter (Parker Society, Cambridge 1849), p. 319; *The Anglica Historia of Polydore Vergil, A.D. 1485–1538*, ed. Denys Hay (Camden Society, London 1950), p. 324.

[35] Henry's awareness of the impediment is shown by his request for a dispensation to marry one related to him in the first degree of affinity (see Hughes, *Reformation*, i. pp. 163–4). The law involved was canon law; Scripture says nothing about marrying a mistress's sister. Henry's case also probably rests on canon law rather than Scripture. Lev. 20: 21 appears only to refer to intercourse with the wife of a living brother, but canon law interpreted it as forbidding marriage with a brother's widow, which was commanded by Deut. 25: 5 if she was childless.

[36] *St. P.* i. 199–200.

[37] George Cavendish, *The Life and Death of Cardinal Wolsey*, ed. R. S. Sylvester (Early English Text Society, London 1959), p. 83.

ber 1527 to Sir Gregory Casale, Henry's agent at Rome, which said that
the scruple derived from the king's own study of scripture.[38] Moreover,
letters to Paris from Turenne, a member of the spring 1527 French
embassy, indicate that the French were eager for a marriage between
Mary and Francis,[39] which would make their questioning of Mary's
legitimacy more than strange.

The charge that Wolsey initiated the divorce should also be rejected.
In 1527 Wolsey was pursuing an anti-Imperial foreign policy based on
a French alliance. The customary way of cementing such an alliance
would have been by contracting Mary to Francis or Orleans, not by
instigating a divorce that would make her legitimacy questionable.[40] At
Blackfriars Wolsey asked Henry to declare whether he had been the
'chief inventor or first mover' of the matter. Henry not only absolved
Wolsey but added: 'Marry indeed, ye have been rather against me in
attempting or setting forth thereof.' [41] The unsolicited addition, which
was hardly to Wolsey's advantage, gives the king's response a sound of
truth. Moreover, according to a Marian account, Longland, Wolsey's
alleged agent, then said that Henry broached 'the matter to him first,
and never left urging of him until he had won him to give his consent . . .'.[42] Henry VIII was certainly capable of deciding to be rid of a
wife without the initiative of Wolsey or anyone else, and it is more than
difficult to believe that he had not learned of the Levitical objection to
his marriage long before 1527; lacking substantial evidence to the contrary, the obvious presumption is that the divorce originated with the
king himself.

The real problem is that of Henry's motivation for the divorce. Was
he primarily concerned with relieving his conscience, satisfying his
passion for Anne Boleyn, or securing the succession? L. B. Smith has
recently argued for the primacy of conscience. He indicates that but for
conscience the king had easier ways than the divorce for achieving his
ends. He could have obtained Anne and the prospect of a son to succeed
him either by having Catherine 'quietly murdered' or by accepting a
papal dispensation to commit bigamy. He might have secured the
succession and achieved the 'creation of Great Britain' by marrying
Mary to James V. It was Henry's 'real and excessively tender' con-

---

[38] *L.P.* iv. 3641.

[39] L.P. iv. app. 104–5.

[40] Vergil, *Anglica Historia*, ed. Hay, p. 327, suggests that Wolsey planned to
cement the alliance via a French marriage for Henry after the divorce. This
requires the doubtful assumption that Wolsey was sure of Henry's matrimonial
plans and of a swift divorce

[41] Cavendish, *Cardinal Wolsey*, pp. 82–3.

[42] Nicholas Harpsfield, *The Life and Death of Sir Thomas Moore, Knight*, ed.
E. V. Hitchcock and R. W. Chambers (Early English Text Society, London
1932), p. 41.

science, based on religious conviction and belief in a king's special accountability to God, which compelled him to atone for the sin of marrying his brother's widow by divorcing her.[43]

Smith's negative arguments for conscience will not do. Murder was against Henry's conscience unless it was done by judicial means, an impossibility in Catherine's case. As for bigamy, the cold fact is that in 1527 and 1528 the king sent agents to Rome with instructions to ask for a dispensation to have two wives, the children of both being legitimate.[44] The argument that Henry might have secured the succession through Mary's marriage fits the case for passion at least as well as it does the case for conscience. Nevertheless, Henry's conviction of conscience that his marriage was sinful was genuine. This was a matter about which he was impervious to any argument throughout the long divorce crisis; indeed, it was his conscience that fortified him to endure that crisis. That it took nearly twenty years for his scruple to appear does not gainsay the reality of his conscience. Nor does his knowledge that his intended marriage to his mistress's sister was as much against canon law as his marriage to his brother's widow. Nor does the likelihood that he later divorced Anne Boleyn on the very ground of the impediment created by his relationship with her sister.[45] That Henry's conscience conveniently adjusted itself to fit his purposes does not deny its reality; it does indicate that conscience was not the origin of the divorce.

Most historians are reluctant to attribute something so momentous as the divorce to a carnal love that did not long outlive its satisfaction. Yet in a matter where the decision to proceed had to come from a self-centred and short-sighted man the force of a basic human urge should not be discounted. Henry VIII's infatuation for Anne Boleyn probably began about early 1526.[46] His passion for her is testified to by seventeen extant love letters, one of which is reproduced below (Doc. 15).[47] That these are all holograph letters is unique evidence of the devotion of a monarch who loathed the task of writing.[48] Their often pathetic and sometimes servile sound reveals a mature sovereign blindly in love with a girl who first left her teens in 1527. Notwithstanding his public

[43] L. B. Smith, 'A Matter of Conscience', in *Action and Conviction in Early Modern Europe*, ed. T. K. Rabb and J. E. Seigel (Princeton 1969), pp. 32–51.

[44] *St. P.* vii. 3; *L.P.* iv. 4977, 4979.

[45] See below, p. 66.

[46] Henry, in one of his earliest letters to Anne, wrote of 'having been now above one whole year struck with the dart of love' (*The Letters of King Henry VIII*, ed. M. St C. Byrne (London 1936), p. 57). The letter probably belongs to the summer of 1527. See ibid. pp. 53, 431.

[47] All of the letters are in Byrne, *Letters of Henry VIII*, pp. 54–85.

[48] See G. R. Elton, *The Tudor Revolution in Government* (Cambridge 1953), p. 68.

protests of preference for Catherine,[49] Anne was, so Henry wrote, 'that she which of all the world I most do esteem'.[50]

Most historians, following A. F. Pollard, while not ignoring conscience or passion, tend to stress Henry's concern over the succession in explaining the divorce.[51] Undoubtedly the king was concerned about the Tudor future depending on a female who only reached her eleventh year in 1527: the succession, like conscience, was not a mere excuse to justify the divorce. But the succession might have been secured without the divorce. The situation in 1527 was quite favourable for arranging a match between Mary and James V.[52] Though most Englishmen would not have been enthusiastic about a union with a Scot, James's being half-Tudor and his youth would have made it worth while for Henry to gamble on living long enough for England to get used to the idea. Or Henry might have secured the succession peculiarly in his own blood by marrying Mary to his bastard son Richmond. A marriage between brother and sister was manifest incest, but Campeggio thought of it as a means of establishing the succession, and Clement VII indicated that he would grant a dispensation for it if Henry would abandon the divorce.[53]

But the king apparently preferred to be succeeded by a legitimate son of his own, and that was only possible via a new wife. Tyndale from abroad asked a pointed question: 'Who hath promised him a prince?' [54] It is difficult to believe that Henry had so deluded himself as to be sure that a new marriage would produce a son. Moreover, if Henry insisted on replacing Catherine, Anne was not a prudent choice. Wolsey, before he learned of the king's real intention in August 1528, evidently had hoped that the divorce would be followed by Henry's marriage to Renée, the daughter of Louis XII.[55] A French princess would have been less objectionable in England as a replacement for a Spanish princess than a 'fetching nobody'.[56] The prospect of such a match doubtless would have assured Henry of Francis I's unqualified support at Rome and against any action that Charles V might take in behalf of his aunt. Henry, however, was no more interested in marrying a French princess than he was in securing the succession without the divorce through Mary's marriage; his passion for Anne determined his 'solution' to his great dynastic problem. Indeed, it may not be amiss to conclude that

[49] Doc. 16 and Cavendish, *Cardinal Wolsey*, p. 83.

[50] Byrne, *Letters of Henry VIII*, p. 56.

[51] See Pollard, *Henry VIII*, pp. 143–50.

[52] See Garrett Mattingly, *Catherine of Aragon* (London 1950), p. 180.

[53] *L.P.* iv. 4881, 5027.

[54] Tyndale, *Expositions*, p. 333.

[55] See *L.P.* iv. 4649.

[56] Hughes, *Reformation*, i. p. 164. Anne may have been 'fetching'; as a granddaughter of a Howard duke of Norfolk and of a daughter of a Butler earl of Ormond, she was not exactly a 'nobody'.

Anne Boleyn was the agent that caused Henry VIII to discover his scruple of conscience, aroused his concern over the succession, and set in motion far-reaching changes that he never intended.

There is no need to attempt to trace in detail Henry's futile efforts to obtain the divorce through Rome. Wolsey initially proposed a case that would have been practically undeniable in canon law,[57] but Henry insisted on basing his suit on the unsure ground of Leviticus, which involved sticky matters such as the question of whether Catherine and Arthur consummated their marriage and Clement VII's reluctance to rule that Julius II had erred in granting his dispensation allowing Henry to marry Catherine. Nevertheless, Henry had a better case than was normally required for a ruler or magnate to gain a divorce.[58] What made his case different, probably impossible, was that Clement dared not give Henry his way while Rome was in the military control of Charles V, who, as Catherine's nephew, was a more than interested party.[59]

Henry's real hope of achieving success via the Pope came in early 1528 when the French invaded Italy, freed Rome, and bottled up the Imperialists in Naples. On 8 June Clement issued a secret decretal commission authorizing Campeggio and Wolsey to hear and decide the divorce case in England. Henry had reason to be sanguine about a judgment to be given by an English cardinal and an Italian cardinal who was also bishop of Salisbury. Campeggio, however, did not reach England until October. By then the Imperialists had driven the French back to northern Italy and Clement had instructed Campeggio to procrastinate.[60] Catherine came to Campeggio's aid by conveniently producing a copy of the so-called Spanish brief, a second dispensation of Julius II, which, if genuine, practically destroyed Henry's case based on the bull of dispensation.[61] This caused Henry to waste months trying to get hold of the original brief which Charles would not let out of Spain, or to get Clement to declare it a forgery.[62] Then the English, fearing that the case would be revoked to Rome, opened the legatine court at Blackfriars on 31 March 1529. Blackfriars, despite its drama, accomplished nothing except to allow Catherine to steal the show.[63] On 23 July,

---

[57] On this case, which cannot adequately be presented here, see the convincing discussion in Scarisbrick, *Henry VIII*, pp. 184–97.

[58] See A. G. Dickens, *The English Reformation* (London 1964), p. 105.

[59] This does not mean that Charles was particularly devoted to his aunt. Both the feelings of his Spanish subjects for a daughter of Isabella and a dynastic interest in maintaining his cousin Mary's place in the English succession, required that Charles take Catherine's side.

[60] *L.P.* iv. 4721, 4736–7, 4857.

[61] See G. de C. Parmiter, *The King's Great Matter* (London 1967), pp. 73–9.

[62] Despite ibid. p. 92, the authenticity of the brief has never been proved. Clement, in a letter to Campeggio, called it 'an evident forgery' (*L.P.* iv. 5181).

[63] The best account of the trial is in Cavendish, *Cardinal Wolsey*, pp. 78–91.

the day when sentence was expected, Campeggio adjourned the court until 1 October. It was never to meet again, for a week before the adjournment Clement had yielded to Charles, who by then had evicted the French from Italy, and revoked the case to Rome where Henry could no more expect justice than Catherine could in England.

The revocation was followed by Wolsey's fall and three unproductive years in the matter of the divorce. The central issues were whether the king could be compelled to attend in person or by proxy a trial at Rome and whether the Pope could be persuaded to return the case to England. On these Henry's negotiators got nowhere and in the end were reduced to trying to prevent or at least delay an adverse decision at Rome. A way out apparently was beyond the ken of Henry and those who had his ear. Henry asserted that as a sovereign prince he recognized no superior authority on earth; he wrung from the English clergy a vague acknowledgment as their supreme head; he allowed rumours to circulate that Parliament would deal with the divorce. But these were little more than futile attempts to coerce Clement; no follow up was made or intended. A positive policy only began to emerge in 1532 with the rise of Thomas Cromwell, who suggested that Henry could make a reality out of his claims to supremacy and get his divorce by evicting the pope from England.[64]

Events of 1532 and early 1533 prepared the way for the divorce and much more. During the first half of 1532 Parliament began to move in an antipapal direction by passing the first Act of Annates, the English Church exchanged its legislative dependence on Rome for legislative dependence on the crown through the 'Submission of the Clergy', and opposition and conservative leaders either left or were excluded from the king's inner circle.[65] On 23 August William Warham, archbishop of Canterbury, died. Warham had been determined not to disobey a papal prohibition against deciding the divorce case in England, and a divorce secured in England without papal sanction practically required the participation of the primate.[66] On 1 September Anne Boleyn was created marchioness of Pembroke, an elevation of a woman to a peerage in her own right that would be uncalled for except as a prelude to a higher title. Probably in January 1533, when she was already pregnant, Anne was secretly married to Henry.[67] Also in January Henry appointed

---

[64] See G. R. Elton, 'King or Minister? The Man behind the Henrician Reformation', *History* (1954), xxxix, pp. 225–30.

[65] See Elton, *History* (1954), pp. 229–30. Sir Thomas More resigned as lord chancellor and Stephen Gardiner was in disgrace.

[66] See Mortimer Levine, 'Henry VIII's Use of His Spiritual and Temporal Jurisdictions in His Great Causes of Matrimony, Legitimacy, and Succession', *Hist. J.* (1967), x, pp. 3–4.

[67] It is possible that the marriage took place in November 1532. See H. M. Smith, *Henry VIII and the Reformation* (London 1948), p. 32.

as Warham's successor at Canterbury Thomas Cranmer, an anti-papalist with close ties to the Boleyn family. Early in March Parliament completed the preparations for the divorce in a revolutionary enactment.

The Act in Restraint of Appeals did not, as had at first been intended, merely preclude an appeal to Rome of an English judgment on the divorce. Cromwell succeeded in turning it into a general statute that stopped nearly all appeals to foreign courts and thereby cut England's judicial ties with Rome. Moreover, its preamble indicated an even larger meaning: England was a territorial empire, a sovereign state 'governed by one supreme head and king' and subject to no outside authority.[68] Henry VIII not only had the means to obtain his divorce; England had declared her independence.

The divorce was not long in coming. On 12 April the king licensed Archbishop Cranmer, 'the principal minister "of our spiritual jurisdiction"', to try the case. On 23 May Cranmer gave sentence that Henry's marriage with Catherine was void; five days later he pronounced valid Henry's marriage to Anne. Cranmer, however, did not declare Mary a bastard. He could not have done so justly as an ecclesiastical judge, for canon law held a child legitimate if its parents were ignorant of the invalidity of their marriage at the time of its birth. Henry's doubt about his marriage came some two decades too late to allow Cranmer to bastardize Mary.[69] As far as the succession was concerned it would hardly matter if the child in Anne's womb turned out to be a son, but on 7 September she gave birth to a daughter, named Elizabeth after her grandmother of York. Two daughters – the younger regarded by the king as his heir but the elder not illegitimate – only complicated the great dynastic problem that the divorce was supposed to solve.

The divorce, the development of the royal supremacy in the Church, and the emergence of the Cromwellian regime produced both opposition at home and the possibility of intervention by Charles V. In 1533 Eustace Chapuys, the Imperial ambassador, indicated that discontent was so great that England was on the verge of civil war; he urged Charles to undertake an invasion which would be easy because the common people and the nobility in general would side with the Emperor; he also suggested that Charles make use of Reginald Pole, a grandson of George of Clarence, 'upon whom, in the opinion of many people here, the succession to the crown would by right devolve' and whom Catherine wanted as a husband for Mary.[70] The Emperor, however, was too preoccupied with French, Turkish, and German Pro-

---

[68] 24. Henry VIII cap. 12; *Stat. Realm*, iii. 427–9; on which see G. R. Elton, 'The Evolution of a Reformation Statute', *English Historical Review* (1949), lxiv, pp. 174–97.

[69] See Levine, *Hist. J.* (1967), pp. 5–6.   [70] *Span. Cal.* iv. Pt ii. 1058, 1130.

testant menaces on the Continent to involve himself in a war with
Henry who probably could count on the aid of Francis I; [71] Charles
prudently concluded that his obligation to his aunt was 'a private matter,
and public considerations must be taken into account'.[72]

If the threat of an Imperial invasion was more apparent than real, so
was Chapuys' appraisal of the situation in England. The nobility in
general may not have liked the divorce or Cromwell, but this does not
mean that many nobles were inclined to face the risks of civil war. A
few northern and western lords who did not realize that the fifteenth
century was over, and perhaps the Poles and the Courtenays, might
have been willing to go all the way, but co-ordination among them was
lacking,[73] and they probably would have found it difficult to unite
behind Chapuys' suggested Yorkist claimant, for the Courtenays, as
descendants of Edward IV, could claim priority over the Poles in the
succession. As for the common people, public opinion reports of a
plotter like Chapuys are hardly reliable evidence. There is evidence that
some loose-tongued individuals made foolish utterances about the
divorce, mainly that Queen Anne was a whore.[74] This last may have
reflected a widely held view, but there was a great distance between
regarding Anne as a whore and rebelling against Henry. After Anne was
dead and gone there would be rebellion, but not of the type or scope
that Chapuys saw as imminent in 1533.

There was, however, a more insidious kind of opposition, an organized one, called a conspiracy by Cromwell, which attempted to influence
Parliament in the interest of Catherine and Rome.[75] The main evidence
of this opposition is a confession made after its break up by Sir George
Throckmorton (Doc. 21). Throckmorton when an MP had done its
bidding, speaking in the Lower House against the important statutes of
Annates, Appeals and Supremacy. He was first moved to work for the
opposition by Friar Peto, who may have been its organizing genius.
Peto alleged that he had told the king both in sermon and conversation
that he could not remarry while Catherine lived. He also embellished
the impediment to Henry's marrying Anne by accusing him of having
'meddled' with her mother as well as her sister.[76] Throckmorton next

[71] Wernham, *Before the Armada*, pp. 120–7.   [72] *L.P.* vi. 568.
[73] See Mattingly, *Catherine of Aragon*, pp. 286–9; Dickens, *English Reformation*, pp. 123–4.
[74] See G. R. Elton, 'The Law of Treason in the Early Reformation', *Hist. J.*
(1968), xi, pp. 223–6.
[75] For a fuller account of this opposition than can be given here see G. R.
Elton, 'Sir Thomas More and the Opposition to Henry VIII', *BIHR* (1968) xli,
pp. 25–34.
[76] Peto's charge may be the basis of the more vicious story of an Elizabethan
polemicist that Anne was Henry's daughter. Nicholas Sander, *The Rise and
Growth of the Anglican Schism*, trans. David Lewis (London 1877), pp. 24–5.

received flattering encouragement from Lord Chancellor More, who implied that Henry would eventually abandon his present course and be grateful to those who had fought against it. Then Throckmorton began seeing John Fisher, bishop of Rochester, who apparently instructed him with regard to proposed legislation and the question of papal supremacy. He also received advice from Nicholas Wilson, formerly the king's confessor. Finally Throckmorton went to the Bridgettine house at Syon where the intransigent Father Reynolds told him that he must speak in Parliament even if he was sure it would do no good.

It seems unlikely that Throckmorton was the only MP at the disposal of Peto and his fellows; motions of the first half of 1532 to petition the king to take back his wife, the reception of which disturbed Henry,[77] may well have been presented by their clients. Until late spring, when Cromwell's ascendancy became clear, the opposition was not ineffective. The resignation and retirement to a life of contemplation in May of More, who had circumspectly worked for the opposition from within the government,[78] probably signifies that its foremost member regarded its cause as lost. The easy passage of the Act in Restraint of Appeals in March 1533 made this obvious. That Throckmorton spoke against the Act of Supremacy, passed in late 1534, shows that the opposition was not dead, but Reynolds' telling him to speak even if he knew it would be of no avail indicates its desperation. That it had already been driven to extremes is shown by Fisher's secret appeals of late 1533 to Charles V to make war on Henry.[79]

Even if the oppositions – noble, popular and organized – were not great immediate threats, the government could not be expected to tolerate them. Nor was it safe to leave the succession unclarified. To deal effectually with the problems of opposition and succession Henry and Cromwell had to turn to Parliament. The law of treason, still basically that enacted in 1352,[80] did not satisfactorily cover the activities of the oppositions of the 1530s,[81] and new treasons could only be created by parliamentary statute. The succession was a matter that had customarily been regarded as ordained by God; its determination required the highest sanction possible. By making Parliament his accomplice, the king gave his determination the appearance, if not the fact, of having the consent of the nation.[82] At any rate, Parliament acted in early 1534.

[77] Edward Hall, *Chronicle*, ed. Henry Ellis (London 1809), p. 788; *L.P.* v. 989.
[78] See Elton, *BIHR* (1968), pp. 25–9, 32–3.
[79] *L.P.* vi. 1164, 1249.
[80] 25. Edward III st. 5 cap. 2; *Stat. Realm*, i. 319–20.
[81] See Elton, *Hist. J.* (1968), 211–13.
[82] Mortimer Levine, 'A Parliamentary Title to the Crown in Tudor England', *Huntington Library Quarterly* (1962), xxv, p. 122.

Henry VIII's first Succession Act (Doc. 17) gave as its justification the dangers of an uncertain succession, calling to remembrance the Wars of the Roses. Invoking Cranmer's judgments, it pronounced Henry's union with Catherine to be void and his marriage with Anne to be valid. It specifically declared Henry's issue by Anne to be his 'lawful children'. And it set the order of succession as the king's sons by Anne and future wives and their heirs, his daughters by Anne and future wives and their heirs, and, lacking such issue, the 'right heirs of your Highness for ever'. The only clear immediate result of all this was that the infant Elizabeth was Henry's heir presumptive – hardly a secure succession.

What if Elizabeth predeceased Henry and he had no other issue by Anne or a future wife? 'Right heirs' meant nothing without their being named, which would be unsafe while the heir presumptive was a mere girl, or without provision as to how they were to be designated. And what of Henry's elder daughter? Lady Shelton, Anne's aunt, probably reflected the view of most contemporaries, the king included, when she, as reported by Chapuys, told Mary that 'her father did not care in the least that she should renounce her title, since by statute she was declared a bastard and incapable'.[83] The first Succession Act, however, stated nothing of the sort; indeed, it did not even mention Mary. Statutory confirmation of Cranmer's judgments against Henry's first marriage and in favour of his second marriage could not make Mary illegitimate; Cranmer, as we have seen, did not bastardize Mary. Nor would the declaration that Henry's issue by Anne were his 'lawful children' establish Mary's illegitimacy. Of course the act, ignoring Mary, vested the succession in Elizabeth, unborn children, and unspecified 'right heirs'. But what if no such succession was possible at Henry's death? Then presumably the succession would revert to where it had been before, that is, to Mary, who, if still living, remained technically legitimate and normally the king's heir.

The act's failure to state that Mary was a bastard and incapable of succession could not have been accidental. Such a slip would be inconceivable in an important statute drafted during the period when Cromwell was in charge of affairs. In fact, the act's neglect of Mary may well have been Cromwell's work. A year before Cromwell had wanted Cranmer to state in his judgment against Catherine's marriage that Mary was born 'in bona fide parentum',[84] that is, that she was legitimate because at the time of her birth her parents were ignorant of the invalidity of their marriage. In 1534 such a pronouncement may no longer have been politic, but an unqualified bastardization was unnecessary. An act of Parliament, according to Cromwell's concept of the

[83] L.P. vii. 530.
[84] Paul Friedmann, *Anne Boleyn* (London 1884), i. p. 231.

supremacy of statute,[85] could make Elizabeth heir presumptive without it. And it would be prudent to provide for future contingencies. The time might come when it might be desirable for the king to have another daughter who, whatever the implications of the first Succession Act, could be shown to be technically legitimate.[86]

The act also created new treasons. Anyone who maliciously did anything by writing, print, deed or act to the peril of the king or to the prejudice of the Boleyn marriage or of the new succession was subject to the dread penalties of high treason. But anyone who committed the same offences by word only or refused to be sworn to the performance of the act was only subject to the lesser penalties of misprision of treason. Misprision doubtless was regarded as insufficient by Henry and Cromwell, who in a time of revolution undertandably feared that treasonable utterances might incite overt acts.[87] The 'defect' was removed in November with the passage of the Treasons Act of 1534. This act made it high treason maliciously to 'wish, will, or desire by words or writing, or by craft imagine, invent, practise, or attempt any bodily harm' to the king, the queen, or their heirs apparent, or to deprive them of their dignities and titles, which would include that of supreme head, 'or slanderously and maliciously publish and pronounce, by express writing or words' the king to be a 'heretic, schismatic, tyrant, infidel, or usurper . . . '.[88]

In 1535 the treason legislation was used to secure the deaths of More, Fisher and eight monks. These executions, especially the judicial murders of More and Fisher, shocked much of Europe but produced neither invasion from abroad nor rebellion at home. Nor did a 1533 papal decision in favour of the Aragon marriage and continuing threats to excommunicate Henry and 'deprive' him of his throne.[89] Then on 8 January 1536, Catherine of Aragon removed the main 'moral' reason for invasion or rebellion by passing away. Except for the lack of a prince, Henry VIII had safely achieved his original dynastic objectives, and new dynastic options were in the offing.

On 29 January Anne Boleyn was prematurely delivered of a dead male child. This, at least her second miscarriage,[90] no doubt sealed Anne's doom. Henry's passion for her was wholly gone and her failure to produce a prince suggested that his second marriage was as sinful as

---

[85] See Elton, *England under the Tudors*, pp. 168–70, 174–5.
[86] This and the preceding paragraph are based mainly on the fuller account in Levine, *Hist. J.* (1967), pp. 6–7.
[87] See Elton, *Hist. J.* (1968), pp. 223, 232–3.
[88] 27. Henry VIII cap. 13; *Stat. Realm*, iii. 508.
[89] Clement VII drew up a sentence of excommunication in July 1533. Paul III published a bull of excommunication, dated 30 August 1535, in December 1538. No bull of deprivation was ever published. Pollard, *Henry VIII*, p. 242.
[90] Cf. Pollard, *Henry VIII*, pp. 150, 274.

his first. Moreover, Anne constituted an unnecessary obstacle to desired better relations with Charles V. On 15 May the queen was convicted on doubtful evidence [91] of having illicit intercourse with five men, one of them her own brother, and conspiring with them to kill the king.[92] She was beheaded on the 19th.

Two days before her execution Cranmer gave sentence that the convicted adulteress had never been Henry's wife.[93] Cranmer stated no grounds for the judgment, but there were two possibilities. One was an alleged precontract between Anne and the current Henry Percy, earl of Northumberland. Northumberland, however, had denied any such precontract on oath and on the sacrament and let Cromwell know of his intention to repeat the denial.[94] The precontract story, therefore, was an unsure ground for nullifying the king's marriage. More likely, Cranmer, as Chapuys was told, 'pronounced the marriage invalid on account of the king having had connection' with Anne's sister Mary. Such a ground could not well be published, for it would imply censure of the king for contracting what he knew was a void union.[95] It would also have implication regarding the statutory heir presumptive: Chapuys also was told that, since Henry and Anne both knew of his liaison with her sister, 'the good faith of the parents cannot make the bastard [Elizabeth] legitimate'.[96]

Anne's fall came as particularly encouraging news to the Imperialists who wanted England as an ally in their impending war with France. Charles V hoped that Henry VIII might marry his niece of Portugal or his niece of Milan and that Princess Mary might be matched with his brother-in-law of Portugal.[97] And Chapuys hoped that Mary would be 'declared true heiress of the kingdom, not as born of lawful marriage, but as legitimate *propter fidem parentum*'.[98] Henry, however, had other plans. He preferred to remain a sought-after neutral in a Habsburg–Valois conflict and to pursue an English solution to his dynastic problem. On 30 May the king married Jane Seymour, the daughter of a Wiltshire knight. In early summer Parliament enacted new succession legislation.

Henry VIII's second Succession Act (Doc. 19) pronounced the invalidity of the king's marriages with Catherine and Anne and declared

---

[91] See *L.P.* x. 799, 908, 965, 1036.

[92] *L.P.* x. 876.

[93] *Concilia Magnae Britanniae et Hiberniae*, ed. David Wilkins, (London 1737) iii. 803. The contradiction implied did not impair Henry's record regarding 'legal' murders, for Anne was still 'guilty' of conspiring to kill him.

[94] *L.P.* x. 864.

[95] See above, p. 55.

[96] *L.P.* x. 909.

[97] *L.P.* x. 888.

[98] *L.P.* x. 909.

the issue of both unions to be 'illegitimate' and 'utterly foreclosed, excluded, and barred to claim . . . any inheritance' from their father 'by lineal descent'. Regarding Henry's first two marriages, Parliament was merely confirming judgments of Cranmer's archiepiscopal courts. Cranmer, by his judgment against the Boleyn marriage, also may in effect have illegitimated Elizabeth, but the definitive bastardization of Mary, which normally should have been done in an ecclesiastical court, was now first accomplished in a parliamentary enactment. Henry VIII, whether he realized it or not, had followed Richard III's precedent of 1484.[99]

Henry apparently had decided to erase the past and start anew. Since Catherine and Anne were both dead, he now had an undoubted wife. He had every hope that Queen Jane would bear him indisputably lawful heirs. Hence he permitted Mary and Elizabeth to be bastardized and excluded from the succession in no uncertain terms. The second Succession Act entailed the succession first on Henry's sons by Jane and future wives and then on his daughters by Jane and future wives. This meant that unborn children were the king's only declared successors, which, left alone, would be a manifestly unsafe succession.

The act, however, did not let all depend on Henry's having lawful issue. In a unique demonstration of the virtual omnicompetence now attributed to statute, Parliament gave the king unqualified authorization to designate a further succession by his letters patent or his last will. This did not mean that Henry had absolute power to dispose of the succession: he could not will the crown away from his lawful issue. But if such issue failed to appear or became extinct in the future, Henry's will was absolute. He did not have to make his designations in accordance with customary rules governing the succession when a direct line became extinct. He could will the crown as he pleased – to his nephew of Scotland, to his bastardized daughters, to his dying bastard son, even to Thomas Cromwell. No English monarch before or since has ever had this statutory power.

Lack of lawful issue was not the only danger that the act attempted to provide against. It empowered Henry to designate by his last will a government for the minority of an under-age successor. This great extension of the authority of statute created the possibility of a dead king governing a living one. The treason provisions of the second Succession Act were much stronger than those of the first, which was neither sur-

[99] See above, pp. 29–30. A basic difference should be noted. Richard's Parliament, which doubted its competence in matrimonial causes, was simply confirming a *fait accompli* in an attempt to give legal sanction to a usurpation. Henry's Parliament did not have to act out of mere expediency. By 1536 the operation of statute was extended 'virtually to omnicompetence'. See Elton, *Tudor Constitution*, pp. 229–33.

prising nor constitutionally questionable after the Treasons Act of 1534. Every offence specified in the 1536 statute was full treason; there were no misprisions. It became high treason for anyone 'by words, writing, imprinting, or by any exterior act or deed' to do anything against the king's new marriage or the new succession, or to 'accept or take, judge or believe' his former marriages to be lawful or to call their issue legitimate. Refusal to take an oath of succession became high treason. So even did protest against declaring one's 'thought and conscience' when questioned about the act or anything in it.

In the last months of 1536 Henry VIII was faced with the most serious rebellion of his reign. The so-called Pilgrimage of Grace was a many-sided rising of diverse discontented elements of northern England. The rebels wanted to overthrow the new regime in Church and State, not the Tudor dynasty. Their loyalty to and naive trust in the word of their king contributed no little to their defeat.[100] Even if Cardinal Pole, sent to Flanders by Paul III with implied authority to use force of arms against Henry if necessary,[101] had succeeded in joining the rebellion, his Yorkist descent would hardly have inspired the rebels to consider a change in dynasty. Indeed, their primary dynastic objective apparently was to ensure the continuance of Tudors on the throne.

The rebels, as later indicated by the examination of the noblest of their leaders, Robert Aske (Doc. 20), had two dynastic demands: repeal of the 'statute of the illegitimacy' of Henry's elder daughter Mary and annulment or qualification of the 'statute of the declaration of the crown of this realm by will'.[102] The evident distinction between two statutes shows that Aske and his fellows shared the probably common view that the first Succession Act bastardized Mary [103] and apparently did not realize that that statute was already repealed by the second Succession Act, which definitively bastardized Mary (Doc. 19). That they also did not know that the Pope had ruled in favour of Catherine's marriage three years before is revealed by Aske's objection that if Rome should find Mary legitimate, it would appear that the statute had been made 'more for some displeasure towards her and her friends than for any just cause' – perhaps evidence of a successful government effort to prevent news of the papal decision from reaching at least the more remote parts of England. Aske's other arguments against the statute are commonplace: Catherine's 'virtue and high peerage', Mary's 'great virtues', and fear that her continued bastardy might cause Charles V to make war on England and stop English trade with Flanders.

More impressive are Aske's objections to the 'statute of the declara-

---

[100] See Scarsbrick, *Henry VIII*, p. 342.
[101] See *L.P.* xii. Pt i. 779.
[102] Also see *L.P.* xi. 1246.
[103] See above, p. 64.

tion of the crown of this realm by will', that is, the second Succession Act. No king since the Conqueror had 'declared his will of the crown',[104] nor had any before Henry VIII been given statutory power to make such a declaration. If the crown should pass by will to other than the 'rightful heir apparent', there would be 'great war risk'. Therefore, the act should be changed so that either an 'heir apparent' – a living one, not merely an unborn child – be designated by statute or the succession should go as it regularly would 'to the very next blood of the King', that is, to Mary. This indicates that the rebels would admit a statutory heir other than Mary if that heir was named in Parliament. They were willing to risk a parliamentary designation, which they probably expected to be in Mary's favour, but they had a genuine fear about what Henry might do by will.

The nature of that fear is made clear by Aske's last objection. While politely expressing doubt that Henry intended to do so, he pointed out that the king might will the crown to an alien. Then he alluded to the common-law rule against aliens inheriting ordinary property, and concluded that the 'voice of the most part of the people is, and I suppose the law is also, that no stranger can claim this crown by no descent of inheritance, unless he were born under the allegiance of this crown'. This foreshadows early Elizabethan arguments against Mary Queen of Scots' claim to the English succession, and like them doubtless was aimed at the Scottish line. Some rebels seem to have had the rather preposterous notion that Henry intended to marry Cromwell to Lady Margaret Douglas, Margaret of Scotland's daughter by her second marriage, and will the crown to them.[105] More sensible rebels, like Aske, probably were thinking in terms of James V. This is implied in the rebels' final, comprehensive petition, which included apparently interconnected demands: repeal of the statute of the declaration of the crown by will and 'That the Lady Mary may be made legitimate, and the former statute therein annulled for the danger of the title that might incur to the crown of Scotland'.[106] In short, the rebels wanted a living and legitimate Tudor to stand in the way of the Scottish king.

The dynastic concerns of the rebels were hardly confined to their number or their region. Dislike of the possibility of a Scot ascending the throne was no doubt a national phenomenon. Most Englishmen probably would have welcomed the naming of a Tudor successor, at least until Henry VIII was blessed with an indisputably legitimate one. And that Tudor successor almost had to be the 20-year-old Mary

---

[104] William the Conqueror seems to have 'willed' the crown to William Rufus, his second son. It is at least possible that Richard I later 'willed' the crown to his brother John.

[105] See *L.P.* xii. Pt i. 532–3.

[106] *L.P.* xi. 1246.

rather than the 3-year-old Elizabeth: a queen regnant would be a risky enough experiment without her also being a tot. On 3 August 1537 the king's council considered the situation. It recommended that Henry's bastard daughters 'be made of some estimation', and Mary first because because she was 'of more age'. The council indicated that this would enhance the value of Mary and Elizabeth on the matrimonial market and expressed its trust that Queen Jane, then pregnant, would 'bring forth many fair children'. Yet it also wanted more to be made of Henry's daughters, 'though not his lawful daughters', so 'as to take away the remainder hanging upon the King of Scots, and the hope which perchance he hath of the same'.[107]

The situation changed on 12 October when Queen Jane gave birth to a son, Prince Edward. Bishop Latimer's report of the great joy this news caused in his diocese of Worcester undoubtedly reflected the general reaction throughout England. The birth of a prince after so many years of waiting must have seemed something of a miracle; Catholics as well as Protestants could agree with Latimer that God had turned English.[108] The queen's death on 24 October mattered little. She had provided the king with a male heir of unquestionable legitimacy. There could be no doubt about Henry's virility. He could marry again and have more children. Mary and Elizabeth, so it seemed, could safely be forgotten.

In 1538 the activities of Cardinal Pole gave Henry VIII the opportunity to commence a purge of Yorkists. Pole was the chief promoter of a papal project to reconquer England. By summer a Franco–Imperial invasion of England seemed a distinct possibility, and the publication of a papal bull depriving the king of his throne seemed imminent. Pole was in correspondence with his relatives in England and possibly also with the Courtenays, and Chapuys was in contact with both families. In August, thanks to the confession of Sir Geoffrey Pole, Henry Pole, Lord Montague, Margaret, countess of Salisbury, Henry Courtenay, marquis of Exeter, and Sir Edward Neville were arrested. Montague, Exeter, and Neville were executed in December. Speaking treason was about all they were guilty of, but Henry and Cromwell, remembering the Pilgrimage of Grace and considering the threats from abroad, could not be expected to be tolerant. Finally, in 1541, after Cromwell's fall, Henry carried out the worst of his judicial murders, that of the aged countess of Salisbury, whose main crimes were her being the daughter of George of Clarence and the mother of Reginald Pole. Surely even Henry could not have really believed that this relic of the fifteenth century constituted a menace to himself or the succession of Prince

[107] *St. P.*, i. 545–6.
[108] See *St. P.*, i. 571.

Edward. At any rate, the king had come close to fulfilling his long-meditated aim of annihilating the house of York.[109]

After Cromwell's fall Henry reverted to a foreign policy of continental involvement. By early 1544 he was preparing to launch an invasion of France which he was to lead in person. His marriages with Anne of Cleves and Catherine Howard had been childless and Catherine Parr, his new wife, was not pregnant. Two years before Prince Edward had suffered a nearly fatal illness.[110] It was unsafe for the king to hazard battle with the succession dependent on the life of a boy. He could have designated a further succession by will but evidently decided that an open declaration by statute would be preferable.

Henry VIII's third Succession Act (Doc. 22) set the order of succession after Edward and his children and any future children of the king as Mary and her lawful heirs, Elizabeth and her lawful heirs, and those Henry might designate by letters patent or will. Mary and Elizabeth were thus restored to their appropriate place in the succession but not to legitimacy. Parliament's authority was now such that it could ignore legitimacy in determining the succession. The king, however, was empowered to set conditions by letters patent or will which his daughters would have to meet to be eligible to assume the royal dignity.

At first glance, this 1544 statute appears to be grist for the mill of those who maintain that there was a Tudor despotism. Not only did Parliament reaffirm Henry's unqualified authorization to designate further successors by letters patent or will; it also gave him unqualified power to set conditions by letters patent or will which Mary and Elizabeth would have to satisfy to be eligible for the succession. This last potentially enabled Henry, for any personal reason whatever, to establish impossible conditions for his daughters and thereby frustrate Parliament's declared succession. Parliament certainly had granted the king exceptional authority.

But was Parliament merely bowing to the will of a despot? It did not grant Henry, nor is it likely that he desired, authority to interfere with the normal succession. Edward and any other indisputably lawful heirs to come would succeed according to the customary law of the land. Placing bastardized females in the succession, however, was both extraordinary and potentially dangerous, and this justified setting conditions. And designating a further succession was difficult and potentially divisive, for it was debatable which line of right came after the Tudors. Parliament's immediate purpose in 1544 was to provide for the succession in the event of the unlikely coincidence of Henry's death in battle

[109] See H. A. L. Fisher, *The Political History of England*, vol. v, *1485–1547* (London 1913), pp. 427–31; Pollard, *Henry VIII*, pp. 298–300; Scarsbrick, *Henry VIII*, pp. 364–5.
[110] See H. W. Chapman, *The Last Tudor King* (London 1961), pp. 51–2.

and Edward's death by illness. It was neither necessary nor desirable for Parliament to set conditions for Mary and Elizabeth and designate a further succession via the open route of statute. It was better to entrust these ticklish matters to the king whose determinations did not have to be published prematurely and could easily be altered in the interval if the need arose. In Parliament the third Succession Act very probably enjoyed willing acceptance, not reluctant acquiescence.

Cromwell's fall was followed not only by a reversion to continental involvement but by a new involvement in Scotland. In October 1542 Henry declared war upon Scotland, ending a formal peace of nearly thirty years. On 24 November the Scots were routed at Solway Moss; on 14 December James V died and his 6-day-old daughter Mary became Queen of Scots. These events seemed to present Henry with God-given opportunities. He induced the many nobles captured at Solway Moss to promise to serve English interests in a Scotland afflicted with disunity and facing the prospect of a long minority. He sought to tie Scotland to England and ultimately create Great Britain by matching Prince Edward with the infant Queen of Scots.

Speaking two decades later to an Elizabethan Parliament, Sir Ralph Sadler, Henry's principal negotiator in Scotland, bitterly recalled what ensued. A marriage treaty was concluded in the summer of 1543 and ratified by Henry and James Hamilton, earl of Arran, the Scottish governor, but no sooner was the treaty made than the Scots began to violate it by failing to send hostages who were to remain in England until the delivery of the young queen when she reached the age of ten.[111] In December, though Sadler did not rehearse it, the Scottish Parliament revoked both the marriage and peace treaties and renewed the 'auld alliance' with France, bringing to an end the 1543 English 'wooing' of Scotland.

Sadler attributed this failure of 1543 to the perfidy of the Scots, and the conduct of many of them, notably Arran, Mary of Guise, the Queen Mother, and the 'assured Scots' whom Henry permitted to return to Scotland, certainly was not beyond reproach. English 'diplomacy', however, practically assured failure. Early in the year, when prospects looked good for the marriage that Henry sincerely desired, he made assertions that were bound to irritate the Scots. The preamble to his Subsidy Act not merely revived the old Plantagenet claim to suzerainty but described James V as the 'late pretensed king of Scots' and declared that Henry VIII had a 'right and title to the . . . crown and realm of Scotland'.[112] During the ensuing months Henry veered back and forth between gentle dealing and bellicose threats culminating in

[111] *The State Papers and Letters of Sir Ralph Sadler*, ed. Arthur Clifford (Edinburgh 1809), ii. pp. 558–9.
[112] 34. and 35. Henry VIII cap. 27; *Stat. Realm*, iii. p. 938.

the seizure of Scottish ships in the Thames. And Sadler, whose diplomatic vision apparently was obscured by his desire to promote the Scottish Reformation, was unable to exploit real divisions among the Scots. In the end, Henry and Sadler played right into the hands of the pro-French Cardinal Beaton and Mary of Guise, whose triumph was registered in the united voice of the Scottish Parliament.[113]

Even if Henry and Sadler had been the ablest of wooers, however, their objective may well have been unattainable. In his speech Sadler also recalled a question put to him by a Scot: 'If . . . your lad were a lass and our lass were a lad . . ., could you be content that our lad should marry your lass and so be king of England?' [114] In the sixteenth century a match between sovereigns, no matter what safeguards were stipulated by treaty, was most likely to result in the rule of their respective realms by the husband, especially in the case of adjacent realms. The English doubtless would not have liked the earlier possibility of James V becoming their king through marrying their own Mary, even though James probably would have been unwilling and unable to subordinate the greater realm to the lesser. The creation of Great Britain via a marriage of the English Edward with the Scottish Mary, on the other hand, might well have meant the absorption of Scotland into England. It was hardly realistic to expect the Scots voluntarily to consummate such an arrangement with their ancient enemy.

The failure of 1543 did not cause Henry VIII to give up the marriage project. Scottish unity was only momentary, and Henry soon found new opportunities to enlist Scottish allies. His one lasting success here was Matthew Stuart, earl of Lennox, whom he matched with his niece, Lady Margaret Douglas. Lennox proved of little use to Henry and soon began a long exile in England, but his marriage was to complicate the dynastic future, for one of its fruits was Henry Stuart, Lord Darnley. At any rate, seeking Scottish allies was but a peripheral aspect of Henry's Scottish policy after 1543.

The king evidently decided that what could not be gained by diplomacy could be won by war. In the spring of 1544 Henry sent an army into Scotland under the command of his brother-in-law, Edward Seymour, earl of Hertford, with instructions to sack and burn Edinburgh, Leith and St Andrews, 'putting man, woman, and child to fire and sword without exception where any resistance shall be made against you'.[115] Except for not reaching St Andrews, Hertford accomplished his terrible mission. In the autumn of 1545 Hertford carried out

---

[113] For a fuller account of the English failure of 1543 see A. J. Slavin, *Politics and Profit: A Study of Sir Ralph Sadler, 1507–1547* (Cambridge 1966), pp. 94–131.

[114] Clifford, *Sadler Papers*, ii. p. 560.

[115] *The Hamilton Papers*, ed. Joseph Bain (Edinburgh 1890–2), ii. p. 326.

a second destructive invasion of south-eastern Scotland. Of course, this 'Rough Wooing' of 1544 and 1545 did not make the Scots think better of the idea of a marriage that would make an Englishman their king. A war policy made no sense at all unless Scotland could be wholly conquered, and such an enterprise was no doubt beyond the capacity of a sixteenth-century English army.[116] Nevertheless, Henry did not abandon that policy. Only death prevented him from witnessing its total defeat, which Hertford was to bring about in the next reign.

On 12 December 1546, six and a half weeks before the king's death, Henry Howard, earl of Surrey, and his father, Thomas, third duke of Norfolk, were arrested. The Howards had more than their share of enemies, but it is difficult to attribute their fall to anyone but Henry VIII. Though both of them were charged with treason, Surrey, through his mother Buckingham's grandson, was doubtless the primary offender and probably the king's principal concern. He evidently was guilty of foolhardy things such as boasting of his Plantagenet blood and quartering his own arms with those of Edward the Confessor. Perhaps most dangerous of all was his alleged words: 'If the King die, who should have the rule of the Prince but my father or I.' [117] Coming from a man so proud of his royal blood, these words could well have inspired in Henry memories of Richard of Gloucester and a boy-king named Edward. Surrey was beheaded for treason on 19 January 1547; Norfolk, who was attainted for concealing his son's offence, was saved from his scheduled execution on the morning of the 28th by Henry's death a few hours earlier.

Henry VIII left a will dated 30 December 1546 (Doc. 23). This will failed to claim statutory authorization for its succession provisions, perhaps an indication of the old king's inflated notion of his authority. Nonetheless, the succession provisions of Henry's will were obviously based on his third Succession Act, without which they scarcely would have been constitutional. Henry reaffirmed the order of succession declared in the 1544 statute, that is, Edward, future indisputably lawful heirs, Mary, and Elizabeth. As authorized by the same act, the king made the places of Mary and Elizabeth in the succession conditional: they would lose their places if they married without the consent of the councillors named by Henry to rule during Edward's minority. Also as authorized by statute, Henry designated a further succession. Here he ignored the Stuarts despite their descent from his elder sister, Margaret of Scotland. Instead he designated the so-called Suffolk line, to wit, the heirs of Ladies Frances and Eleanor Brandon, the daughters of his younger sister Mary, the French queen. After the Suffolk line the suc-

[116] See A. F. Pollard, *The Political History of England*, vol. vi, *1547–1603* (London 1910), p. 10.
[117] *St. P.* i. 981.

cession was to go to the 'next rightful heirs', which considering their being ignored in their hereditary place, probably did not mean the Stuarts.

What can be said of Henry VIII's use of his extraordinary statutory authority? The requirement that Mary and Elizabeth obtain conciliar consent before marrying or lose their places in the succession was doubtless exactly the type of thing the Parliament of 1544 had in mind when it empowered the king to set conditions governing the eligibility of his daughters to succeed to the crown. Females in the line of succession were risk enough; if they made 'wrong' marriages, that might mean undesirable kings for England. Henry's real reason for ignoring, if not excluding, the Stuarts may have been a silly one. It is conceivable that the king had so deluded himself about Scotland as to think that loss of hope of their queen coming to the English throne on her own might induce the Scots to want her to share it by marrying Edward. But whatever Henry VIII's motive, considering the English dislike of Scots and the fact that England and Scotland were at war, the designation of a purely English line descending from Henry VII rather than a Scottish line with slightly senior descent from the same king probably reflected the contemporary English preference. The dynastic policies and actions of the second Tudor were often wrong, but in the succession provisions of his will he did not violate the trust placed in him by his Parliament of 1544.

4

The Reigns of Edward VI and Mary I

The accession of the 9-year-old Edward VI in 1547 stands out in sharp contrast to that of the 12-year-old Edward V in 1483. In 1547 a repetition of 1483 was almost an impossibility. The great reason for this no doubt was that Henry VII and Henry VIII had so firmly established the Tudor dynasty that England would have nothing but Edward VI, child though he was. Another, but lesser, reason was that there was no pretender able or even inclined to attempt a usurpation. Henry VIII had dispatched all those of Plantagenet blood who conceivably might have tried to displace Edward VI, but it is most unlikely that any of them, if they had been spared, would have got very far. The young king indeed had an ambitious and powerful uncle in Edward Seymour, earl of Hertford, but, lacking any claim to the throne, he could not assume the role of Richard of Gloucester; Hertford could only aspire to exercise regal power during his nephew's minority.

Henry VIII in his will had named sixteen executors who were to serve as a council of regency until Edward VI reached his eighteenth year. Hertford was but one of them, which was no indication of the pre-eminence that his kinship to Edward and his prominence seemed to call for. Moreover, government by sixteen equals without a leader was unlikely to be workable. On 1 February the executors chose Hertford, shortly thereafter created duke of Somerset, as protector of the realm with the express provision that he should 'not do any act but with the advice and consent of the rest of the co-executors'. This obvious step was not forbidden by Henry's will, which apparently was only intended to prevent any individual from assuming the regal power during Edward's minority. On 1 March those designated by Henry as assistant executors were joined with the executors in a privy council of twenty-six plus Somerset. This may or may not have been a violation of Henry's will, but the will was not overthrown. That, however, was to come before March expired.

Negotiations were in progress for a defensive alliance with France.

The French indicated their concern that Edward, when he came of age, might legitimately repudiate a treaty concluded by a protector and council whose authority derived not from himself but from his late father's will. This provided an excuse for the councillors to petition the living king to grant them a new commission empowering them to govern during his minority. Edward not only granted the commission; he also granted Somerset a large measure of control over the council and power to act without its advice and consent if he so chose. In effect, this established the one-man regency that Henry's will was intended to prevent; Somerset had 'seized unfettered the royal power of the Tudors'.[1] More was overturned than a provision of a will. Henry had statutory authority to designate by will a government for his successor if a minor (Doc. 19). Whatever its justification, the competence of statute had been limited by the will of a boy at the instigation of his uncle and a handful of councillors.[2]

Somerset's main task of a dynastic nature was to carry out Henry VIII's Scottish policy. He was not the ideal man for the job, for the Scots remembered him as the general who led the destructive invasions of 1544 and 1545. Nevertheless, Somerset's intentions with regard to Scotland were nobler than those of his late master. He prefaced his invasion of Scotland in September 1547 with a proclamation in which he made no mention of any claim of suzerainty and declared that his great purpose was simply to obtain the performance of the marriage contract between Edward and Mary. On 10 September, at Pinkie, he inflicted on the Scots the bloodiest defeat they had ever suffered at the hands of England. Pinkie and the occupation of strongholds that followed, contrary to Somerset's naive hope that they would make the Scots more amenable to the marriage, only served to confirm Scottish suspicions that the soft words of England's new leader were merely a refinement of her late king's brutal stick. Somerset was successfully driving Scotland into the receptive arms of France.[3]

In early 1548, when the sending of French forces to Scotland was in the offing, Somerset published his 'Epistle of Exhortation' (Doc. 24). This last plea to the Scots reflects its author's admirable foresight and his reluctance to accept contemporary reality. Somerset recalled the long history of hostilities between the English and the Scots. Since they both spoke the same language [4] and lived on the same island, he saw the way

---

[1] For detailed accounts of Somerset's movement to regal power see A. F. Pollard, *England under Protector Somerset* (London 1900), pp. 20–38; W. K. Jordan, *Edward VI* (Cambridge, Mass. 1968–70), i. pp. 51–74.

[2] Perhaps an instance of Tudor despotism, but not in the reign where it is usually looked for.

[3] J. D. Mackie, *The Earlier Tudors* (Oxford 1952), pp. 483–5.

[4] Gaelic was still spoken in the Highlands and the Isles, but Somerset perhaps

out of this sad state in the union of the two peoples under one rule.[5] This happy conclusion could be accomplished by the marriage of Edward and Mary. Despite their triumph in war, the English were willing to relinquish their rights as conquerors. They intended not to disinherit Scotland's queen but 'to make her heirs inheritors also to England'. They would allow the Scots to keep their own laws and customs and offered them the prospect of unimpeded 'intercourse of merchandises' and 'interchange of marriages' with England. The English would even relinquish their identity as a nation and 'take the old indifferent name of Britons again'. All this was a remarkable forecast of the ultimate solution to the Britannic problem in 1707, but in 1548 it was simply unrealistic.

Though the idea of union may have been attractive to some Scots, it is difficult to see how Scotland could have accepted Somerset's sincerity in offering it. For several years to come union would mean that the rule not of Edward VI, an unknown quantity, but of Somerset, the man who had thrice brought devastation to Scotland. It was only natural for Scots to suspect hypocrisy in Somerset's statement that England's aim was 'not to conquer but to have in amity, not to win by force but to conciliate by love, not to spoil and kill but to save and keep . . .'. Right after these sweet words came the threat that refusal of England's offer would be followed by a terrible war of conquest for which the Scots would only have themselves to blame. Moreover, this time Somerset revived the irritating claim to suzerainty by writing of the 'title which we have to the crown of Scotland',[6] words reminiscent of Henry VIII's extreme assertion of 1543.[7] Finally, Somerset warned the Scots of the consequences if they married Mary to anyone other than Edward. He wisely indicated that her marriage to a Scot was likely to produce disastrous quarrels among Scottish factions. He saw Mary's marriage to a 'foreign prince' as very possibly resulting in her removal and that of protecting foreign troops from Scotland, which would be left a prey to England and a 'true conquest' instead of a union of brethren.

Somerset's well-intentioned but impolitic appeal did not alter the course of events. In June 1548 French troops arrived in Scotland. On 13 August the Queen of Scots landed in France where she was to marry the Dauphin. A little over a year later the English, not the French as Somerset had forecast, evacuated their last remaining strong-point in

---

preferred to ignore those areas which made a total English conquest of Scotland impossible.

[5] The assumption that neighbouring peoples who speak a common language should unite into one country is an article of faith that history does not always justify.

[6] These words refute the argument of Pollard, *Somerset*, pp. 172–4, that Somerset was reluctantly forced into reviving the claim to suzerainty by Mary's later removal to France.

[7] Above, p. 72.

Scotland. On the day of Mary's arrival in France Henry II had boasted that 'France and Scotland are now one country'.[8] This would never be entirely true, but for the next decade French influence would predominate in Scotland. Somerset had brought Henry VIII's Scottish policy to its logical conclusion.

At home Somerset's main problem with dynastic implications was his jealous younger brother, Thomas, Baron Seymour of Sudeley. Sudeley evidently sought to gain via matrimonial schemes the power that his elder brother would not share with him. At the beginning of Edward's reign he considered taking as his wife Anne of Cleves, Princess Mary, or Princess Elizabeth.[9] A match with Anne, Henry VIII's divorced wife, would have been rather innocuous, but marrying either of Henry's daughters without the consent of the council, which Somerset no doubt would have been able to withhold, would have upset the established succession. Then Sudeley probably seduced Catherine Parr, Henry's widow, whom he wedded in May 1547.[10] This was fraught with danger, for if Catherine gave birth too early it could be alleged that the child was Henry's and therefore Edward's heir presumptive. Though seemingly happy with his marriage, Sudeley engaged in an improper flirtation with young Elizabeth, who resided with Catherine. He also took into his custody little Lady Jane Grey, the senior Suffolk claimant according to Henry's will, promising her parents that he would marry her to Edward. After Catherine's death in September 1548 Sudeley sued for Elizabeth's hand, continued to keep Jane Grey in his household, and recklessly plotted treasons.[11] In March 1549 he was attainted and beheaded.

The erratic matrimonial scheming of Sudeley, an unscrupulous man of questionable sanity, may well have been aimed not only at gaining power in the government of Edward VI but at least equally at overturning the established succession in the event of the young king's premature demise. It is not inconceivable that Sudeley did hope that Catherine Parr would bear him a child that could be alleged to be Henry VIII's. A marriage to Elizabeth probably would not have enabled Sudeley to displace Somerset in Edward's government, but he may have anticipated that the zealously Protestant king could be induced to attempt to displace his Catholic sister Mary in the succession. Particularly suspect is Sudeley's taking charge of Lady Jane Grey. Somerset, who had his own matrimonial plans for the king, doubtless would have been able to prevent a match between Edward and Jane, but

---

[8] R. B. Wernham, *Before the Armada: the Growth of English Foreign Policy, 1485–1558* (London 1966), p. 173.

[9] Pollard, *Somerset*, p. 181; Jordan, *Edward VI*, i. p. 369.

[10] Jordan, *Edward VI*, i. p. 370.

[11] For an extensive documentation of Sudeley's activities see *Burghley Papers*, ed. Samuel Haynes and William Murdin (London 1740–59), i. pp. 62–109.

the senior Suffolk claimant was a logical second choice for Sudeley if his
projected marriage with Elizabeth failed to materialize. Jane had
already begun the Protestant upbringing [12] which was to make her
attractive to Edward as his successor.

Sudeley's fall was an embarrassment to Somerset, but the latter's
brotherly grief could hardly have been overwhelming. It is not too
much of an exaggeration to say that Sudeley was to Somerset what
Clarence had been to Edward IV. In particular, Sudeley's control of
and apparent matrimonial plan for Lady Jane Grey must have irritated
Somerset. One of the accusations later made against Somerset was that
he 'plotted' to marry his own daughter Jane to Edward VI.[13] He may
well have intended such a union after the projected match between
Edward and Mary of Scotland fell through. By making Edward his son-
in-law, Somerset might ensure the continuance of his influence after the
king came of age. If it had ever become an open question whether
Edward should marry Sudeley's Jane or Somerset's Jane, the former
was clearly the more appropriate bride for the king. Jane Grey, a great-
granddaughter of Henry VII, was a princess of the blood royal of
England; Jane Seymour was not and in addition was Edward's first
cousin, an undesirable consanguinity. Moreover, Somerset had a
matrimonial plan of his own for Jane Grey. He sought to marry her to
his son Edward, earl of Hertford, but Sudeley successfully blocked the
match.[14] One wonders about Somerset's intention here. Was he merely
interested in marrying his son highly? Or did he consider the possibility of keeping the crown in his own family by attempting to bring
about a Suffolk succession in the event of Edward's death without issue?

On 22 January 1552 Somerset suffered the death that Tudor political
life offered to incompetent idealists, leaving Edward and England under
the rule of the abler but unpopular John Dudley, duke of Northumberland. Northumberland antagonized the rural poor by replacing Somerset's well-meant but ill-advised agrarian policy with one obviously
intended mainly to satisfy his own greed and that of his associates.
Somerset, following his own religious convictions, had fostered the
development in England of a moderate Protestantism, but Northumberland, doubtless for non-religious reasons, moved what was still basically
a Catholic country in the more radical direction of the Swiss Reformation. Nor did Northumberland help his image by pursuing, quite
sensibly considering England's weakness and more proximate dangers,
a foreign policy that involved appeasement of France and a reversal of
the 'traditional' Habsburg alliance. Such a widely disliked ruler had

[12] See H. W. Chapman, *Lady Jane Grey* (Boston 1962), pp. 21–40.
[13] *The Chronicle and Political Papers of King Edward VI*, ed. W. K. Jordan
(Ithaca 1966), p. 93.
[14] Haynes and Murdin, *Burghley Papers*, i. p. 80.

small hope of even surviving the accession of the Catholic and half-Spanish Princess Mary, a prospect that grew more and more imminent as consumption took command of the fate of Edward VI.

Consequently, Northumberland decided on a bold gamble that might, if successful, ensure the continuance of both his life and his power. He would secure the throne for his own family by marrying his son Guilford to a princess of the blood royal and inducing the compliant young king to name their male heir as his successor. Mary obviously could not be expected to be a party to such a scheme. And Elizabeth almost had to be rejected for the role, since, as we shall see, the 'legal' arguments for Mary's exclusion were equally applicable to her half sister. Nor could Northumberland find a suitable candidate in the Catholic Stuart line. Mary Queen of Scots, in France and betrothed to the Dauphin, was out of the question. Also unavailable was the already-married Margaret, countess of Lennox. Northumberland's only possibilities were the unmarried daughter of the house of Suffolk. Lady Margaret Clifford, Lady Eleanor Brandon's daughter by Henry, earl of Cumberland, evidently was the first of that line to be considered, but her father, perhaps a Catholic and probably afraid of the consequences of unsuccessful kingmaking, prevented the match from taking place.[15] Eventually Northumberland arrived at the more sensible conclusion that Lady Jane Grey, the eldest daughter of the senior Suffolk branch and a definite Protestant, was his best choice.[16]

The marriage of Lady Jane and Lord Guilford Dudley, which was solemnized in May 1553, 'with a display truly regal',[17] brought with it the involvement of Jane's father, Henry Grey, duke of Suffolk, but more than one important ally would be required if Northumberland was to execute his dangerous design. Consequently, he arranged four more matches through which he hoped to involve other great nobles. Lady Margaret Clifford was betrothed to Northumberland's brother Andrew,

[15] BM, Royal MS. 18 C XXIV, fo. 236; A. F. Pollard, *Political History of England*, vol. vi, *1547–1603* (London 1910), p. 82.

[16] Jordan, *Edward VI*, ii. pp. 494–504, 510–32, argues against the usual view followed here that Northumberland was the prime mover in the attempt to alter the succession. He assigns that role to Edward VI and sees Northumberland as one who loyally but reluctantly went along with his king's design. While allowing that Jordan could be right, I find his case unconvincing. It makes it quite difficult to explain Edward's by-passing Elizabeth in favour of Northumberland's daughter-in-law. Edward obviously was not too concerned about 'legal' arguments; his great concern was religion. Surely his shrewd sister gave him no reason to doubt her Protestantism. Someone else most likely induced Edward to turn away from Elizabeth, and that someone would almost have to be Northumberland. In any case, the identity of the prime mover in the attempt to alter the succession is not of vital import to our discussion, the main point of which is the illegality of that attempt.

[17] *Ven. Cal.* v. p. 536.

a man whom the earl of Cumberland could accept as a safer husband for
his daughter; Lady Catherine Grey, Jane's younger sister, was engaged
to Lord Henry Herbert, son of William, earl of Pembroke; Lady Mary,
the youngest Grey sister, was pledged to her kinsman Arthur, son of
William, Lord Grey of Wilton; Lady Catherine Dudley, Northumberland's daughter, was married to Lord Henry Hastings, son of Francis,
earl of Huntingdon. Before the first three of these matrimonial projects
could be completed – they never would be – the king's rapidly de-
teriorating condition made it necessary for Northumberland to proceed
to the alteration of the succession with haste.[18]

He now had to abandon his original plan of having his hoped-for
grandson succeed Edward VI and adopt the expedient of making Lady
Jane Grey next in line. This shift from the role of kingmaker to that of
queenmaker was not to his advantage. Jane might prove too inde-
pendent when she assumed the regality; it would be better to have a
baby on the throne with Northumberland as regent. Moreover, the
change destroyed his best chance for excluding Mary and Elizabeth,
namely the establishment of a variation of the Salic law that would
forbid the succession of a woman but permit her son to become king.
Precedents for this could be found in Henry II and Henry VII ascending the throne while their mothers were still living. Englishmen could
hardly have awaited the impending experiment of a queen regnant with
enthusiasm; they might well have been willing to accept even Northumberland's grandson as a lesser evil. But this one real chance of success
had practically faded away; the crucial wording in the king's 'devise for
the succession' had to be changed from 'to the Lady Jane's heirs male'
to 'to the Lady Jane and her heirs male'.[19] Northumberland had
anticipated taking a bold gamble; he was now committed to playing a
more desperate game.

He found it no problem to convince Edward VI to accept Lady Jane
as his successor. The bigoted king only had to be assured that the
Reformation was in jeopardy if anyone else followed him on the throne.
It proved more difficult to gain the approval of the councillors and
judges, but all of the dissidents save one[20] were soon enough brought
into line by what amounted to little more than pure and simple bully-
ing.[21] In the end, eighty-five notables of the realm subscribed to the

[18] See ibid.

[19] There are several printed versions of Edward's 'devise', the latest being
that in *English Historical Documents*, vol. v, *1485–1558*, ed. C. H. Williams
(London 1967), p. 460. None of these are entirely satisfactory. It is better to
consult the facsimile of the Inner Temple MS. in H. W. Chapman, *The Last
Tudor King* (London 1961).

[20] Sir James Hales, justice of the Common Pleas.

[21] See the respective testimonies of Chief Justice Montague, Archbishop
Cranmer, and Secretary Cecil in Thomas Fuller, *Church History of Britain*, ed.

settlement that the 15-year-old king agreed to make in order to bring about a Suffolk succession.[22]

Northumberland attempted to cloak his illicit plan with the trappings of legality by having Edward VI lend his royal name to two documents: the 'devise for the succession'[23] and the letters patent for the limitation of the crown (Doc. 25). The 'devise' need not detain us. It was little more than a recital of provisions for a new succession and was superseded by the letters patent. The 'devise' has attracted much attention because of its many emendations which record the futile efforts of Edward and Northumberland to escape from the dichotomy involved in their desire to hold on to their conception of a Salic law and yet permit Lady Jane to succeed to the throne.[24] The letters patent was the more important document, however, in that it was the final and official limitation of the crown and presented the arguments designed to give the appearance of right to that which could never be right.

The letters patent (Doc. 25) began rather innocuously by indicating the king's concern over the succession due to his failing health, but this was immediately followed by the damaging admission that his half-sisters were to be deprived of their claims to the crown despite the fact that the Succession Act of 1544 (Doc. 22) had vested the succession in Mary and then Elizabeth should Edward die without issue. This constituted a virtual acknowledgment of the illegality of Edward's intended settlement. The succession provisions of the 1544 statute had never been repealed; indeed, they had been corroborated by Henry VIII's will. Moreover, the 1544 statute had declared it high treason to be a party to the 'interruption, repeal, or annulment of this act, or of any thing therein contained, or of anything that shall be done by' Henry 'in the limitation and disposition' of the crown. And this had been confirmed in the eighth clause of Edward VI's Treasons Act of 1547.[25] Those who subscribed to the exclusion of Mary and Elizabeth were guilty of high treason if it ever was treason to obey the wishes of a living monarch. And the entire limitation of the crown that was to follow was dependent upon the validity of their exclusion.

Now there was nothing accidental about the illegality of the letters patent. The young king had been duly warned by his highest judges and

---

J. S. Brewer (Oxford 1845), iv. pp. 137–46; John Strype, *Memorials . . . of Thomas Cranmer* (London 1853), ii. app. lxxiv; P. F. Tytler, *England under the Reigns of Edward VI and Mary* (London 1839), ii. pp. 171–204.

[22] The notables are listed according to rank and office in *The Chronicle of Queen Jane*, ed. J. G. Nichols (Camden Society, London 1850), p. 100.

[23] Above, n. 19.

[24] For an interesting discussion of the changes in the 'devise' see Pollard, *Political History*, pp. 64, 84–5.

[25] 1. Edward VI cap. 12; *Stat. Realm*, iv. 20.

law officers that his 'devise' was 'directly against the Act of Succession',
which, as a parliamentary statute, could not be repealed by royal fiat.
None the less, Edward insisted that the reluctant lawyers draw up his
letters patent.[26] Here was the great difference between the succession
arrangements of Henry VIII and Edward VI. Henry had thrice dealt
with the succession through parliamentary enactments, thereby providing a constitutional means of settling the succession. Edward attempted
to flout the standing legislation on the subject and deny the competence
of statute via a deliberate exercise of despotic will.[27]

Of course, the authors of the letters patent contrived arguments in
favour of overturning the established succession. The first and most
obvious was that Mary and Elizabeth were bastards and therefore unable
to claim the crown, statute notwithstanding. This argument might have
worked if its premise had been really credible. It must have been difficult for Englishmen to believe that Henry VIII had not been lawfully
married to either Catherine of Aragon or Anne Boleyn. The ground of
his divorce from Catherine was well known and certainly questionable;
the ground of his divorce from Anne had never been made public.
These things allowed men to accept one or the other marriage according
to their prejudices. If the Aragon match was valid, Mary was legitimate;
if the Boleyn union was valid, Elizabeth was legitimate and Mary could
also be deemed so on the ground of the lawful ignorance of her parents
of the invalidity of their marriage at the time of her birth. Moreover, an
implication of legitimacy could be read into Henry's restoration of his
daughters to the succession by statute and will: the king could not very
well have been expected to call his own justice in question by specifically
restoring his daughters in blood. Two weeks after Edward's death
Charles V's ambassadors in England reported to Prince Philip that
since Henry made his will Mary 'has always been regarded here as
legitimate'.[28] The same may well have applied to Elizabeth, whom
Philip was not particularly interested in at the time. Consequently,
the reaffirmation of their bastardy in the letters patent was not likely
to be received favourably; on the contrary, most people were
probably shocked when they learned of this cruel act done in Edward's
name.

The second argument devised by the authors of the letters patent to
debar the king's half sisters was even less likely to be effective than the
first. Edward VI was made to say that Mary and Elizabeth 'be unto us
but of the half blood, and therefore' according to English law 'be not
inheritable unto us, although they were legitimate, as they be not

[26] See Montague's testimony in Fuller, *Church History*, iv. p. 139.
[27] Surely an instance of attempted Tudor despotism, but not the work of
Henry VIII or Thomas Cromwell.
[28] *Span. Cal.* xi. p. 101.

indeed'. This attempt to apply the common-law rule against inheritance by the half blood to the royal succession was most probably unprecedented.[29] Moreover, the one precedent at the time for the succession of the half blood was an inappropriate and perhaps dangerous one for a Tudor to contravene, for Henry VII's claim to the crown had come from his descent from John Beaufort, earl of Somerset, a legitimated half brother of Henry IV. At any rate, England could hardly be expected to see the argument that Mary and Elizabeth were excluded from the succession because they were Edward's half sisters as much more than mere legal trickery.

The last objection raised against Mary and Elizabeth was that after their accessions they might marry aliens, and such unions might lead to the subversion of the laws and customs of England. This might have made some impression if Northumberland had seriously tried to arrange English matches for Mary and Elizabeth as he had done for their Suffolk second cousins. The marriage of a queen regnant to a foreign prince was indeed potentially dangerous for England. So, however, was the marriage of a queen regnant to a domestic nobleman, which might provoke baronial jealousies and even factional strife in England. A spinster queen regnant was apparently unthinkable.

After disposing of the king's sisters, the letters patent made Edward call to his remembrance certain things about his second cousins of the Suffolk line. Ladies Jane, Catherine, and Mary Grey and Lady Margaret Clifford were 'very nigh of our whole blood, of the part of our father's side'; they were 'natural-born here within the realm'; they had been 'very honourably brought up and exercised in good and godly learning and other noble virtues', which promised that they would be 'very well inclined to the advancement and setting forth of our commonwealth'. Out of these recollections two qualifications besides legitimate and whole blood emerged for the kingship: the wearer of the crown must be English and must be a zealous Protestant.

The first of these undoubtedly arose out of another bit of remembering. Edward had cousins of the Stuart line who not only were very nearly of his whole blood on his father's side but also had priority over the Suffolks in the hereditary order. This obstacle would be eliminated if only those who were 'natural-born here within the realm' were eligible for the succession. Mary Queen of Scots was a foreigner and Lady Margaret Lennox, though born in Northumberland, could be considered an alien on the ground that her parents were not under the allegiance of England at the time of her birth.

[29] It is remotely possible that this rule played some part in Henry IV's refusal to include the royal dignity in his confirmation of the legitimation of the Beauforts. See T. P. Taswell-Langmead, *English Constitutional History*, 11th edn (Boston 1960), p. 495.

The second qualification indicated Edward's objective in becoming the instrument of Northumberland's design. His cousins of Suffolk had been 'very honourably brought up and exercised in good and godly learning'. This did not refer to education *per se*. Elizabeth, like Lady Jane Grey and Edward himself, had received a 'good and godly' training in the new humanism as it came from Cambridge, but it had not caused her to adopt the new religious doctrines that were coming from Switzerland. It was Jane who had embraced the ideas of the Zürich reformers, who had called Henry Bullinger, Zwingli's successor, the 'intrepid . . . champion of true religion', the 'brightest ornament and support of the whole church of Christ'.[30] Jane was Edward's spiritual sister; she was 'very well inclined to the advancement and setting forth of our commonwealth'. As queen she could be counted on to uphold and further the cause of Protestantism in England. That was what the king expected of his successor; that was why he evidently had no compunction about ignoring the rights of his real sisters.

Next in the letters patent came the main business of the limitation of the crown. If Edward was to die without issue, the succession was first to go to sons who might be born to Lady Francis Brandon during the king's lifetime. This was a meaningless gesture since Edward's life expectancy precluded the possibility of a woman who was not pregnant having a son. The next places, the only significant ones, went to Ladies Jane, Catherine and Mary Grey and their respective heirs male. Then followed a real jigsaw-puzzle of unborn males which did not always conform to proper hereditary order and which, thanks to its insignificance, may safely be left to those fascinated by studies in confusion. There were incongruities enough in the proximate settlement.

These arose out of the desire of Edward and Northumberland to have a Salic law and yet ensure a Suffolk succession when there was no existing male claimant in the Suffolk line. The answer of the king's 'devise' had been to make Lady Jane Grey the exception to the rule and then vest the succession in her heirs male, her sisters' heirs male, and those of Lady Margaret Clifford.[31] This was unsafe because Jane might die before a male Suffolk had been produced. The letters patent corrected this by also making exceptions out of Ladies Catherine and Mary Grey, but this was a surrender to expediency and not to logic. It was illogical to exclude future sisters. Nor was it reasonable to ignore Margaret Clifford, who, like the Grey sisters, was a great-granddaughter of Henry VII and who but a few sentences before had been referred to as having the same qualifications as the Ladies Grey.

[30] *Original Letters relative to the English Reformation*, ed. Hastings Robinson (Parker Society, Cambridge 1846–7), i. pp. 5, 7.
[31] Williams, *English Historical Documents*, v. 460.

But the outstanding defect in the new limitation of the crown was the exclusion of Lady Frances Brandon. Assuming that the king's sisters and the Stuarts had been rightfully deprived of their places in the succession, Frances, not her daughter Jane, came first hereditarily among the Suffolks. Frances's claim, however, almost had to be disregarded. If she became queen, her husband most probably would become king in fact if not in name. Henry Grey was valuable to Northumberland as a junior partner, but he did not intend to make him head of the firm. Henry VIII's will, which had assigned the succession to Frances's heirs and not to Frances herself, might have provided a way out, but it evidently was deemed best to forget a document that might remind England that her late king of famous memory had named Mary and Elizabeth to the succession before the Suffolks. The ignoring of the prior claim of Lady Frances was an injustice of Edward VI's arrangements for the succession that would be visibly brought home to the English people when Queen Jane arrived at the Tower accompanied by her mother who was bearing her train.[32]

The conclusion of the letters patent went beyond despotism to tyranny. The 15-year-old king, who was not old enough to make a will for any purpose, was made to charge all Englishmen, high and low, to see that his will regarding the succession was carried out, which amounted to a command to commit what by statute law was high treason.[33] They were also to see that his limitation of the crown was validated by Parliament and all laws to the contrary repealed. If there was any real hope that Edward would live long enough to have another Parliament, this might have made sense. But if, as must have been expected, the king died within a few weeks, his successor and her Parliament would only be committed to the manifest absurdity of taking illegal steps to legalize their own existence. What could be a clearer admission of the invalidity of the entire settlement?

Doubtless the main reason for the failure of Northumberland's plan was its illegality. Discontent with the Reformation may well have been a factor, but Protestants as well as Catholics embraced Mary's cause.[34] Northumberland's unpopularity may also have been involved, but England had tolerated his rule under Edward VI and probably would have continued to do so if he could have provided a lawful successor. By 1553 the Tudor version of fifteenth-century history, then readily available in two or perhaps three editions of Hall's *Chronicle*, had acquired almost the status of an article of faith. Its message was that

---

[32] *The Diary of Henry Machyn*, ed. J. G. Nichols (Camden Society, London 1848), p. 35.

[33] Above, p. 83.

[34] See Nichols, *Chronicle of Queen Jane*, pp. 110–11; Pollard, *Somerset*, pp. 311–12; Jordan, *Edward VI*, ii. pp. 524–5, 527.

usurpations inevitably led to anarchy, and anything was preferable to that. The accession of Henry VIII, the heir to both Lancaster and York, was seen as settling a succession question that had troubled England since 1399. The indisputably lawful king had left only a frail son of undoubted legitimacy and two daughters of debatable legitimacy, but by statute and will authorized by statute he had set a succession that would remain in the Tudor line until it was extinct. The English people were not inclined to reject this Tudor succession established by law because of dubious arguments presented in the name of a boy. Mary seems to have sensed this in her letters demanding allegiance in which she based her claim to the crown not on hereditary right but on the Succession Act of 1544 and the 'testament and last will of our late dearest father, King Henry VIII' (Doc. 26).[35]

When Edward VI died on 6 July 1553, the odds seemed to be on the side of Northumberland's attempt to alter the succession. Council, armed force, and treasure were all at his command. The king's death was kept secret for three days to allow Northumberland to consolidate his position. When Queen Jane was proclaimed in London on the 10th Northumberland's success seemed assured. True, Mary had fled to friendly Howard country and sent out letters as queen demanding allegiance, but Charles V's ambassadors in London, doubtless reflecting the general view there, practically despaired of her chances.[36] But Mary, uncharacteristically for her, knew England better. Northumberland's forces dwindled as he moved towards Mary's rapidly growing army. All over England Mary I, the unengaging but lawful Tudor successor, was being proclaimed; on the 19th the council followed suit in London and on the next day Northumberland, facing certain doom whichever way he turned, proclaimed Queen Mary in Cambridge.

England now had a queen regnant, and an unmarried one at that. Cardinal Pole seems to have been alone in his opinion that Mary, because of her age which made childbearing unlikely, should remain single, 'leaving the affairs of the succession of the realm to take their course'.[37] Pole himself, not yet a priest, was a possible husband for Mary, but the main English candidate for her hand was Edward Courtenay, earl of Devon. Courtenay's sole qualification was his Yorkist descent; otherwise his ambition was only exceeded by his lack of ability and his cowardice. A choice of Courtenay might well have had similar consequences for Mary Tudor as the choice of Darnley was to have for Mary Stuart. But there was no danger that Mary I would marry Courtenay; from the start she was determined to take a Habsburg

---

[35] Also see her letter to the council in Raphael Holinshed, *Chronicles of England, Scotland, and Ireland*, ed. Henry Ellis (London 1807–8), iii. p. 1066.

[36] *Span. Cal.* xi. p. 89.

[37] *Ven. Cal.* v. p. 404. Also see Tytler, *Edward VI and Mary*, ii. pp. 303–4.

husband. When Charles V offered his son, Philip of Spain, the matter was settled as far as the queen was concerned.

Mary's decision to marry Philip, which was hardly a well-kept secret,[38] was bound to arouse concern about the succession. What if the queen died without issue? Would the Spaniard then be left as king of England? Fears of the possibility of a Spanish succession had to be allayed if the marriage was to be made at least tolerable to the English. It was in this connexion that Mary and Lord Paget, the principal supporter of the Spanish match on the council, conferred late in November with Simon Renard, the Imperial ambassador (Doc. 28).

Both Mary and Paget apparently hoped to make a succession settlement, presumably excluding Philip, part of the marriage treaty. Paget thought that if the succession were so settled, 'the people and the nobility might easily be brought to accept the marriage'. Be that as it may, the immediate problem was the designation of an heir presumptive. Mary Queen of Scots and Lady Frances Brandon were mentioned as having hereditary claims, but neither of them could have been given serious consideration, the Scottish queen owing to her French match and Lady Frances on account of her family's recent association with Northumberland. Then there was Elizabeth who, according to statute and Henry VIII's will, was already heir presumptive. But Mary I scrupled 'to allow her to succeed because of her heretical opinions, illegitimacy, and characteristics in which she resembled her mother'; the queen also feared that her sister would be a French partisan. Mary evidently preferred Lady Margaret Lennox, 'the person best suited to succeed'.

Paget obviously favoured Elizabeth's being declared heir presumptive in the marriage treaty, that is, a confirmation of the succession already established by law. He also suggested that Elizabeth be matched with Courtenay. This union, so Paget thought, would satisfy Courtenay and keep Elizabeth Catholic. And keeping Elizabeth in the succession would prevent her from becoming a French partisan, which would be unsafe 'because it was impossible to make the heart of the kingdom French except by the utmost violence'. The difficulty of making the heart of the kingdom Spanish apparently was not considered. At any rate, Paget failed to overcome Mary's reluctance to allow her sister to succeed, and inducing Parliament to repeal the Succession Act of 1544, which entailed the crown upon Elizabeth after Mary and her issue, would be, as Paget implied, well-nigh impossible. This meant that Mary, who had originally based her own claim to the throne on the 1544 statute and the will authorized by it (Doc. 26), could only attempt to alter the succession in defiance of statute.

---

[38] See D. M. Loades, *Two Tudor Conspiracies* (Cambridge 1965), pp. 12–18.

Whether due to inclination or necessity, Mary I, unlike those who ruled in her brother's name, showed much respect for the supremacy of statute in matters dynastic. When Mary ascended the throne it was only to be expected that she would secure reversals of Cranmer's sentence against her mother's marriage and her subsequent statutory bastardization. These things were accomplished in an act of 1553 (Doc. 27). Parliament, not an ecclesiastical court, pronounced void the judgment of Cranmer's archiepiscopal court against the Aragon marriage and declared that marriage to be valid. The Succession Act of 1536 (Doc. 19) was repealed insofar as it bastardized Mary. This left Elizabeth illegitimate, but the great significance of the 1553 statute derived from its voiding of a royal divorce and legitimation of a queen without citing any ecclesiastical authority. Mary doubtless would have preferred the inclusion of some reference to the papal decision in favour of her mother's marriage, but this might have been taken to imply a restitution of papal supremacy. The implied message for the queen, which she accepted, was that she would have to await a more compliant Parliament to restore the Pope in England. The Parliament of 1553 had done more than to establish a legal basis for Mary I to claim to rule by hereditary right; in effect, it had, with the queen's acquiescence, confirmed and consolidated the position of virtual omnicompetence to which statute had been elevated during the reign of Henry VIII.

The next Parliament, that of 2 April–5 May 1554, considered the authority of a queen regnant. The resulting statute (Doc. 29) declared that 'the law of this realm is and ever hath been' that all regal powers of the kings of England, 'being invested either in male or female, are and be and ought to be taken in the one as in the other'. Though the wording of the act indicated that it was merely confirmatory, kingly power in fact was conferred upon Mary I and future queens regnant by statute. Past statutes, as the act indicated, specifically referred to kings only in connexion with regal power, and this might lead 'malicious and ignorant persons' into denying Mary the authority of her predecessors. If we may believe an Elizabethan account, however, Parliament feared the opposite because of a tract that urged the queen to claim that she ruled by right of conquest and therefore was not bound by the laws of former kings. If so the fear was groundless, for Mary, according to the story, showed her rejection of the absolutist tract by burning it.[39] At any rate, the date of the act suggests that Parliament's main concern was the impending Spanish match. The vesting of kingly power in Mary would legally bar Philip, no matter what his title, from claiming it for himself.

Mary's respect for statutory authority was at least questionable in the case of Henry VIII's will. Early in her reign Mary seems to have

[39] See W. H. Dunham, Jr, 'Regal Power and the Rule of Law: a Tudor Paradox', *Journal of British Studies* (1964), iii, no. 2, pp. 45–6.

ordered the destruction of the chancery enrolment of the will. In
Elizabeth I's reign advocates of the Stuart claim alleged that Mary so
acted because the will was found to be invalid. If the queen really had
the enrolment destroyed on the ground that the will was invalid, however, it is difficult to see why she did not also order the destruction of the
original will instead of leaving it in the safe-keeping of the discreet Lord
Treasurer Paulet. More likely, Mary had the record of the will destroyed
in the interest of the Spanish match. Henry VIII had statutory authorization to set conditions by will governing the eligibility of his daughters
to assume the royal dignity (Doc. 22); the will required that they obtain
the consent of a majority of the surviving councillors and executors
named therein to marry (Doc. 23). Mary I surely had no intention of
placing the question of her marriage before the remainder of Edward
VI's original council of regency, but if she did not, it was possible to
allege that she had thereby forfeited her crown to Elizabeth.[40] This
doubtless was what Renard had in mind when he predicted that Mary
would have the will 'annulled for the sake of avoiding all the difficulties
that Elizabeth would make if she were able'. Indeed the Dudley conspirators later tried to make trouble for Mary along these lines despite
any destruction of the enrolment: they exhibited a copy of Henry's will
and pretended that the queen 'having done contrary thereto, has forfeited the crown . . ., and therefore they may rebel against her'.[41]

The Spanish match, both before and after its completion, was the
main reason for the conspiracies of Mary's reign. The marriage treaties,
signed on 12 January 1554, were obviously designed in the hope of dis-
pelling English fears about the match and indeed making it attractive.
Spaniards were to hold no offices in England. Philip was not to involve
England in his current war with France. He was to be given the title of
king during Mary's lifetime and might assist her in government, but his
connexion with England was to end if she died childless. If they had
children, their eldest son was to inherit England, the Netherlands, and
Franche-Comté, and if Don Carlos, Philip's son by a former wife, were
to die without issue, Spain and its dependencies as well.[42] That Philip
had signed a secret protestation absolving himself from full observance
of the treaties [43] was not known in England.

Nevertheless, the treaties were received with suspicion in England.
When their terms were revealed to an assembly of notables, Lord

[40] The question of whether the consent requirement of the will was meant to
apply to reigning queens as well as daughters in the line of succession does not
seem to have come up.
[41] See Mortimer Levine, *The Early Elizabethan Succession Question, 1558–
1568* (Stanford 1966), pp. 151, 152–3, 155.
[42] The treaties are in *Foedera*, ed. Thomas Rymer (London 1726–35), xv. pp.
377–81, 393–403.
[43] Loades, *Tudor Conspiracies*, p. 18.

Windsor, who ordinarily was slow to grasp anything, quickly asked what would happen if Philip failed to keep his promises. Despite much distrust of the Spaniards, however, most of the great men of the realm were prepared to acquiesce, since, with the privy council already committed to the marriage and Parliament dissolved, resistance would have to take the form of open rebellion. Only a few extremists, mainly lesser men, were ready to take that dangerous course.[44]

Four simultaneous risings were planned for 18 March. Outbreaks were to be led by Sir Thomas Wyatt in Kent, by the duke of Suffolk in Leicestershire, by Sir Peter Carew and presumably Courtenay in Devon, and by Sir James Crofts in Herefordshire. Leaks about the impending risings and revelations to Lord Chancellor Gardiner by the cowardly Courtenay, however, forced those conspirators who were to act at all to do so before January was over. No rising occurred in Herefordshire, and those in Devon and Leicestershire were abortive. Only the Kentish rising assumed the proportions of a serious rebellion, Wyatt's forces actually reaching London. In the end, the rebellion collapsed thanks to Mary's courage and the military aid provided by former allies of Northumberland, notably the earls of Pembroke and Huntingdon.[45]

The primary objective of the rebels of 1554, as indicated by Wyatt in his proclamation to the men of Kent, was to stop the Spanish match: 'no earthly cause could move us unto this enterprise but this alone'.[46] They sought, so Wyatt protested, 'no harm to the Queen, but better counsel and councillors'.[47] Saving England from Spain and meaning no harm to the queen was the obvious formula to give the risings the widest possible popular appeal, but a month before the leading conspirators had agreed upon a policy of marrying Elizabeth to Courtenay and supplanting Mary I with them.[48] The course of events had not ruled out the idea of deposing Mary; indeed, that might well have been a logical or necessary consequence of a rebel victory. Suffolk's joining the conspiracy did not mean that he or anyone else now intended to re-proclaim Queen Jane,[49] though his involvement was to result in his innocent daughter's execution as well as his own. The only practicable replacement for Mary remained Elizabeth with or without that weakling Courtenay.

While the success of the 1554 risings might have put Elizabeth on the throne prematurely and perhaps disastrously with Courtenay, their

[44] Wernham, *Before the Armada*, pp. 213–14. Also see Loades, *Tudor Conspiracies*, pp. 15–17.

[45] A full account of the 1554 risings is in ibid. pp. 21–88.

[46] Any view that the rebels were mainly inspired by zeal for Protestantism will not stand up (see ibid. pp. 16–17, 87–8).

[47] *Tudor Tracts*, ed. A. F. Pollard (Westminster, 1903), pp. 212–13.

[48] Loades, *Tudor Conspiracies*, p. 19.

[49] See ibid. pp. 27–8.

failure threatened to upset the succession established by law. It was suspected that Elizabeth and Courtenay were implicated in the conspiracy and Renard pressed for their trial and execution. Courtenay's involvement could not be proved, probably due to Gardiner's suppressing incriminating evidence against him. Courtenay was not tried and in 1555 was released and went into exile on the Continent.[50] The danger to Elizabeth was greater, for she was Spain's principal target. When Elizabeth was committed to the Tower in March 1554, Hurtado de Mendoza, Charles V's envoy, indicated the need for her execution, 'as while she lives it will be very difficult to make the Prince's entry here safe'.[51] And Gardiner and Mary had most likely no desire for Elizabeth's survival. Efforts to get Wyatt and other traitors to implicate her failed, however. In April Renard reported that 'the judges can find no matter for her condemnation,[52] and Mary was not one to murder her sister judicially without some evidence of guilt.[53] In May Elizabeth was transferred from the Tower to house-arrest at Woodstock in Oxfordshire. Her reception by the people in the course of her journey to Woodstock turned what was supposed to be a retreat into disfavour into a veritable royal progress,[54] an indication of the continuing popularity of the heir presumptive.

Though the risings failed to stop the Spanish match, they doubtless helped to increase public concern about the possible consequences of that match for England. This concern was reflected in the doings of Mary's second Parliament, which was summoned primarily for the purpose of ratifying the marriage treaties. In its first act this Parliament removed any doubt that all regal powers of the kings of England now resided in the queen, thus, as previously suggested, legally barring the coming King Consort from claiming those powers for himself.[55] In its next act Parliament not merely confirmed the marriage treaties but rehearsed their terms. Thus it was stated by statute that if Mary predeceased Philip and they had no children, he was to have no claim to the crown and was to 'permit the succession thereof to come unto them to whom it shall belong and appertain by the right and laws' of England. This last was an implied statutory guarantee of Elizabeth's status as heir presumptive. In addition, the act declared that Mary, 'as a sole queen', was to have 'the crown and sovereignty of and over' her 'realms,

[50] See ibid. pp. 89–95.
[51] *Span. Cal.* xii. p. 162.
[52] Tytler, *Edward VI and Mary*, ii. p. 375.
[53] It is difficult to believe that the shrewd Elizabeth would have allowed herself to become unnecessarily involved with conspirators who, if successful, probably would have had to turn to her anyway.
[54] See Neville Williams, *Elizabeth the First, Queen of England* (London 1968), pp. 35–6.
[55] Above, p. 90.

dominions, and subjects'.[56] Clearly Parliament sought to provide every feasible statutory bar against Spanish rule and against a Spanish succession.

Gardiner seems to have hoped that the Parliament would assure Elizabeth's removal from the succession. According to Paget, someone, presumably Gardiner, proposed that, 'since matters against Madame Elizabeth do not take the turn which was wished, there should be an act brought into Parliament to disinherit her'. Paget would not consent to the proposal,[57] which probably never reached Parliament. More likely Gardiner decided to substitute a seemingly subtle scheme to replace Elizabeth, that is, to have Parliament empower Mary to leave the crown by will.[58] This, however, was not likely to fool many; it was almost bound to be viewed as intended to enable Mary, if she had no children, to designate Philip as her successor. If the proposal was put before Parliament – Paget may well have stopped it in the council – it probably was rejected overwhelmingly. Elizabeth, unless she allowed herself to become implicated in a conspiracy, was not going to be deprived of her place in the succession by legal means.

On 25 July 1554, the marriage of Philip and Mary was solemnized and Philip, as provided in the marriage treaties, had his title of king. Now Philip and especially Charles V had not accepted what to them must have been unfavourable treaties for a mere title. Their real objective was to bring England into the Habsburg orbit not only for the duration of the marriage but permanently. Developments of the first few months of the marriage seemed to promise success for the enterprise. The King Consort's correct and prudent behaviour won him some popularity in England. By autumn Mary was thought to be with child, a child who would be three-quarters Spanish by blood and whose upbringing Philip might expect to have charge of. Philip had hopes of getting most, if not all, of what he wanted out of the third Parliament of the reign, that of 12 November 1554–16 January 1555, the 'Catholic' Parliament that restored papal supremacy. Its compliance, however, was limited when it came to matters of a dynastic nature.

Early moves to get Elizabeth declared a bastard and to turn the succession to Philip in the event of Mary's death without issue had to be abandoned.[59] In January 1555, after the King Consort's popularity had practically evaporated, the Parliament did produce a statute dealing with his position in England. This act gave Philip the protection of the treason laws as if he were fully king. Of greater potential importance, it

[56] I. Mary st. 3 cap. 2; *Stat. Realm*, iv. 222–5.
[57] Tytler, *Edward VI and Mary*, ii. p. 382.
[58] See Pollard, *Political History*, p. 119; P. Hughes, *The Reformation in England*, rev. edn (New York 1963), ii. p. 211.
[59] *Span. Cal.* xiii. 131.

gave Philip, in the event of Mary's death, the government of the realm during the minority of their issue. For the duration of such minority, however, the marriage treaties and the act confirming them were to be observed,[60] an implied stipulation that, should the heirs fail to reach majority, the succession would revert to Elizabeth and not go to Philip. About the same time a bill for Philip's coronation was unanimously rejected by the Commons.[61]

The question of Philip's coronation became the main issue as 1555 progressed and Mary's pregnancy proved a false one. The Imperialists lost all hope that the 37-year-old queen would ever have children and gave some thought to the idea of securing the future by matching Elizabeth with a Habsburg.[62] This, however, would require both Elizabeth's co-operation and English acceptance of another Habsburg match, neither of which were by any means certain. The Imperialists apparently decided that their most promising course would be to press for the coronation of Philip, who left England in September to join Charles V in the Netherlands.

On the surface the coronation proposal was innocuous. A coronation would bring back to the queen her 'loving' husband and would not alter his position according to law. But those opposed to the Spanish connexion succeeded in rousing English fears about the consequences of a coronation. They saw it as changing a king consort, which was an unprecedented and vague position, into an anointed king. As such Philip, contrary to treaties and statutes, might with some justification claim to be a full king, to possess the crown and the regalia with or without Mary and with the succession to the same belonging to his heirs whoever their mother.[63] What Philip, if crowned, would have done probably would have been determined by circumstances, but, considering the zeal of the Imperialists for his coronation, the fears of the English were not groundless.

Mary intended to have the coronation proposal presented to her fourth Parliament which met in late 1555. She found the opposition so strong that she dared not make the proposal. Philip seems to have been willing to let the matter rest, but Charles V goaded him on. No sooner was Parliament dissolved than Philip began to press Mary to have him crowned by her prerogative power. Only if she did this would he return to England. As much as the queen wanted her husband back, she could not risk a step that was opposed by her councillors as well as the country at large. Nor could she induce the council to declare war on France. By March 1556 Philip was openly expressing his disgust with England.[64]

[60] 1. and 2. Philip and Mary cap. 10; *Stat. Realm*, iv. 255–6.
[61] Loades, *Tudor Conspiracies*, p. 140.
[62] See *Span. Cal.* xiii. 249.
[63] See Loades, *Tudor Conspiracies*, pp. 138–40.
[64] See ibid. pp. 140–1.

In the same month Mary had to deal with a serious conspiracy that was in no small measure a product of Philip's demands for his coronation and English aid against France.

The conspiracy, the leadership of which was assumed by Sir Henry Dudley, a distant cousin of Northumberland, had its origin during the last months of 1555. The heated parliamentary opposition to the queen's policies no doubt was taken by extremists as indicative that the time was ripe for the overthrow of the Marian regime. Dudley and his associates received encouragement from Antoine de Noailles, the French ambassador, and hoped to use France as a source of money and a base from which to launch an invasion of England. They expected that a successful landing would inspire discontented gentry first in the west country and then in the southern shires to lead risings. After the conclusion of a Franco-Spanish truce in February 1556 destroyed the possibility of effective aid from France, the conspirators hit upon the bold plan of securing funds by seizing the exchequer. The plan was betrayed to the council in March, arrests began, and, though there were a few disturbances,[65] Dudley's conspiracy was soon over. Mere luck had saved Mary I from having to face a rebellion potentially more dangerous than Wyatt's.[66]

If Dudley's plans for rebellion were more sophisticated than those of the conspirators of 1554, his plan for replacing Mary and Philip was by 1556 rather naive. Apparently all he and his fellows could conceive of was the old idea of Elizabeth married to Courtenay. While the need for Elizabeth was obvious, past performances should have ruled out the inclusion of the unreliable Courtenay. In any case, sad experiences and fear of assassination by Spanish agents [67] had made Courtenay wary. There is no evidence that emissaries sent to Venice by Dudley succeeded in implicating Courtenay, whose death later in the year merely removed an unnecessary dynastic complication. Nor could any proof be produced that Elizabeth even knew of the conspiracy. Nevertheless, Mary wanted to get her sister out of English reach by sending her overseas. Philip managed to put a stop to this idea, the carrying out of which, considering Elizabeth's popularity, would have been extremely dangerous.[68] Elizabeth had survived another major conspiracy with her position as heir presumptive intact.

In March 1557 Philip, now, since his father's abdication early in the previous year, Philip II of Spain, returned to England to seek English involvement in his recently renewed war with France. Initially the

[65] Pollard, *Political History*, p. 161.

[66] For a full study of Dudley's conspiracy see Loades, *Tudor Conspiracies*, pp. 176–237.

[67] *Ven. Cal.* vi. 328.

[68] See Loades, *Tudor Conspiracies*, pp. 198–9.

council resisted all efforts of Philip and Mary in this behalf. Then in late April Thomas Stafford, a grandson of Buckingham, and a band of exiles made a landing at Scarborough and seized the castle there. Their two ships and their arms had been supplied by Henry II of France. It is possible that Stafford, who lacked Dudley's understanding of English realities, intended to assert his own remote claim to the crown. At any rate, the invaders drew next to no support and were easily defeated. French backing of this foolhardy enterprise, however, proved the provocation that broke the council's resistance.[69] By June England's war with France was under way, a war fought in Spanish interests that cost England Calais and brought to full bloom English dislike of the Spaniards and their king.

By the fall of 1558, when Mary I's demise was obvious, any attempt on the part of the queen to turn the succession away from Elizabeth to Philip or anyone else would have been against Spanish interests as well as English. The ensuing crisis would have presented Henry II of France with an irresistible opportunity to invade a weakened England with the purpose of placing his daughter-in-law, Mary Queen of Scots, on the throne of the Tudors. French hegemony over the British Isles was a possibility that Philip II of Spain could not risk, no matter what the alternative. Therefore, his main English objective became that of persuading his wife to accept her sister as her successor. On 6 November Mary I acceded to her council's request that she 'make certain declarations in favour of the Lady Elizabeth concerning the succession'.[70] Three days later Count Feria, Philip's ambassador, paid a secret visit to Elizabeth, told her that her succession was assured, and implied that she owed the same to Philip.[71] That Mary, who never got over the disillusioning experience of the loss of Calais, merely yielded to the influence of her absentee husband is surely questionable. The queen, whose original claim to the crown was based on her father's statute and will, may well have been governed mainly in her decision by respect for the law of the realm. Be that as it may, when Mary I died on 17 November, Elizabeth I, unlike her sister after the death of their brother, enjoyed a peaceful accession: the Henrician succession settlement had managed to survive the troublous reigns of a child and a half-Spanish woman.

[69] Pollard, *Political History*, p. 164; Wernham, *Before the Armada*, pp. 230–1.
[70] *Span. Cal.* xiii. 498.
[71] Tytler, *Edward VI and Mary*, ii. p. 498.

5

The Reign of Elizabeth I to 1571

Philip II's expedient advocacy and Mary I's late 'declarations' did not make Elizabeth I queen; they merely assured that the inevitable happened peacefully. Elizabeth had been essentially correct at the secret meeting of 9 November when she told Feria that she would owe her crown to the people of England.[1] The mistakes and crises of Mary's reign had served to elevate Elizabeth's popularity. That she was Anne Boleyn's daughter had become more an asset than a liability, for it made her a fully English Tudor. Even the Catholic north was enthusiastic over the accession of 'a princess . . . of no mingled blood of Spaniard, or stranger, but born mere English here among us, and therefore most natural unto us'.[2] True, Elizabeth remained bastardized by her father's Succession Act of 1536 (Doc. 19), but what really mattered was that the crown was now hers according to his Succession Act of 1544 (Doc. 22) and his will (Doc. 23) authorized by that statute. In 1558, as in 1553, the English people would have none other than the lawful Tudor succession set by King Henry VIII of famous memory.

This statutory succession was in fact the only legal basis for Elizabeth I's title that her first Parliament, which met in early 1559, put forward in its act recognizing her right to the throne (Doc. 30). The tactful statement of this act that the queen was 'rightly, lineally, and lawfully descended and come of the blood royal' did not change her status in blood according to law. That would have required repeal of the 1536 bastardization, something that Elizabeth, whatever her reason, never sought. The determinative declaration of the 1559 statute was that the crown now belonged to Elizabeth as rightfully as it did to Henry VIII, Edward VI, or Mary I 'at any time since' the enactment of the Succession Act of 1544. This implied that Elizabeth had had no claim to the succession from her exclusion in 1536 to her restoration in 1544, that

[1] P. F. Tytler, *England under the Reigns of Edward VI and Mary* (London 1839), ii. p. 499.
[2] N. Williams, *Elizabeth the First, Queen of England* (London 1968), p. 50.

her present title was statutory rather than hereditary. Moreover, the 1559 statute stated that 'the limitation and declaration of the succession' established by the 1544 statute 'shall stand, be, and remain the law of this realm for ever'. This last would apply not only to Elizabeth's issue but to the further succession designated in Henry VIII's will authorized by the 1544 statute, that is, if the will was valid. The foregoing analysis may seem to involve reading too much into an act of recognition, but the Parliament of 1559, which forced on the queen a religious settlement more Protestant than she had wanted, was surely not beyond using such an act as a means of asserting the supremacy of parliamentary statute in the determination of the succession.

The question of the succession was indeed a cause for wide concern, for Elizabeth I was the last remaining Tudor. The ideal solution was for the queen to marry and have issue. And Elizabeth, as the greatest matrimonial prize in Christendom, had her choice of no end of potential consorts, foreign and domestic. The queen's statement to the Parliament of 1559 that she preferred to live and die a virgin [3] could not have been taken too seriously at the time. Most contemporaries doubtless shared the view expressed by an Imperial agent: 'that she should wish to remain a maid and never marry is inconceivable'.[4] But Elizabeth could not be expected to marry hastily and there was no guarantee that her marriage would be fruitful.

The next best and hopefully temporary solution was to designate the heir presumptive, but his or her identity was problematic. Elizabethans, like their predecessors, no doubt desired above all that a lawful successor be named, but, since the succession after the queen's non-existent issue was debatable in law, other considerations – male or female, Protestant or Catholic, foreign or domestic – also influenced men in their preferences. The result was a confused situation during the early years of Elizabeth's reign.

Hereditarily the next place after Elizabeth and her issue belonged to Mary Queen of Scots. The common-law rule against alien inheritance and Henry VIII's will, however, made Mary's claim doubtful in law. Moreover, Mary's position was complicated by her French marriage. England and France concluded their war at Cateau-Cambrésis in April 1559, but Henry II followed up the peace by having his daughter-in-law publicly assume the title and arms of England.[5] This signified that Mary's claim was asserted not for the succession to Elizabeth but for her

[3] R. Holinshed, *Chronicle of England, Scotland, and Ireland*, ed. Henry Ellis (London 1807–8), iv. p. 179.
[4] Victor von Klarwill, *Queen Elizabeth and Some Foreigners*, trans. T. H. Nash (London 1928), p. 94.
[5] *Burghley Papers*, ed. Samuel Haynes and William Murdin (London 1740–1759), i. pp. 277–8.

very crown. The pretension was not dropped after her husband became Francis II in July; indeed, her Guise kinsfolk, temporarily ascendant in France and Scotland, threatened to attempt to make a reality of Mary's immediate claim to the English throne.[6] Elizabeth by proclamation placed the blame for the 'injurious pretence' on the Guises and excused Francis and Mary as being too young to be 'capable of such an enterprise'.[7] Be this last as it may, Mary's claim, whether immediate or in remainder, must have enjoyed next to no support in England, even among Catholics, during her stay in France.

A more expedient succession choice for English Catholics at the time was the junior Stuart line represented by Lady Margaret Lennox and her son, Henry, Lord Darnley. Though the title of the Lennox Stuarts was hereditarily inferior to that of Mary Stuart, it was possible to argue that their claim was better because both mother and son were born in England. But it could be objected that the Englishness of their descent was broken because Lady Margaret's parents were not under allegiance to the king of England at the time of her birth.[8] And the Lennox Stuarts, like Mary Stuart, were ignored in Henry VIII's will. Moreover, Margaret's legitimacy was doubtful.[9] Nevertheless, the Lennox claim was the most feasible one for English Catholics to favour while the Scottish queen remained in France, and even after Mary's return to Scotland it still was backed by those Catholics who doubted her orthodoxy.[10]

If the Henrician succession settlement was to be followed, Lady Catherine Grey was the heir presumptive according to Henry's VIII's will. But the validity of that document, the original of which remained in concealment, was open to question. So was the legitimacy of Lady Catherine's descent from Henry VII.[11] And rumour had it that Catherine, despite the Protestant tradition of the Greys, was favourable to Catholicism. Indeed, Philip II hoped to marry her to a Habsburg and in early 1559 even considered having her spirited to the Continent for the accomplishment of such a match.[12] As late as October 1560, Bishop Quadra, the Spanish ambassador, reported to Philip that the English heretics feared 'that if the Queen were to die without issue your

---

[6] See J. B. Black, *The Reign of Elizabeth* (Oxford 1936), p. 34; Wallace MacCaffrey, *The Shaping of the Elizabethan Regime* (Princeton 1968), p. 71.

[7] *Tudor Royal Proclamations*, ed. P. L. Hughes and J. F. Larkin (New Haven and London, 1964–9), ii. p. 141.

[8] This objection was raised officially in 1562. See *For. Cal., Eliz.* v. 26.

[9] Investigations of 1562 and 1563 produced a strong case for her bastardy. See ibid., v. 25, vi, 483, 485; Haynes and Murdin, *Burghley Papers*, i. p. 381.

[10] *Span. Cal., Eliz.* i. 189.

[11] See below, p. 111.

[12] See M. Levine, *The Early Elizabethan Succession Question, 1558–1568* (Stanford 1966), pp. 13–15.

Majesty would get the kingdom into your family by means of Lady Catherine'.[13] Obviously there were doubts and suspicions about Catherine that had to be allayed before she could attract the backing that one might expect her to have in England as the leading Suffolk claimant.

A possible alternative to Catherine Grey was the former Lady Margaret Clifford, since 1555 wife of Henry Stanley, Lord Strange. Though her claim was hereditarily junior to those of Catherine and her younger sister Mary, Lady Margaret Strange reportedly alleged that her cousins of Grey were debarred from the succession because their sister Jane had corrupted their blood by her treason; hence she was next in line by Henry VIII's will and 'as the nearest in blood . . . legitimately of English birth'.[14] This application of the common-law rule against inheritance by persons of attainted blood to the succession was legally untenable.[15] Lady Margaret doubtless never had more than small support for her claim, and that probably came mainly from Lancashire where the Stanleys were an important Catholic family.

Wider backing was undoubtedly given to the claim of Henry Hastings, earl of Huntingdon, who after his mother was the heir of George of Clarence and whose paternal grandmother was Buckingham's sister. Huntingdon's lack of descent from Henry VII stood against him, but this no longer had to matter quite so much, since, in any case, Elizabeth's successor could not be a Tudor. One thing that made Huntingdon attractive to an England still unenthusiastic about women rulers was his sex. Another attraction to some was that he, though a nephew of Cardinal Pole, was a definite Protestant, indeed a Puritan. Moreover, Huntingdon, himself a Leicestershire magnate, had an influential connexion at Court in the person of his brother-in-law, Lord Robert Dudley. Huntingdon had the potential of being a serious contender for the succession, but he, perhaps warned by the fates of too many of his Yorkist and Stafford ancestors, apparently was not ambitious for the crown.[16]

A succession settlement was practically an impossibility with Englishmen so divided and confused about the claimants. Elizabeth I, as we shall see, was even less inclined to allow the succession to be determined than she was to marry. Only the strongest political necessity could have forced her to do either. It would take the course of events to clarify the situation somewhat and indicate that the most expedient succession choice, depending whether one's prejudices favoured hereditary right

[13] *Span. Cal., Eliz.* i. 120.

[14] *Ven. Cal.* vi. p. 1077.

[15] See above, pp. 30–35.

[16] See Claire Cross, *The Puritan Earl: the Life of Henry Hastings, Third Earl of Huntingdon* (London 1966), pp. 143–7.

and Catholicism or statutory right and Protestantism, was between Mary Queen of Scots and Lady Catherine Grey. That course of events began to unfold in August 1561.

On 12 August Sir William Cecil, Elizabeth's principal secretary, wrote of the discovery two days before of a 'great mishap'. Lady Catherine Grey was 'big with child'. She said that Edward Seymour, earl of Hertford, was responsible for the pregnancy and that 'she was married to him secretly before Christmas last'.[17] Hertford, the son that Protector Somerset had planned to match with Lady Jane Grey,[18] was described by Quadra as 'very heretical'.[19] The news of his union with Catherine brought to an end both Spanish interest in her and English misconceptions about her religion. It was now clear that there was a Protestant succession candidate without foreign connexions who descended from Henry VII.

What really made the affair of Catherine and Hertford a 'great mishap' was the queen's reaction to it. Elizabeth, due to past experiences with the Seymours and the Greys, no doubt would have been suspicious about the business under any circumstances, but the clandestine marriage evidently took place not long after the mysterious death of Amy Robsart, Lord Robert Dudley's wife.[20] It was suspected that she was murdered to open the way for Elizabeth to marry Dudley. This made plausible the conjecture that Dudley's enemies matched Catherine and Hertford with the idea of placing them on the throne in the event that Elizabeth aroused popular indignation by making what would surely have been regarded as a scandalous marriage with a son of the notorious Northumberland.[21] On 17 August the queen wrote: 'It is certain that there hath been great practices and purposes.' [22] By September Quadra was naming those allegedly responsible for the supposed plot: the earls of Arundel and Bedford, the bishop of Salisbury, and Cecil, who was 'at the bottom of it'.[23]

Early in 1562 Elizabeth commissioned Archbishop Parker and others 'to examine, inquire, and judge of the infamous conversation and pretended marriage' between Catherine and Hertford.[24] The record of the ensuing trial and examinations gives evidence neither of a plot nor of

[17] Thomas Wright, *Queen Elizabeth and Her Times* (London 1838), i. pp. 68–9.
[18] See above, p. 80.
[19] J. M. B. C. Kervyn de Lettenhove, *Relations politiques de Pays-Bas et de l'Angleterre sous le règne de Philippe II* (Brussels 1892–1900), ii. p. 608.
[20] She died on 8 September 1560. Catherine and Hertford testified that they were married sometime between November 1st and December 25th (BM, Harleian MS. 6286, pp. 41, 48–9).
[21] See Lettenhove, *Relations politiques*, ii. pp. 529–33.
[22] Haynes and Murdin, *Burghley Papers*, I. p. 370.
[23] Lettenhove, *Relations politiques*, ii. 619–20; *Span. Cal.*, *Eliz.* i. pp. 213–24.
[24] Haynes and Murdin, *Burghley Papers*, i. p. 378.

advocacy of the match by any of Quadra's 'conspirators'. Rather it indicates that the union was probably the result of an ordinary romance of long standing. Though Catherine and Hertford were unable to produce responsible witnesses, circumstantial evidence makes it likely that they did conclude a valid but secret Anglican marriage. Nevertheless, Parker and his fellows, understanding the implication of their queen's commission, dutifully found against the 'pretended marriage'.[25] This meant that Edward and Thomas Seymour, the sons that Catherine gave birth to in 1561 and 1563 respectively, were legally bastards and ineligible for the succession. Catherine was to remain in custody for the rest of her days. In its result her love match with Hertford both clarified and exacerbated the succession situation: it revealed her as a claimant Protestants could support; it made her and her claim enduringly loathsome to Elizabeth.

On 19 August 1561, but nine days after the discovery of Lady Catherine Grey's pregnancy, the widowed Mary Queen of Scots returned to Scotland. Since power in France had passed from her Guise relatives to the unfriendly Queen Mother, Catherine de Medici, Mary could regard herself as entirely free of the French connexion that had made her claim so unpopular in England. She wisely chose as her principal Scottish advisers Lord James Stuart, her bastard half brother, and William Maitland of Lethington. These statesmen proposed that Mary give up her previously announced immediate claim to the English crown in exchange for a present recognition as next in line; indeed, Lord James had sent advance notice of the proposal to Elizabeth some two weeks before Mary's arrival in Scotland.[26] Mary apparently accepted the proposal, and in early September sent Maitland on a mission to Elizabeth in its behalf.

Maitland's negotiation with Elizabeth (Doc. 31), though a failure in so far as its objective was concerned, turned out to be significantly revelatory of the queen's attitude toward the succession. Elizabeth confessed to Maitland her love for his queen as her 'next kinswoman', reminding him that she had never hated or blamed Mary for the 'injurious pretence' of 1559.[27] This last contrasts suggestively with Elizabeth's refusal to forgive Catherine Grey, who was as much her 'next kinswoman' as Mary,[28] for a far lesser offence than claiming her very crown. Elizabeth also indicated to Maitland that, failing issue of her own, Mary was her preferred successor and implied her contempt for the other claimants as powerless creatures. Moreover, Elizabeth suc-

[25] The trial and examinations are recorded in BM, Harleian MS. 6286; analysed in Levine, *Early Elizabethan Succession*, pp. 19–28.
[26] *Scot. Cal.* i. 999.
[27] See above, pp. 99–100.
[28] Catherine, like Mary, was Elizabeth's second cousin.

ceeded in convincing the not easily deceived Maitland of her preference
for Mary.

Nevertheless, Elizabeth rejected Maitland's proposal that Mary be
designated her heir presumptive and spoke of three main considerations
that deterred her from so doing. First, she implied that settling the succession would need an inquiry as to who had the best title, and that
would provoke a debate that she wanted to avoid. She preferred to let
the matter rest until she was dead; then 'they shall succeed that has
most right'. If Mary had such right, Elizabeth would 'never hurt her';
but if someone else had 'better right', it was unreasonable to require her
'to do a manifest injury'. Elizabeth protested that she did not know if
there was any law debarring Mary for she was 'not curious to inquire of
that purpose', but if there was any such law, she was sworn when she
was crowned 'not to alter the laws' of the realm. This protest of lack of
knowledge and curiosity may have been a deception in Mary's interest.
Elizabeth certainly had access to the concealed original of Henry VIII's
will and, as we shall see, probably believed it to be valid.[29] If the will
authorized by the Succession Act of 1544 was valid, Catherine Grey was
by law Elizabeth's heir presumptive. Then the will could only be overthrown by repeal of the 1544 statute, and the statement in this regard by
the Parliament of 1559 in its act recognizing Elizabeth's title (Doc. 30)
surely suggested that it would be difficult to obtain such repeal from a
future Parliament. Moreover, Elizabeth's failure to mention Parliament
in this connexion may well signify an inclination on her part to ignore if
at all possible her father's precedents for settling the succession by parliamentary statute.

Secondly, Elizabeth expressed her fear that acceptance of Maitland's
proposal would result in the reverse of friendship between herself and
Mary. It was too much to expect Elizabeth to love her 'own winding-
sheet'. Since 'princes cannot like their own children, those that should
succeed them', she could hardly like her cousin as her declared successor. Maitland could not have have been favourably impressed by this
revelation of the queen's selfish and jealous nature, but also involved may
have been an understandable distrust of Mary that Elizabeth deemed it
undiplomatic to bring up. Once Mary's *right* of succession was promulgated, 'it could never be rescinded with any show of justice or hope of
real effect'.[30] Then the Scottish queen might feel free to embark on
hostile policies, including even a reassertion of her immediate claim,
most likely with French and/or Spanish support. The prospect of the
succession served as a restraint on Mary; an actual designation as heir
presumptive might well have unleashed her.

[29] See below, p. 113.
[30] J. E. Neale, *Queen Elizabeth* (London 1938), p. 126.

The third and 'most weighty' consideration, so Elizabeth told Maitland, was the 'inconstancy' of the English, 'how they ever mislike the present government and have their eyes fixed upon the person that is next to succeed'. She feared that dissatisfied subjects, 'if they knew a certain successor of our crown. . . , would have recourse thither'. It would be particularly dangerous if that successor was Mary, 'she being a puissant princess and so near our neighbour'. No guarantee from Mary on this point would be satisfactory to Elizabeth: 'it is hard to bind princes by any security where hope is offered of a kingdom'. Though Elizabeth was speaking primarily about Mary, her conclusion suggests that she would not even tolerate the lesser risk involved in designating as heir presumptive one of those 'poor souls', the English claimants: 'if it were certainly known in the world who should succeed her, she would never think herself in sufficient surety'. That a declaration of the succession might give the English people some feeling of security about the future did not really matter to their queen; her own anxieties were all that counted.

Maitland returned to Scotland encouraged by Elizabeth's implied preference for Mary over the other claimants and hence not disposed to regard his proposal as dead. To further it, he wrote a letter to Cecil on 7 October in which he presented a case for the justice of Mary's claim. About the same time Francis, duke of Guise, Mary's uncle, had an interview with Sir Nicholas Throckmorton, Elizabeth's ambassador to France, during which he also argued in favour of his niece's claim. Neither Maitland nor Guise made too impressive cases for Mary, both failing to deal adequately with the main matters of the common-law rule against alien inheritance and the will of Henry VIII,[31] but at least they were getting their arguments to influential Englishmen who might be expected to transmit them to their queen. The long campaign to secure Mary's recognition as Elizabeth's heir presumptive was under way.

A counter-campaign was begun openly with the performance of Thomas Sackville and Thomas Norton's *Gorboduc* by the gentlemen of the Inner Temple before the queen at Whitehall on 18 January 1562.[32] *Gorboduc* was ostensibly a play about a succession problem in the mythical Britain of long ago, but its fifth act obviously referred to the contemporary situation. The villain of the piece who attempted to seize the crown after the extinction of the direct royal line was a Scot whom the audience could easily identify with Mary Stuart. Her accession would subject England to the 'unnatural thraldom of stranger's reign';

[31] For Maitland's case see Haynes and Murdin, *Burghley Papers*, i. p. 373; for Guise's see *For. Cal.*, *Eliz.* iv. 592.
[32] A. W. Green, *The Inns of Court and Early English Drama* (New Haven 1931), p. 140.

'foreign titles' should 'yield to public wealth'.[33] The preferable and rightful successor, so *Gorboduc* implied, was Catherine Grey:

> Right mean I his or hers, upon whose name
> The people rest by mean of native line,
> Or by the virtue of some former law,
> Already made their title to advance.[34]

Catherine came of an unobjectionably 'native line'; her claim was primarily based on Henry VIII's will authorized by 'former law'. The principal and most urgent message of *Gorboduc*, however, was the need for an immediate settlement of the succession in Parliament; letting the matter rest until the direct Tudor line was extinct would expose England to civil war and leave her an 'open prey' for conquest by a foreign prince.[35]

It has lately been argued that there may have been more behind the Whitehall performance of *Gorboduc* than previously suspected. Lord Robert Dudley, whom the Inner Templars had recently chosen as their Christmas Prince, was probably responsible for taking the play to Court. The performance of the play was followed by that of a masque which by implication offered Dudley to the queen as an appropriate husband. This suggests an accommodation between Catherine Grey's supporters and Dudley: they would advocate his marriage to Elizabeth; he would use his influence to press for a parliamentary settlement of the succession, which was Catherine's best chance.[36] If any such arrangement existed, however, there is no indication that the queen was aware of it. In any case, *Gorboduc* gave notice to Elizabeth of anti-Stuart sentiment and warned her about what might happen if Parliament was allowed to deal with the succession.

In November 1562 financial need caused Elizabeth to call for the election of a Parliament to meet in January. The resulting House of Commons contained only twenty-seven Catholics; its predominant voice, according to a contemporary lampoon, was to come from forty-three radicals, most of whom probably were Puritans.[37] No sooner did the Parliament of 1563 get under way than the Commons began dealing

[33] Thomas Sackville and Thomas Norton, *Gorboduc*, in *The Minor Elizabethan Drama*: (1) *Pre-Shakespearean Tragedies* (London and New York 1913), p. 51.

[34] Ibid.

[35] Ibid. pp. 51–3. For a fuller consideration of *Gorboduc* as a succession play see Levine, *Early Elizabethan Succession*, pp. 38–44.

[36] See Marie Axton, 'Robert Dudley and the Inner Temple Revels', *Hist. J.* (1970), xiii, pp. 365–78.

[37] See J. E. Neale, *Elizabeth I and her Parliaments* (London 1953–7), i. pp. 85–86, 90–2.

with the succession. Before January was over they presented to the
queen a petition concerning her marriage and the succession.

In their petition, which may well have been written by Thomas
Norton, the Commons set forth the dangers of an uncertain succession
in words reminiscent of *Gorboduc*. They made obvious allusions to the
foreign and domestic threats emanating from the claim of Mary Queen
of Scots. They made a humble and sincere request that Elizabeth marry,
the fulfilment of which would not provide the immediate security they
desired. That would require a present succession settlement. Here the
Commons pledged themselves to uphold the Succession Act of 1544
(Doc. 22) and asked if a further succession after Elizabeth and her issue
was already made in accordance with that statute – an implied request
for a determination of the validity of Henry VIII's will. If there was such
a succession, they desired the queen to have it declared, which would
mean the designation of Catherine Grey as heir presumptive. If there
was no 'such certainty already provided', they desired a 'limitation of
some certainty . . . to provide a most gracious remedy in this great
necessity'.[38]

Neither the Commons' petition nor a similar but somewhat weaker
one presented by the Lords [39] could get far with the queen. Elizabeth's
disinclination to marry was too strong to be overcome by mere parliamentary requests. Nor could her even greater reluctance to permit a
succession settlement be budged by a Parliament that was apparently
unable to advocate a specific settlement. That majorities in both Houses
most likely were opposed to the Scottish queen's claim was merely
negative. That Parliament doubtless would have been willing to declare
Catherine Grey heir presumptive if Henry VIII's will was shown to be
valid does not necessarily signify that she was its preferred claimant.
Indeed, what little evidence we have indicates that Parliament was a
house divided when it came to succession preferences. Catherine Grey,
Huntingdon, Margaret Strange, Mary Stuart, and the Lennox Stuarts
all had some supporters. The first two probably had the largest parties,
but neither came close to having majority backing. Considering the
queen's attitude and Parliament's division over the claimants, there was
no real chance of achieving an outright succession settlement.[40]

Realization of this may well have inspired two propositions which
apparently came up towards the end of the session. The first, for which
Quadra is our only source, was a proposal to the House of Lords to limit
the succession to 'four lines or families in the kingdom, leaving to the

[38] The petition is printed in John Harington, *Nugae Antiquae*, ed. Thomas
Park (London 1804), i. pp. 69–80; considered more fully in Levine, *Early
Elizabethan Succession*, pp. 48–51.
[39] See Neale, *Parliaments*, i. pp. 109–10.
[40] See Levine, *Early Elizabethan Succession*, pp. 49–57.

queen the nomination of the one that has to succeed out of these four'.[41]
This would impose on Elizabeth the burden of making a choice among
the English claimants which the divided Parliament would have had
difficulty making on its own. The phrase 'in the kingdom' would give
Parliament its likely main objective by excluding the Queen of Scots,
Elizabeth's probable preferred successor and the only claimant whose
reaction she had real cause to fear. This 'compromise' solution, if
actually proposed, could hardly have been attractive to Elizabeth.[42]

The second proposition is recorded in an abortive bill prepared for
Parliament (Doc. 32), probably by councillors who despaired of achieving any succession settlement at the time. It provided that if the queen
died without issue or before Parliament had settled the succession by
law, her last privy council plus any additional members she might name
to it by will would govern England until her rightful successor was proclaimed by Parliament, which, according to Quadra, was to meet within
thirty days as last constituted.[43] This proposal raised difficulties. It was
debatable in law whether even statute could establish continued
authority for Elizabeth's privy council and Parliament after her demise.[44]
The potential dangers of an interregnum of a months or more were such
that it probably would have been a better gamble for those in control on
the queen's death to proclaim one of the pretenders and then face
eventualities with a sort of *fait accompli*. In any case, the proposal could
hardly have been attractive to Elizabeth. Its enactment would likely
have produced hostile reactions from the Scottish queen whose chances
for the succession would have been slim indeed if the decision was to be
made by an English Parliament on its own. If, instead of the mere right
to name additional councillors, Elizabeth had been offered statutory
authority to designate *any* succession by will, it might have been a different story, but significantly there is no evidence that council or Parliament ever seriously considered entrusting her with Henry VIII's power.

On 10 April Elizabeth prorogued Parliament, leaving the Lords and
Commons with an answerless response to their petitions: it was a
mistake to believe that she was determined never to marry; the succession was too great a cause for her to speak on until she had further
advice. Perhaps the main reason for this abrupt postponement was the
problem of Mary Stuart. During the session Elizabeth doubtless learned
that the Scottish queen was seeking for herself a Habsburg marriage of

[41] *Span. Cal.*, *Eliz.* i. 216.
[42] Cf. Neale, *Parliaments*, i. p. 112, who holds that the proposal, if made,
came from the queen.
[43] *Span. Cal.*, *Eliz.* i. 218.
[44] A contrary precedent could be found in Somerset's getting a new commission from Edward VI for the council of regency named in Henry VIII's will. See
above, pp. 67, 76–7.

obvious potential menace to England. Elizabeth's response was to offer
Lord Robert Dudley to Mary as a preferable mate. The delicate
negotiations for the Dudley match could best be conducted without
Parliament around to get involved.[45]

That proposed match had the potential of producing a succession
settlement. Parliament might have been prevailed upon to accept Mary
with the English and Protestant Dudley as her consort. Mary was
favourable to the marriage provided that Elizabeth promise to have
Parliament declare her heir presumptive.[46] It was over this point that
negotiations dragged on. In a letter of late 1564 Cecil informed Mary's
principal advisers of the difficulties involved. Elizabeth, even if she was
willing to act, could not promise automatic parliamentary assent. But
she was not ready to proceed: it was a ticklish matter 'for princes to be
provoked to determine of their successors – *Durus enim est sermo* – and
such as nature scantly sometimes will bear it for her own children with
patience or without jealousy'. All that could now be offered to the Scots
was to trust in what Elizabeth might eventually do 'of her frank good
will'.[47] In July 1655, the exasperated Mary married her cousin Darnley:
a match that ended the division among English Catholics over the
succession and opened the possibility of both French and Habsburg
support for the Stuart claim.

Meanwhile, a pamphlet war over the succession question developed.
The opening gun was fired during the session of 1563 by John Hales, a
radical MP, in a manuscript tract defending Catherine Grey's claim and
attacking Mary Stuart's.[48] Probably early in 1565 Anthony Browne, a
prominent Catholic judge, supplied a manuscript answer to Hales's
tract [49] which four years later became the basis of the succession book of
Bishop Leslie's more famous defence of Mary Stuart.[50] Late in 1565 an
anti-Stuart tract appeared in print.[51] This was answered in a manuscript
tract of 1566.[52] Also in 1566 there appeared an anti-Suffolk tract
which may have been printed [53] and a manuscript answer to

[45] See Levine, *Early Elizabethan Succession*, pp. 59–60.
[46] BM, Cotton MS. Caligula B X, fo. 282. I owe this reference to Dr Katharine Frescoln.
[47] *Scot. Cal.* ii. 126.
[48] Printed in Francis Hargrave, *The Hereditary Right of the Crown of England Asserted* (London 1713), pp. xx–xliii.
[49] BM, Harleian MS. 555, fos. 11–16.
[50] John Leslie, *A Defence of the Honour of . . . Mary, Queen of Scotland* (London 1569), pp. 51–119.
[51] The only extant printed copy (BM ref. C. 55 c. 3) is illegible in places due to wear. It is better to use BM, Harleian MS. 4627, No. 2. pp. 1–32.
[52] Bodleian Library, Ashmolean MS. 829, fos. 31–6.
[53] Printed in William Atwood, *The Fundamental Constitution of the English Government* (London 1690), Appendix, pp. 1–19. No printed copy of 1566 is extant.

it.[54] Early in 1567, just after the next parliamentary session, Edmund Plowden, an eminent Catholic jurist, produced a manuscript answer to both Hales's tract and the printed anti-Stuart tract.[55]

These succession tracts were obviously written to influence public and parliamentary opinion. Since their subject matter related chiefly to the claims of Catherine Grey and Mary Stuart, they doubtless helped to make the succession question primarily one of choosing Catherine or Mary. Three main legal issues were raised by the tracts as the determinants of that choice.

One was whether the common-law rule against an alien inheriting ordinary property applied to the succession and to Mary Stuart. The pamphleteers were on unsound ground in considering the applicability of the rule to the succession. Their debates over alleged precedents for and against aliens succeeding to the crown really showed that history afforded no answer. Rather complicated legal arguments by Plowden and Leslie that the succession did not follow common-law rules of inheritance generally proved nothing and probably passed the understanding of most of their readers.[56] The pamphleteers were on more substantial ground in discussing the applicability of the rule against alien inheritance to Mary Stuart.

Here their debate centred on an act of Edward III's Parliament of 1351 (Doc. 1).[57] This statute declared two general exceptions to the common-law rule against alien inheritance: 'the children of the kings of England' whenever and wherever they were born, and children afterwards born abroad of parents in the allegiance of the king of England. A few pro-Stuart writers maintained that the latter exception applied to the Queen of Scots due to the English claim of suzerainty over Scotland, but their opponents could point out that James V, Mary's father, was at war with Henry VIII at the time of her birth and that she had never done homage to Elizabeth I.[58] Moreover, honour forbade Mary's claiming Englishness by acknowledging suzerainty. As she was to put it at her trial in 1586, she 'would not offend against her progenitors the kings of Scots by acknowledging herself a subject of the crown of

[54] Printed in Mortimer Levine, 'A "Letter" on the Elizabethan Succession Question, 1566', *Huntington Library Quarterly* (1955), xix, pp. 26–38.

[55] BM, Harleian MS. 849, fos. 1–38.

[56] On these matters see Levine, *Early Elizabethan Succession*, pp. 100–15. Significantly, the pro-Stuart tract writers of the 1560s did not argue that there was a divinely ordained hereditary right that overruled English law.

[57] Leslie saw the reference in the title of this act to 'those who are born in parts beyond sea' as showing that Scots were not aliens but there is considerable evidence that Scots were legally aliens in Tudor England. See ibid. pp. 122–4

[58] See ibid. pp. 121–4.

England, for this were nothing else but to profess them openly to have been rebels and traitors' in their English wars.[59]

More debate was waged over the 1351 statute's exemption of 'the children of the kings of England'. If 'children' was meant to include not only sons and daughters but remoter descendants, Mary Stuart as a great-granddaughter of Henry VII was not subject to the rule against alien inheritance. Tract writers for and against her claim argued this point mainly by attempting to read the minds of the makers of the act of 1351, who, knowing exactly what they meant by the word children, did not realize that their language would not be so clear to later ages. A more productive approach would have been to give the statute a closer reading, for first among those named therein as previously born abroad but specially exempted from the common-law rule was 'Henry son of John de Beaumond'. Henry Beaumond or Beaumont was a great-great-grandson of Henry III, so there was no reason for his being specially designated if he was regarded by the statute makers as included among 'the children of the kings of England'. The naming of Beaumont practically settled the matter against Mary, but none of the anti-Stuart writers of the 1560s perceived this.[60]

Another legal dispute of the pamphlet war was over the legitimacy of the Suffolk descent from Henry VII. Here only the perhaps printed anti-Suffolk tract raised the question of the validity of Catherine Grey's marriage and the legitimacy of her sons, which legally was not a matter of immediate concern. It did not touch Catherine's claim, and her designation as heir presumptive might be expected to be accompanied by a reversal of the doubtful verdict against her marriage. And none of the anti-Suffolk writers challenged Catherine's legitimacy, an indication that an old tale that Henry Grey, duke of Suffolk, and Lady Frances Brandon were not lawfully married was worthless. The main pamphlet debate dealt with the charge that Lady Frances was a bastard because Charles Brandon, duke of Suffolk, had another wife when he married Mary, the French queen. The Suffolk side had the advantage in this argument due to a papal bull issued prior to the break with Rome, which stated that Charles Brandon had secured a divorce in England before he married Mary Tudor. In any case, Frances Brandon's bastardy would not overturn Catherine Grey's title by Henry VIII's will, which, as Hales pointed out, assigned the succession not to Frances but to her heirs (Doc. 23).[61]

Probably the crucial legal question debated by the pamphleteers was that of the validity of the will of Henry VIII. Those who challenged the

---

[59] *A Complete Collection of State Trials*, ed. William Cobbett and T. B. Howell (London 1816–98), i. p. 1171.

[60] Levine, *Early Elizabethan Succession*, pp. 116–20.

[61] See ibid. pp. 126–46.

will not only accepted but insisted on the competence of statute in the matter. As one of them put it, 'it is . . . certain that King Henry should have had no authority or power to dispose of the crown by will if by Parliament it had not been given him'.[62] What they claimed was that the will was void because it was signed with a stamp and not, as prescribed by statute, signed with Henry's 'most gracious hand' (Docs. 19, 22). They and their opponents, however, were only able to get into often bewildering conjectural disputes over whether the will was signed with a stamp or with Henry's hand,[63] since none of the tract writers had ever seen the original document which Elizabeth kept concealed. Recent examinations of the original[64] yield no positive conclusions about the signatures at its beginning and end. They lack the indentations one would expect to be left by a dry stamp, but such impressions could have disappeared over the centuries. L. B. Smith thinks that the signatures were made with a stamp and I that they were made with Henry's hand, but both of us admit that the calligraphic evidence is inconclusive.[65]

The weightiest evidence of a stamped will is the inclusion of Henry's testament in a list of documents stamped at the king's order by one William Clerc during January 1547.[66] This has been explained as either a mistake on Clerc's part or indicative of a well-nigh deathbed replacement of a stamped will by another hastily drawn up and signed in writing by the king.[67] The possibility of a mistake is quite remote, but the penmanship of the extant original, which even contains some interlineations, does suggest that it was written in haste.[68] The question of a stamped will or one signed in writing may well be irrelevant, however, for it is not unlikely that a stamped signature ordered by Henry was regarded in law as equivalent to subscription with his 'most gracious hand'.[69]

The most telling evidence of the validity of Henry VIII's will, whether stamped or signed in writing, is its acceptance without serious challenge for some two decades after Henry's death. At Edward VI's accession consequential legalists with reason to dislike some of its

---

[62] Atwood, app. p. 13.

[63] e.g. cf. ibid. app. pp. 13–17; Hargrave, *Hereditary Right*, pp. xxi–xxix.

[64] PRO, Royal Wills, E. 23, iv.

[65] Cf. L. B. Smith, 'The Last Will and Testament of Henry VII: A Question of Perspective', *Journal of British Studies* (1962), ii, no. 1, pp. 22–3; Mortimer Levine, 'The Last Will and Testament of Henry VIII: A Reappraisal Appraised', *Historian* (1964), xxvi, pp. 478–80. More recently, W. K. Jordan, *Edward VI* (Cambridge, Mass. 1968–70), i. p. 55, has stated that the two signatures 'are certainly the King's'.

[66] *L.P.* xxi. Pt ii. 770.

[67] A. F. Pollard, *England under Protector Somerset* (London 1900), p. 7.

[68] Levine, *Historian* (1964), pp. 480–1.

[69] See J. J. Scarisbrick, *Henry VIII* (London 1968), pp. 492–3. Also Hargrave, *Hereditary Right*, pp. xxii–xxiii.

terms – Stephen Gardiner, Thomas Wriothesley, and probably Richard Rich – certainly would have raised objections to the will if there had been any doubt of its authenticity.[70] True, early in Mary I's reign the chancery record of the will seems to have been destroyed, most likely in the interest of the Spanish match, but significantly the queen preserved the original.[71] And late in the reign Mary's judges found it safe to show due respect for the will in a case involving the queen's property. That Elizabeth I kept the original concealed hardly signified that she doubted its validity. In 1559 that reputedly penurious and Protestant queen commanded that £600 per annum be allocated to execute a Catholic provision of the will. Perhaps most significant was Elizabeth's failure to permit a judicial examination of the original, even after assuring the Queen of Scots in 1566 that she would have one. If, as Elizabeth may well have expected, such an investigation showed the will to be valid, even she might not have been able to resist a parliamentary demand for a declaration of Catherine Grey, the claimant she hated most, as her heir presumptive.[72] We may safely conclude that those who challenged Henry VIII's will in the middle 1560s on the ground that it was stamped merely invented an expedient legal technicality. The tract of Plowden, the most learned of them in the law, makes it clear that he only reluctantly impugned the will after the urging of others.[73]

The pamphlet debate over legal issues – at times bewildering, sometimes misdirected or misinformed, and usually inconclusive – could hardly have been the determinant for very many readers in choosing between Catherine Grey and Mary Stuart. Of likelier influence on the average reader were the appeals to common prejudices made by the author of the printed anti-Stuart tract (Doc. 33). First, he maintained that Mary's accession would make the English 'bound and subject unto a foreign nation'. Mary would bring England government by Scots. This would be insufferable, for the Scots were 'a people by custom and almost nature our enemies, thirsty of our blood, poor and miserable by their country and envious of our welfare'. A Scottish regime would undermine England's well-being and dignity by introducing such 'tyrannies' as allowing Scots to 'trade and communicate the commodities of our country'. That Mary Stuart's love for the Scots was hardly such that she would have ruled England in their interest was beyond the ken of prejudiced Elizabethans; so was the shrewd prediction attributed to Henry VII that the accession of a Scot would not mean Scottish dominion over England but the reverse (Doc. 12). Secondly, the author

[70] Jordan, *Edward VI*, i. p. 55.
[71] Above, pp. 90–1.
[72] See Levine, *Historian* (1964), pp. 483–4.
[73] Cf. BM. Harleian MS. 849, fos. 1, 31.

brought up the threat of 'corrupt religion'. Many of the Scottish queen's English supporters were open Papists or feigned Protestants who wished 'to wash their hands in the blood of the faithful'. Their prospects of accomplishing this were raised by Mary's recent troubling of Scottish Protestants and dealings with Catholic Europe. The suggestion to true English Protestants, no matter how small its justification, was obvious: Mary Stuart should be equated with the fanatical Mary Tudor. In nationality and religion the author surely found effective grounds on which to attack the Queen of Scots' claim, and the one pro-Stuart attempt to refute him was too feeble to require rehearsal here.[74]

On 30 September 1566 the Parliament that had been in prorogation for over three years reassembled. Financial need had forced Elizabeth to recall Parliament at what for her was a most unpropitious time. Parliament was bound to demand to deal with the succession and likely to press for a settlement more vigorously than in the last session. The pamphlet war had helped to increase national concern over the question and to centre attention on the claims of Lady Catherine Grey and Mary Queen of Scots. The latter's marriage with Darnley had ended the main cause of division among English Catholics over the succession by uniting the Stuart claims. And Elizabeth had some reason to fear that Mary and Darnley might secure French and Habsburg backing for hostile acts against England. In August 1565 Mary and Darnley had informed Elizabeth of their terms. They would do nothing against her title and enter a league with England if she by act of Parliament established the succession, failing herself and her issue, in Mary and her issue, and then in Lady Margaret Lennox and her line, 'as the persons by the law of God and nature next inheritable to the crown of England'.[75] Even if Elizabeth had been eager for such a succession, she probably would have been unable to obtain parliamentary consent. If the session of 1563 showed anything, it was the apparent aversion of the majority of the Parliament men to Mary Stuart's claim. Had Mary married the Protestant Dudley that aversion might have been overcome in time, but her match with the Catholic Darnley could only have augmented it, especially after she gave birth to Prince James in June 1566, thus promising a continuing Catholic dynasty. With Mary and Darnley seemingly in a position to make threats and seeking a succession settlement in their favour, and Parliament wanting to act on the succession but most likely in a contrary way, Elizabeth was committing herself to a difficult holding operation when she called the Parliament of 1566.

Inauspicious for Elizabeth were certain outside activities which took

[74] See Bodleian Library, Ashmolean MS. 829, fos. 62–3, 67.
[75] *Scot. Cal.* ii. 230. Though making an hereditary claim, Mary and Darnley evidently accepted Parliament's jurisdiction.

place shortly after Parliament's opening and were certainly intended to influence its proceedings. In October the law students at Lincoln's Inn held a disputation on the succession in the presence of at least one senior. They found that the Scottish queen as an alien could not legally 'succeed to the crown, even if she were the nearest in birth and the ablest'. This resulted in Elizabeth's receipt of a formal protest from Mary.[76] Equally serious, the finding was doubtless acceptable to the alumni of the Inns of Court who were prominent in the radical leadership of the Commons.

Also in October there appeared a pamphlet purporting to be a 'common cry of Englishmen' (Doc. 34), probably written by Thomas Sampson, an eminent Puritan divine whom Elizabeth had deprived of the deanship of Christ Church.[77] The 'cry' first addressed the queen. It spoke not of a matter private to her but of one which touched all, for if she should die without issue and lacking a recognized successor, 'England runneth to most certain ruin and destruction'. Elizabeth could not provide a solution by marrying, 'for a certain ruin cannot be stayed by an uncertain means'. England's salvation depended on her having the succession settled promptly in Parliament. Then the 'cry', implying little faith in the queen, turned to the Lords and Commons. They knew Elizabeth's answer to their laudable request for a succession settlement in 1563. If it was a promise, 'it is time to claim the performance'. If it was a delay to test their zeal, 'show forth again that affection which the cause requireth'. If it was a refusal and another refusal was forthcoming, 'bestow your wisdom and power to put your country out of . . . peril'. If princes 'go astray', it is particularly the duty of Parliament men to 'stand instead'. They should exert their privilege of 'free speaking'. 'Good princes', because they have their authority with their parliaments, 'are counted not to rule without them, but with them. Yea, ofttimes to be ruled by them.' The revolutionary implication that Parliament could rule the queen against her will could only have appealed to a few extremists, but otherwise the pamphlet no doubt expressed a 'common cry' of countless Englishmen which reached receptive ears in Parliament.

The Lords and Common of 1566 were certainly determined to secure a succession settlement. Our only information on what settlement they preferred comes from the reports sent to Spain during the session by Guzman de Silva. Though Spanish ambassadors were often misled, Silva was more discerning than most and his appraisals of Parliament's succession sentiments make sense in light of the situation in general. His reports indicate, as one would expect, that Parliament was no

[76] Neale, *Parliaments*, i. p. 133.
[77] Ibid. i. p. 132; W. MacCaffrey, *The Shaping of the Elizabethan Regime* (Princeton 1968), p. 210.

longer impossibly divided over too many claimants. The Common were 'nearly all heretics and adherents of Catherine' Grey. Mary Stuart had her share of supporters among the lay peers, but the greatest of their number, Thomas Howard, fourth duke of Norfolk, seems to have been lured into the Suffolk camp by the prospect of matching his daughter with one of Catherine's sons.[78] If Norfolk was for Catherine, many moderate peers were probably with him. Add to this the Protestant zealots among the nobles and the bishops, whose succession activities would antagonize Elizabeth particularly,[79] and it becomes likely that the majority of the Lords would have gone along with the Commons in a declaration for Catherine.

On 18 October, following the government's introduction of the subsidy bill, the fight for a succession settlement began in earnest. The Commons threatened to withhold supplies until the succession was dealt with. On the 22nd a delegation of prominent peers approached the queen and implored her to yield to the Commons. She told them angrily that the succession was too important a matter to be brought before 'a knot of hare-brains'. Parliament could do as it pleased; its bills had no effect without her authority. This and Elizabeth's subsequent personal display of rage against Norfolk and a few other great peers failed to prevent the Lords from joining with the Commons. On 4 November both Houses resolved 'to petition the Queen by common consent to deal with the matter of the succession'. On the next day Elizabeth resourcefully summoned deputations from both Houses to answer their petition before it was made. After singling out the Commons and the bishops for blame and excusing the lay peers for their 'simplicity', she indicated that the time was 'not convenient' for dealing with the succession. She did promise to marry, adding that the petitioners would 'mislike him with whom I shall marry'. This last no doubt meant the Habsburg Archduke Charles, a match with whom would serve as a diplomatic counterpoise to Mary's union with Darnley but hardly be pleasing to English Protestants. The queen's 'answer' seems to have been enough for the Lords. The Commons, however, continued the suit for a succession settlement, thus provoking a royal command for silence. This led to the raising of the dangerous question of parliamentary liberties, on which Elizabeth managed a skilful 'surrender'. Shortly thereafter the queen pleased the Commons further by not acting on a formal complaint from the Scottish ambassador against James Dalton, an alumnus of Lincoln's Inn, for doubtless making, though he denied it, a direct attack on the Stuart claim in open Parliament. Elizabeth's belated tact finally got her a third of the subsidy she

[78] *Span. Cal., Eliz.* i. 385, 387, 390, 396.
[79] Ibid. i. 388; Neale, *Parliaments*, i. pp. 146–7.

asked for. On 2 January 1567, the queen dissolved Parliament with an intemperate chiding that only served to show her colours.[80]

Parliament's dissolution must have been a disappointment to Catherine Grey's supporters, but they had reason to regard 1566 more as a delay than a defeat. Elizabeth's financial needs, which had only been satisfied in part by the recently granted subsidy, would almost certainly force her to call on Parliament for funds again in due season. Dissolution instead of prorogation meant an election, but a new Parliament would probably be much like its predecessor in its membership and succession sentiments. And it was questionable how long the queen could continue to resist public and parliamentary pressure for a succession settlement. It was Mary Stuart's backers rather than Catherine Grey's who had real cause for despair over how the situation was developing.

Maitland of Lethington indicated this to Cecil in a letter dated but two days after the dissolution. He complained about the Lincoln's Inn disputation and about 'the speeches by sundry in this last session of Parliament, tending all to my Sovereign's disherision, and nothing said to the contrary by any man'. He suggested, probably correctly, that his side was losing the pamphlet war, if only because Hales's tract and the printed anti-Stuart tract were enjoying the most circulation. Moreover, the Suffolk side had apparently devised a form of propaganda more effective than any of the tracts, that is, the publishing of numerous exemplifications of Henry VIII's will, which 'do run abroad in England, and do carry away many men's minds as great presumptions of great verity and veracity'. And now, so Maitland claimed, Elizabeth intended to stop 'by proclamations all books and writings containing any discussion of titles',[81] which would make it most difficult to combat 'a settled opinion against my Sovereign to the advancement of the Lady Catherine's title'.[82]

If things did not look good for the Scottish queen in January 1567, her position would soon reach almost the point of no return as a result of the well-known events of the ensuing months: Darnley's murder under circumstances suggesting Mary's complicity; Mary's marriage in a Calvinist ceremony to the earl of Bothwell, Darnley's probable murderer; revolt by the Scots against their queen; Mary's defeat, imprisonment and forced abdication in favour of her son who became James VI at the age of one. By summer Mary Stuart had not only lost Scotland but practically all of her Catholic supporters in England and on the Con-

[80] For documentation and fuller accounts see ibid. i. pp. 134–64, 183–6; Levine, *Early Elizabethan Succession*, pp. 174–94.

[81] The first proclamation aimed at pro-Stuart writings appeared late in 1570 (see Hughes and Larkin, *Tudor Proclamations*, ii. p. 347).

[82] *The Egerton Papers*, ed. J. P. Collier (Camden Society, London 1840), pp. 47–9.

tinent. With Mary seemingly helpless and those in control in Scotland too busy consolidating their own position to care about James VI's claim to the English crown, Elizabeth had lost her best excuse for telling Parliament that the time was 'not convenient' for dealing with the succession. Never did the chances for a Suffolk succession look better than they did in the second half of 1567.[83]

In 1568, however, the situation changed considerably. On 27 January Lady Catherine Grey died. Her sons, who had reached the ages of only six and four, were still legally bastards and ineligible for the succession. The disclosure two years before of the secret marriage of Lady Mary Grey, Catherine's dwarfish younger sister, to a huge but lowly servant at the Court made the remaining senior Suffolk claimant unthinkable as a prospective queen.[84] The junior Suffolk line of Lady Margaret Strange, Catherine's cousin, was Catholic and therefore unacceptable to Protestants. Outside the Suffolk line there was only the Puritan earl of Huntingdon, whose reluctance to be a succession candidate was such that even Elizabeth would soon overcome her distrust of him,[85] and the alien James VI, whose religious upbringing depended on the uncertainties of Scottish politics. Catherine's death really left English Protestants without a feasible claimant to back.

In May Mary Stuart escaped from her Scottish captivity and fled to an English one. That resourceful lady did find means of communication and soon managed to convince Catholics in England and abroad of both her innocence in the Darnley murder and her religious orthodoxy. Indeed, Mary was so successful in attracting adherents that by the end of 1568 she could have high hopes not only of regaining the crown of Scotland but of sooner or later wearing that of England. Mary's recovery, however, was as dangerous as it was remarkable.

The leadership of her English faction included not only Catholic noblemen but nominally Protestant ones like Norfolk who saw Mary as a means to bring about a feudal reaction and remove Cecil and his ilk from the positions of power. Their followers consisted mainly of humble folk north of the Trent who espoused Mary's cause to express their economic, social and religious grievances. All in all, it was a potentially explosive faction, and it received encouragement and promises of outside aid from Guerau de Spes, the reckless Spanish ambassador.[86] A plan for Mary to marry Norfolk and a plot to overthrow Cecil developed. Then in late autumn of 1569 the Northern Rebellion broke out.

The defeat of this rising of northern earls and their following and the strong measures taken afterward decisively broke the back of feudalism

[83] See Levine, *Early Elizabethan Succession*, pp. 200–2.
[84] Ibid. p. 203.
[85] See Cross, *Puritan Earl*, pp. 145–58.
[86] See Black, *Reign of Elizabeth*, pp. 97–102.

north of the Trent, but the threat of Mary Stuart remained. The situation in Scotland was more uncertain than usual, and there was real danger that Mary's supporters there would gain the upper hand. In February 1570 Pius V did what his predecessors had never done against Henry VIII and promulgated a bull depriving Elizabeth I of her 'pretended title' to the English throne and releasing her subjects from their allegiance.[87] In February 1571, Mary, with papal approval, gave her assent to Roberto Ridolfi's plot for domestic rebellion and foreign invasion aimed at replacement of Elizabeth by Mary with Norfolk as her consort.[88] In April and May Elizabeth's long-overdue third Parliament met.

This first English Parliament in which no avowed Catholic sat was probably more strongly anti-Stuart than its predecessor, but it did not renew the fight for an immediate succession settlement, most likely because of the lack of a suitable Protestant claimant.[89] The main succession event of the Parliament was the attempt by Thomas Norton, who surely would have worked for a Suffolk succession if Catherine Grey was still available, to exclude the Stuarts. Norton proposed an 'addition' to the government's treasons bill that would debar any person – and his or her children – who 'hath [made] or hereafter shall make claim to the crown' during Elizabeth's lifetime, 'or shall say she hath not lawful right, or shall refuse to acknowledge her to be undoubted Queen'. It would be treason to support those so deprived, or to deny the right of the queen, with Parliament, to determine the succession. Norton's retroactive 'hath' could be said to have already caught Mary and her innocent son due to her assumption of the title and arms of England in 1559. Even though Parliament knew nothing of Mary's far more serious dealing with Ridolfi, it probably would have adopted Norton's 'addition' as proposed but for the certainty that it would produce a royal veto.[90]

The resulting compromise was embodied in the Treasons Act of 1571 (Doc. 35). Norton's grounds for debarment from the succession were made law, but refusal to acknowledge Elizabeth's title required the queen's demand to disable. The provision would only apply to offences committed after the Parliament had been prorogued or dissolved for thirty days and would only exclude the offender 'as if such person were naturally dead'. This was acceptable enough to Elizabeth: Mary Stuart's status would depend on her future conduct and James VI would not be disqualified by his mother's misdeeds. But Parliament may have won from Elizabeth something more than she liked to give in the

[87] Printed in P. Hughes, *The Reformation in England*, rev. edn (New York 1963), iii. pp. 418–20.
[88] Black, *Reign of Elizabeth*, pp. 117–18.
[89] Cf. Neale, *Parliaments*, i. pp. 178–9, for a different view.
[90] Ibid. i. pp. 226–33.

inclusion of another of Norton's points. The statute made it high treason during her lifetime and a lesser offence after her demise to deny the queen's right, 'with and by the authority of the Parliament of England', to determine the succession. This did not specifically preclude Elizabeth's making a determination without Parliament, but it clearly indicated that the proper and most lawful way to settle the succession was by parliamentary statute. The point had even been recognized by Mary Stuart and her supporters.[91] Now, at long last and no matter how reluctantly, Henry VIII's precedents had been accepted by his younger daughter.

Tudor England had now achieved solutions to the two great dynastic problems that developed out of Richard of York's assertion of his claim to the throne in 1460, namely, the lack of a constitutional means to settle a disputed succession and the potential power of noble factions to decide the issue on the field of battle. The crushing of the northern earls in 1569 practically ended the threat of succession questions being determined by feudal warfare. And the Treasons Act of 1571 virtually established parliamentary statute as the constitutional way to settle questions of succession. Its enactment marks the culmination of Tudor dynastic progress.[92]

The remainder of Elizabeth's reign is, for our purposes, an epilogue. The queen had formally acknowledged parliamentary statute as a constitutional means of settling the succession, but getting her necessary permission to proceed was another matter. When the next Parliament met in the spring of 1572 the Ridolfi plot had been unfolded and Norfolk had been found guilty of high treason. A Spanish agent reported that Parliament's purpose was to choose a successor and that it was believed that its choice would be a son of Catherine Grey.[93] Be that as it may, Elizabeth did not allow Parliament to do a thing about the succession, not even to exclude the discredited Mary Stuart.[94] By 1584 Elizabeth's refusal to be budged on the succession caused Cecil, now Lord Burghley, to draft a futile bill along the lines of the doubtful interregnum proposal of 1563,[95] an indication of the desperation of the councillor who knew the queen best.[96] Mary Stuart's execution in 1587 and the defeat of the

[91] See above, pp. 109, 112, 114.

[92] If the Britannic question that arose out of Margaret Tudor's marriage to James IV is to be regarded as a third great dynastic problem, it was not to enjoy a Tudor solution. When James VI of Scotland also became James I of England in 1603, his own wishes notwithstanding, Great Britain was not born. The final solution to the Britannic question would have to await the Anglo-Scottish Union of 1707.

[93] *Span. Cal., Eliz.* ii. 383.

[94] See MacCaffrey, *Elizabethan Regime*, pp. 429–37.

[95] Above, p. 108.

[96] See Neale, *Parliaments*, ii. pp. 44–8.

Spanish Armada in the next year did not alter Elizabeth's reluctance to settle the succession, as Peter Wentworth would learn to his cost when he tried to bring up the matter in the Parliament of 1593.[97] Elizabeth remained stubborn to the end. Even the story of her deathbed signification of a preference for James VI, by then her obvious successor, is probably apocryphal.[98] That James VI of Scotland peacefully became James I of England in 1603 has produced the conclusion: 'the conundrums of life sometimes impose a gamble; and Elizabeth's gamble ultimately succeeded'.[99] Ignoring the suggestive but unanswerable question of whether the Stuart dynasty was the best outcome for England, the accident of Elizabeth I's long reign of forty-five years, during which her subjects lived in a dangerous state of insecurity about their future, hardly enhances the fame of the gambler.[100]

[97] See Neale, *Parliaments*, ii. pp. 251–66.
[98] See A. F. Pollard, *Political History of England*, vol. vi, *1547–1603* (London 1910), pp. 479–80.
[99] Neale, *Parliaments*, i. p. 131.
[100] One might add that Elizabeth's failure to secure a statutory designation of James, which Parliament probably would have taken during her last years, made it easier for her successors to claim to rule by an hereditary divine right. The statutory succession that the Tudor development was leading to would not be achieved until after the Revolution of 1688.

DOCUMENTS

1. A Statute for those who are born in Parts beyond Sea (1351).

FROM 25. Edward III st. 1; *Stat. Realm* i. 310.

... Because that some people be in doubt if the children born in parts beyond the sea and out of the ligeance of England should be able to demand any inheritance within the same ligeance or not ..., our lord the King, willing that all doubts and ambiguities should be put away and the law in this case declared and put in a certainty, hath charged the said prelates, earls, barons, and other wise men of his Council assembled in Parliament to deliberate upon this point; all which of one assent have said, That the law of the crown of England, is, and always hath been such, that the children of the Kings of England, in whatsoever parts they be born, in England or elsewhere, be able and ought to bear the inheritance after the death of their ancestors; which law our said lord the King, the said prelates, earls, barons, and other great men, and all the Commons assembled in this Parliament do approve and affirm for ever. And in the right of other children born out of the ligeance of England in the time of our lord the King they be of one mind accorded that Henry son of John de Beaumond, Elizabeth daughter of Guy de Bryan, and Giles son of Ralph Dawbeny, and other which the King will name, which were born beyond the sea out of the ligeance of England, shall be from henceforth able to have and enjoy their inheritance after the death of their ancestors in all parts within the ligeance of England as well as those that should be born within the same ligeance. And that all children inheritors which from henceforth shall be born without the ligeance of the King whose fathers and mothers at the time of their birth be and shall be at the faith and ligeance of the King of England shall have and enjoy the same benefits and advantages to have and bear the inheritance within the same ligeance as the other inheritors aforesaid in time to come. ...

2. The Crown of England and France Entailed upon King Henry IV and his Sons (1406).

FROM 7. Henry IV cap. 2; *Stat. Realm* ii. 151.

Item, at the request and of the assent of the said Lords and Commons, in the said Parliament, it is ordained and established, That the inheritance of the crown, and of the realms of England and France, and of all the other dominions of our lord the King beyond the sea, with all the appurtenances, shall be settled and remain in the person of the same our lord the King, and in the heirs of his body begotten; and especially at the request and of the assent aforesaid, it is ordained and established, pronounced, decreed, and declared, That the lord the Prince Henry, eldest son to our lord the King, be heir apparent to the same our lord the King, to succeed him in the said crown, realms, and dominions, to have them with all the appurtenances after the decease of the same our lord the King, to him and his heirs of his body begotten. [The order of succession after Prince Henry and his issue shall be the King's second son Thomas and his issue, the King's third son John and his issue, and the King's fourth son Humphrey and his issue.]

3. The Duke of York's Claim to the Crown (16–31 October 1460).

FROM *Rot. Parl.* v. 375–80.

10. Memorandum, that the 16 day of October . . . the counsel of the right high and mighty prince, Richard, duke of York, brought into the Parliament Chamber a writing containing the claim and title of the right that the said duke pretended unto the crowns of England and of France, and lordship of Ireland, and the same writing delivered to the right reverend father in God, George, bishop of Exeter, chancellor of England, desiring him that the same writing might be opened to the Lords spiritual and temporal assembled in this present Parliament, and that the said duke might have brief and expedient answer thereof. . . . [The Lords agreed] that the said writing should be read and heard, not to be answered without the King's commandment, for so much as the matter is so high, and of so great weight and poise. . . .

[11. The tenor of the writing in which York bases his claim on his descent from Lionel of Clarence, third son of Edward III, which gives him priority over any descendant of John of Gaunt, fourth son of Edward III. The writing also specifies that Edward I was the eldest son of Henry III.]

12. [On 17 October the Lords went to Henry VI] and thereunto opened and declared the said matter by the mouth of his said chancellor of England. And the same matter by the King's Highness heard and conceived, it pleased him to pray and command all the said Lords that they should search for to find inasmuch as in them was, all such things as might be objected and laid against the claim and title of the said duke. And the said Lords besought the King that he would remember him if he might find any reasonable matter that might be objected against the said claim and title, in so much as his said Highness had seen and understood many divers writings and chronicles. [They also asked the King's justices] to search and find all such objections as might be laid against the same, in fortifying of the King's right.

[On 20 October the justices told the Lords that] the matter was so high and touched the King's high estate and regalie, which is above the law and passed their learning, wherefore they durst not enter in to any communication thereof, for it pertained to the lords of the King's blood, and the peerage of this his land, to have communication and meddle in such matters; and therefore they humbly besought all the Lords to have them utterly excused of any advice or counsel by them to be given in that matter.

[Next the Lords asked the King's sergeants and attorney to assume the task, and on the 22nd received a similar answer. Then the chancellor reminded the Lords of their duty to obey the King's commandment to find objections to York's title, which they proceeded to do.]

[13. Five heads of objections to York's title. These are repeated before each of York's answers in nos. 14–17 below.]

14. Here under follow the answers of Richard Plantagenet, called commonly duke of York, etc., to certain reasons and colours alleged as it is said against the matter of his right and title, etc.

First, where it is said it is thought that the Lords must needs call to their remembrance the great oaths which they have made to the King, which may be laid to the said duke, and that they may not break those oaths.

The said Richard answereth . . . that every man [must obey God's law, according to which] truth and justice owe to be preferred and observed, and untruth and injustice laid apart and repressed; and so it is, that of this bond and duty of obedience to God's law, no man may discharge himself by his own deed or act, promise or oath, for else of the contrary would ensue innumerable inconveniences. Wherefore sith it is so that the matter of the title and claim of the said Richard Plantagenet is openly true and lawful, and grounded upon evident truth and justice, it followeth that man should have rather consideration to truth, right, and justice in this matter accordingly with the will of the law of God than to any promise or oath made by him to the contrary. . . .

15. Over this, where it is thought also that it is to be called to remembrance the great and notable Acts of Parliament made in divers Parliaments of divers of the King's progenitors, the which acts been sufficient to be laid against the title of the said duke, and of more authority than any chronicle, and also of authority to defeat any manner title made to any person.

And also where it is said that it is to be laid against the said title divers entails made to heirs males as for the crown of England, as it may appear by divers chronicles and Parliaments.

The said Richard Plantagenet answereth . . . that in truth there been none such acts and tailles [1] made by any Parliament herebefore, as it is surmised; but only in the 6th year of King Harry IV a certain act and ordinance was made in a Parliament by him called, wherein he made the realms of England and France amongst other to be unto him and to the heirs of his body coming, and to his four sons and the heirs of their bodies coming, in manner and form as it appeareth in the same act. And if he might have obtained and rejoiced the said crowns, etc. by title of inheritance, descent, or succession, he neither needed nor would have desired or made them to be granted to him in such wise, as they be by the said act: the which taketh not place, neither is of any force or effect

[1] i.e. entails.

against him that is right inheritor of the said crowns, as it accordeth
with God's law and all natural laws. . . .

16. Item, where it is thought that if the said duke should make any
title or claim by the line of Sir Lionel,[2] he should bear the arms of the
same Sir Lionel, and not the arms of Edmund Langley, late duke of
York.

The said duke answereth . . . that the truth is that he might lawfully
have borne the arms of the said Sir Lionel herebefore, and also the same
arms that King Edward III bore, that is to say, the arms of the realms of
England and France; but he abstained of bearing the said arms, like as
he abstained for the time of purposing and pursuing of his right and
title, etc., for causes not unknown to all this realm, for though right for
a time rest and be put to silence, yet it rotteth not nor shall not perish.

17. Item, where it is alleged against the title of the said duke, that the
said Harry of Derby,[3] at such time as he took upon him the crown of
England, and that he entered and took the same crown upon him as
right inheritor to King Harry III, and not as a conqueror.

The said duke thereto saith, that such saying of the said King Harry
IV may in no wise be true, and that the contrary thereof, which is truth,
shall be largely enough shewed, approved, and justified by sufficient
authority and matter of record. And over that, that his said saying was
only to shadow and colour fraudulently his said unrighteous and violent
usurpation, and by that means to abuse deceivably the people standing
about him.

18. Item, [on 25 October] it was shewed unto the Lords spiritual and
temporal being in this present Parliament, by the mouth of the said
chancellor, that the said duke of York called busily to have hasty and
speedy answer of such matters as touched his title abovesaid, and how
that forasmuch as it is thought by all the Lords that the title of the said
duke cannot be defeated, and in eschewing of the great inconveniences
that may ensue, a mean was found to save the King's honour and estate,
and to appease the said duke, if he would, which is this: That the King
shall keep the crowns, and his estate and dignity royal, during his life,
and the said duke and his heirs to succeed him in the same, exhorting
and stirring all the said Lords that if any of them could find any other or
better mean, that it might be shewed. [After some deliberation the
Lords agreed] that sith it was so, that the title of the said duke of York
cannot be defeated, and in eschewing the great inconveniences that
might ensue, to take the mean above rehearsed, the oaths that the said
Lords had made unto the King's Highness at Coventry and other places
saved, and their consciences therein cleared. [The Lords also agreed to
present the 'mean' to Henry VI at his palace of Westminster.] And in

[2] Lionel of Clarence.
[3] Henry IV.

their going out of the Parliament Chamber, the said chancellor asked of the said Lords, that sith it was so, that the said mean should be opened by his mouth to the King's good grace, if they would abide by him how so ever that the King took the matter, and they all answered and said yea.

[When the matter was presented to the King, he] condescended to accord to be made between him and the said duke, and to be authorized by the authority of this present Parliament. The tenor of which accord hereafter ensueth in manner and form following:

[19. Primarily a restatement of York's title as in no. 11 above.]

[20. York agrees to accept the compromise in the interest of peace, his immediate right to the crown notwithstanding.]

[21. A solemn oath not to molest Henry VI to be taken by York and his elders sons, the earls of March and Rutland.]

22. Item, it is accorded, appointed, and agreed, that the said Richard, duke of York, rejoice, be entitled, called, and reputed from hence forth, very rightful heir to the crowns, royal estate, dignity, and lordship abovesaid; and after the decease of the said King Harry, or when he will lay from him the said crowns, estate, dignity, and lordship, the said duke and his heirs shall immediately succeed to the said crowns, royal estate, dignity, and lordship.

[23–6. Provisions that York and his sons, March and Rutland, be given estates yielding a yearly income of 10,000 marks; that it be high treason to 'imagine or compass' York's death; that the Lords spiritual and temporal take oaths to York and his heirs, and to the settlement made; and that York, March, and Rutland take oaths to assist the Lords in any quarrel arising out of their acceptance of the settlement. Henry VI's assent to the settlement.]

28. And furthermore ordaineth, granteth, and establisheth, by the said advice and authority, that all statutes, ordinances, and acts of Parliament made in the time of the said King Harry IV, by the which he and the heirs of his body coming, or Harry, late king of England the fifth, the son and heir of the said King Harry IV, and the heirs of the body of the same King Harry V coming, were, or be inheritable to the said crowns and realms, or to the heritage or inheritment of the same, be annulled, repealed, revoked, damned, cancelled, void, and of no force or effect. . . .

29. Memorandum, that after the agreement of the said act of accord by the King and the three estates in this present Parliament assembled, the said duke of York and earls of March and Rutland, in the vigil of All Hallows,[4] come personally in to the chamber of the same Parliament before the King, in the presence of the Lords spiritual and temporal, and there and then every of the said duke and earls severally made

---

[4] 31 October.

promise and oath according to the said agreement and accord, with protestation that if the King for his party duly kept and observed the same accord and act thereupon made, which the King at that time promised to do. And then the said duke and earls instantly desired that this here protestation, and also the said promise made by the King, might be entered of record.

4. Edward IV's Title to the Throne Declared in Parliament (November 1461).

FROM *Rot. Parl.* v. 463–7.

[Statement of Edward IV's title by descent from Henry III and Edward III through Lionel of Clarence, third son of Edward III. Edward IV also declared heir of Richard II, the last previous lawful King.] . . . Henry, late earl of Derby, son of . . . John of Gaunt, the fourth gotten son of the said King Edward III and younger brother of the said Lionel, temerously against rightwiseness and justice, by force and arms, against his faith and ligeance, reared war at Flint in Wales against the said King Richard, him took and imprisoned in the Tower of London of great violence; and the same King Richard so being in prison and living, usurped and intruded upon the royal power, estate, dignity, pre-eminence, possessions, and lordship aforesaid, taking upon him usurpingly the crown and name of king and lord of the same realm and lordship; and not therewith satisfied or content, but more grievous thing attempting, wickedly of unnatural, unmanly, and cruel tyranny, the same King Richard, king anointed, crowned, and consecrate, and his liege and most high lord in the earth, against God's law, man's ligeance, and oath of fidelity, with uttermost punition and tormenting, murdered and destroyed, with most vile, heinous, and lamentable death; whereof the heavy exclamation in the doom of every Christian man soundeth into God's hearing in heaven, not forgotten in the earth, specially in this realm of England, which therefore hath suffered the charge of intolerable persecution, punition, and tribulation, whereof the like hath not been seen or heard in any other Christian realm by any memory or record; then being on live . . . Edmund Mortimer, earl of March, son and heir of . . . Roger, son and heir of . . . Philippa, daughter and heir to the said Lionel, the third son of the said King Edward III. To the which Edmund, after the decease of the said King Richard, the right and title of the same crown and lordship then by law, custom, and conscience descended and belonged, and of right belongeth at this time unto our said liege and sovereign lord King Edward IV as cousin and heir to the said King Richard in manner and form abovesaid. Our said sovereign and liege lord King Edward IV, according to his right and title of the said crown and lordship, after the decease of the . . . right noble and famous prince, Richard, duke of York, his father, in the name of Jesu, to his pleasure and loving, the fourth day of the month of March last past, took upon him to use his right and title to the said realm of England and lordship, and entered into the exercise of the royal estate, dignity, pre-eminence, and power of the same crown, and to the reign and governance of the said realm of England and lordship; and the same fourth day of March amoved Henry, late called King Henry VI, son to Henry, son to the said Henry, late earl of Derby, son to the said John of Gaunt, from the occupation, usurpation, intrusion, reign, and governance of the same realm of England and lordship to the universal comfort and consolation of all his subjects and liegemen, plenteously joyed to be amoved and departed from the obeisance and governance of the unrightwise usurper in whose time not plenty, peace, justice, good governance, policy, and virtuous conversation, but unrest, inward war and trouble, unrightwiseness, shedding and effusion of innocent blood, abusion of the laws, partiality, riot, extortion, murder, rape, and vicious living, have been the guiders and leaders of the noble realm of England. ... [Closes with a detailed account of Henry VI's violations of the settlement made with Richard of York in October, 1460.] ... And over this, it be declared and judged ... that the abovesaid agreement, concord, and act, in all things which been in any wise repugnant or contrary to the said right, title, entry, state, seisin, and possession of our said sovereign lord King Edward IV in and to the crown, royal estate, dignity, and lordship abovesaid, be void and of no force ne effect. ...

5. The Attainder of George, Duke of Clarence (*c.* January 1478).

FROM *Rot. Parl.* vi. 193–4.

. . . [The King calls to remembrance his tender love for Clarence, the large grants he has given him, and how he has forgiven his brother's past offences.] . . . The said duke nevertheless, for all this no love increasing but growing daily in more and more malice, hath not let to confeder and conspire new treasons . . ., how that the said duke falsely and traitor-ously intended and purposed firmly the extreme destruction and dis-heriting of the King and his issue, and to subvert all the politic rule of this realm, by might to be gotten as well outward as inward, which false purpose the rather to bring about, he cast and compassed the means to induce the King's natural subjects to withdraw their hearts, loves, and affections from the King . . . by many subtle contrived ways. . . . And over this, the said duke, being in full purpose to exalt himself and his heirs to the regality and crown of England, and clearly in opinion to put aside from the same for ever the said crown from the King and his heirs, upon one the falsest and most unnatural colored pretence that man might imagine falsely and untruly noised, published and said, that the King our sovereign lord was a bastard and not begotten to reign upon us. . . . And over this, the said duke . . . obtained and got an exemplifica-tion under the great seal of King Harry VI, late in deed and not in right King of this land, wherein were contained all such appointments as late was made between the said duke and Margaret, calling herself Queen of this land, and other; amongst which it was contained that if the said Harry and Edward, his first begotten son, died without issue male of their body, that the said duke and his heirs should be King of this land; which exemplification the said duke hath kept with himself secret, not doing the King to have any knowledge thereof, thereby to have abused the King's true subjects for the rather execution of his said false pur-pose. . . . For which premises and causes the King, by the advice and assent of his Lords spiritual and temporal, and the Commons, in this present Parliament assembled, and by the authority of the same, ordaineth, enacteth, and establisheth that the said George, duke of Clarence, be convicted and attainted of high treason . . . [and shall] forfeit from him and his heirs for ever the honour, estate, dignity, and name of duke [and all his properties and possessions].

6. An Act for the Settlement of the Crown upon Richard III and his Issue, with a Recapitulation of his Title (January or February 1484).

FROM *Rot. Parl.* vi. 240–2.

[Before Richard assumed the throne 'a roll of parchment' was presented to him] on the behalf of and in the name of the three estates . . .; to the which roll and instant petition comprised in the same, our said sovereign lord, for the public weal and tranquillity of this land, benignly assented.

[Since the three estates were not] assembled in form of Parliament . . . diverse doubts, questions, and ambiguities [have] been moved and engendered in the minds of diverse persons. . . . Therefore . . ., be it ordained, provided, and established in this present Parliament that the tenor of the said roll, with all the continue of the same, presented . . . to our before said sovereign lord the King in the name and on the behalf of the said three estates out of Parliament, and by authority of the same, be ratified, enrolled, recorded, approved, and authorized into removing the occasion of doubts and ambiguities, and to all other lawful effect that shall move thereof ensue, so that all things said, affirmed, specified, desired, and remembered in the said roll . . ., in the name of the said three estates, to the effect expressed in the same roll, be of like effect, virtue, and force as if all the same things had been said, affirmed, specified, desired, and remembered in a full Parliament, and by authority of the same accepted and approved. [The tenor of the roll follows.]

To the high and mighty prince, Richard, duke of Gloucester.

Please it your noble grace to understand the considerations, election, and petition underwritten of us, the Lords spiritual and temporal and Commons of this realm of England, and thereunto agreeably to give your assent, to the common and public weal of this land, to the comfort and gladness of all the people of the same.

First, we consider how that heretofore in time past this land many years stood in great prosperity, honour, and tranquility, which was caused forasmuch as the Kings then reigning used and followed the advice and counsel of certain Lords spiritual and temporal and other persons of approved sadness, prudence, policy and experience, dreading God, and having tender zeal and affection to indifferent ministration of justice and to the common and politic weal of the land; then our Lord God was dreaded, loved, and honoured; then within the land was peace and tranquility, and among neighbours concord and tranquility; [then victories were won, trade flourished, and the people were prosperous.] But afterward, when such as had the rule and governance of this land,

delighting in adulation and flattery, and led by sensuality and concu-
piscence, followed the counsel of persons insolent, vicious, and of
inordinate avarice, despising the counsel of good virtuous and prudent
persons . . ., the prosperity of this land decreased, so that felicity was
turned into misery, and prosperity into adversity, and the order of
policy and of the law of God and man confounded. . . .

Over this, amongst other things more specially we consider how that
the time of the reign of King Edward IV, late deceased, after the
ungracious pretended marriage . . . made betwixt the said King and
Elizabeth, sometime wife to Sir John Grey, knight, late naming herself,
and many years heretofore, Queen of England, the order of all politic
rule was perverted, the laws of God and of God's Church, and also the
laws of nature and of England, and also the laudable customs and
liberties of the same, wherein every Englishman is inheritor, broken,
subverted, and contempted against all reason and justice, so that this
land was ruled by self-will and pleasure, fear and dread, all manner of
equity and laws laid apart and despised, whereof ensued many inconveniences and mischiefs as murders, extortions, and oppressions, namely
of poor and impotent people, so that no man was sure of his life, land ne
livelihood, ne of his wife, daughter, ne servant, every good maiden and
woman standing in dread to be ravished and defouled. And besides this,
what discords, inward battles, effusion of Christian men's blood, and
namely by destruction of the noble blood of this land, was had and committed within the same, it is evident and notary through all this realm,
unto the great sorrow and heaviness of all true Englishmen. And here
also we consider how that the said pretensed marriage betwixt the above
named Edward and Elizabeth Grey was made of great presumption,
without the knowing and assent of the lords of this land, and also by
sorcery and witchcraft, committed by the said Elizabeth and her mother,
Jacquetta, duchess of Bedford, as the common opinion of the people and
the public voice and fame is through all this land, and hereafter, if and
as the case shall require, shall be proved sufficiently in time and place
convenient. And here also we consider how that the said pretensed
marriage was made privily and secretly, without edition of banns, in a
private chamber, a profane place, and not openly in the face of the
church after the law of God's Church, but contrary thereunto and the
laudable custom of the Church of England. And how also, that at the
time of contract of the same pretensed marriage, and before and long
time after, the said King Edward was and stood troth plight to one Dame
Eleanor Butler, daughter of the old earl of Shrewsbury, with whom the
said King Edward had made a precontract of matrimony, long time
before he made the said pretensed marriage with the said Elizabeth
Grey in manner and form abovesaid. Which premises being true, as
in very truth they been true, it appeareth and followeth evidently that

the said King Edward during his life and the said Elizabeth lived together sinfully and damnably in adultery against the law of God and of His Church; and therefore no marvel that the sovereign lord and head of this land, being of such ungodly disposition, and provoking the ire and indignation of our Lord God, such heinous mischiefs and inconvenients, as is above remembered, were used and committed in the realm amongst the subjects. Also it appeareth evidently and followeth that all the issue and children of the said King Edward been bastards and unable to inherit or to claim anything by inheritance by the law and customs of England.

[Moreover, the children of George, duke of Clarence, Richard's elder brother, are barred by his attainder for high treason from any claim to the crown.]

Over this, we consider how that ye be the undoubted son and heir of Richard, late duke of York, very inheritor to the said crown and dignity royal, and as in right king of England by way of inheritance; and that at this time, the premises duly considered, there is none other person living but ye only that by right may claim the said crown and dignity royal by way of inheritance, and how that ye be born within this land, by reason whereof, as we deem in our minds, ye be more natural inclined to the prosperity and common weal of the same; and all the three estates of the land have, and may have, more certain knowledge of your birth and filiation. . . .

[Considering the aforesaid, the three estates choose Richard as the lawful successor and ask him to accept the crown] as to you of right belonging, as well by inheritance as by lawful election. . . .

[Though Richard's title is justly grounded on the laws of God, of nature, and of England, all of the people may not understand these. Experience teaches that the best way of establishing certainty and removing doubts is a declaration of any truth or right made by the three estates assembled in Parliament. Therefore, the three estates in this present Parliament ask that the King's title be declared and his son be made heir apparent.]

7. Opinion of the Judges regarding Henry VII's Attainder under the Yorkists (1485).

FROM *The Reign of Henry VII from Contemporary Sources*, ed. A. F. Pollard, London 1913–14, ii. 10–11.[1]

. . . And then a question was raised. What should be said for the King himself inasmuch as he was attainted? And then, discussing him among themselves, all agreed that the King was responsible and discharged of any attainder by the fact that he took on himself the reign and was King. And then this was the opinion of Sir Richard Choke, and the other judges concurred, as was said.

Townsend said that King Henry VI in his readeption held his Parliament; and also this [2] was not reversed. And the other justices said he was not attainted,[3] but was deposed of his crown, realm, dignity, lands and tenements. And they said that by the fact that he had taken on himself the royal dignity and was King, all this was void. And then he that was King was himself able to invest himself, and there was no need of any act for the reversal of his attainder. . . .

[1] My translation.
[2] i.e. his attainder.
[3] He was 'convicted and attainted of high treason'. *Rot. Parl.* v. 478.

8. Henry VII's Title to the Throne Confirmed in Parliament (1485).

FROM *Rot. Parl.* vi. 270.

To the pleasure of Almighty God, the wealth, prosperity, and surety of this realm of England, to the singular comfort of all the King's subjects of the same, and in avoiding of all ambiguities and questions, be it ordained, established, and enacted, by authority of this present Parliament, that the inheritance of the crowns of the realms of England and of France, with all the pre-eminence and dignity royal to the same pertaining, and all other seigniories to the King belonging beyond the sea, with the appurtenances thereto in any wise due or pertaining, be, rest, remain, and abide in the most royal person of our now sovereign lord King Harry VII and in the heirs of his body lawfully come, perpetually with the grace of God so to endure, and in none other.

9. Henry VII's Repeal of the Act Confirming Richard III's Title [1]
(1485).

FROM *Rot. Parl.* vi. 289.

Where afore this time Richard, late duke of Gloucester and after in deed
and not of right king of England called Richard III, caused a false and
seditious bill of false and malicious imaginations, against all good and
true disposition, to be put unto him, that beginning of which bill is thus:

Please it your noble grace to understand the considerations, election,
and petition underwritten, etc.

Which bill, after that with all the continue of the same by authority of
Parliament holden the first year of the usurped reign of the said late
King Richard III, was ratified, enrolled, recorded, approved, and
authorized, as in the same more plainly appeareth. The King, at the
special instance, desire, and prayer of the Lords spiritual and temporal
and Commons in this present Parliament assembled, will it be ordained,
established, and enacted, by the advice of the said Lords spiritual and
temporal and the Commons in this present Parliament assembled and
by authority of the same, that the said bill, act, and ratification and all
the circumstances and dependents of the same bill and act for the false
and seditious imaginations and untruths thereof be void, annulled,
repealed, irrite,[2] and of no force ne effect. And that it be ordained by the
said authority that the said bill be cancelled, destroyed, and that the said
act, record, and enrolling be taken and avoided out of the roll and
records of the said Parliament of the said late King and burnt and
utterly destroyed. And over this, be it ordained by the same authority
that every person having copy or remembrances of the said bill or act
bring unto the chancellor of England for the time being the same copies
and remembrances, or utterly destroy them, afore the feast of Easter
next coming upon pain of imprisonment and making fine and ransom to
the King at his will. So that all things said and remembered in the said
bill and act thereof may be for ever out of remembrance and also forgot.
And over this, be it ordained and enacted by the said authority that this
act ne any thing contained in the same be any way hurtful or prejudicial
to the act of establishment of the crown of England to the King and to
the heirs of his body begotten.

[1] Doc. 6.
[2] i.e. invalid.

10. The Bull Confirming Henry VII's Title and Marriage (1486).

FROM Francis Hargrave, *The Hereditary Right of the Crown of England Asserted*, London 1713, pp. xvi–xvii.

Our Holy Father the Pope, Innocent VIII, etc., by his proper motion, without procurement of our sovereign lord the King or of any other person, for conservation of the universal peace and eschewing of slanders as should gender the contrary of the same, understanding of the long and grievous variances, dissensions, and debates that hath been in this realm of England between the house of . . . Lancaster . . . and the house of . . . York . . ., willing all such divisions in time following to put apart, by the counsel and consent of his College of Cardinals approveth, confirmeth, and stablisheth the matrimony and conjunction made between our sovereign lord King Henry VII of the house of Lancaster . . . and the noble princess Elizabeth of the house of York . . . with all the issue lawfully born between the same. And in likewise his Holiness confirmeth, stablisheth, and approveth the right and title of the crown of England of the said our sovereign lord King Henry VII and the heirs of his body lawfully begotten to him and them pertaining as well by reason of his nighest and undoubted title of succession as by the right of his most noble victory, and by election of the Lords spiritual and temporal and other nobles of this realm, and by the act, ordinance, and authority of Parliament made by three estates of the land. Furthermore he approveth, confirmeth, and declareth that if it pleased God that the said Elizabeth . . . should decease without issue between our sovereign lord and her of their bodies born that then such issue as between him and her whom after that God shall join him to shall be had and born right inheritors to the same crown and realm of England. . . .

11. Roderigo Gonsalez de Puebla to Ferdinand and Isabella (London, 11 January 1500).

FROM *Letters and Papers Illustrative of the Reigns of Richard III and Henry VII*, ed. James Gairdner, Rolls Series, London 1861–3, i. 113–14.

After kissing the royal feet and the hands of your Highnesses, I cause you to know that by the good fortune of your highnesses and of the lady princess of Wales, this kingdom is at present so situated as has not been seen for the last five hundred years till now, as those say who know best and as appears by the chronicles; because there were always brambles and thorns of such a kind that the English had occasion not to remain peacefully in obedience to their king, there being divers heirs of the kingdom and of such a quality that the matter could be disputed between the two sides. Now it has pleased God that all should be thoroughly and duly purged and cleansed, so that not a doubtful drop of royal blood remains in this kingdom except the true blood of the King and Queen and above all that of the lord Prince Arthur. And since of this fact and of the execution which was done on Perkin and on the son of the duke of Clarence I have written to your Highnesses by various ways, I do not wish to trouble you with lengthy writing. . . .

12. A Comment Attributed to Henry VII on the Projected Marriage of his Elder Daughter, Margaret, to James IV of Scotland (*c.* 1501).

FROM Polydore Vergil, *Urbinatis Anglicae Historiae Libri Vigintisex*, Basel 1546, p. 608.[1]

[Some of Henry's councillors expressed the fear that such a marriage might, if the King's two sons died without issue, lead to the absorption of England into Scotland.] To that the King replied, what then? If it should by accident (which God forbid) be seen in the future, then our realm would not be hurt thereby because England would not come to Scotland but Scotland to England as by far the most superior end of the entire island, since the lesser always is wont for glory and honour to be adjoined to that which is very much greater, after the manner that Normandy formerly came into the dominion and power of our English ancestors.

[1] My translation.

13. A Discussion held at Calais (c. 1503).

FROM *Letters and Papers, Richard III and Henry VII*, i. 233.

. . . Sir Hugh [1] said that 'we be here now together the King's true servants to live and die and also to spend all that we have in the world to do his grace service. Therefore, whatsoever we speak or commune for his surety and for the surety of this his town can be no treason; so good it is that we look and speak of things to come as well as those present. I do speak this for a cause that is good that we look sadly to, for the King's grace is but a weak man and sickly, not likely to be no long lives man. It is not long sithens his Highness was sick and lay then in his manor of Wanstead. It happened the same time me to be amongst many great personages, the which fell in communication of the King's grace and of the world that should be after him if his grace happened to depart.' Then he said that some of them spake of my lord of Buckingham, saying that he was a noble man and would be a royal ruler. Others there were that spake, he said, in likewise of your traitor Edmund de la Pole, but none of them, he said, that spake of my lord prince.[2]

[1] Sir Hugh Conway, treasurer of Calais.
[2] Prince Henry.

14. Henry VIII to Cuthbert Tunstal and Sir Richard Wingfield (March 1525).

FROM *St. P.* vi. 412–36 *passim*.

[Tunstal and Wingfield are to remind Charles V of Henry's right to the crown of France 'by just title of inheritance'. They are to remind Charles of the territories that Francis I wrongfully keeps from him and of Francis's ambitions in Italy. Now, with Francis in captivity, the French army defeated, and France in disarray, it is feasible 'utterly to extinct the regiment of the French King and his line, or any other Frenchman, from the crown of France'. Therefore, Charles and Henry should invade France in the coming summer.

When they both reach Paris Henry should receive the French crown. After he is crowned he will, if required, hand over Princess Mary 'without any surety how she should be entreated and ordered touching her marriage to the Emperor when she cometh to full age'. From Paris Henry will accompany Charles to Rome 'to see the crown imperial set on his head'.

The ambassadors are to tell Charles that out of all this] is like to ensue unto the Emperor the whole monarchy of Christendom. For on his own inheritance he hath the realm of Spain and a great part of Germany, the realms of Sicily and Naples, with Flanders, Holland, Zeeland, Brabant, and Hainault, and other his Low Countries; by election he hath the Empire, whereunto appertaineth all the rest of Italy and many towns imperial in Germany and elsewhere; by the possibility apparent to come by my Lady Princess he should hereafter have England and Ireland, with title to the superiority of Scotland, and in this case all France with the dependencies: so as the said Emperor, performing this voyage and taking this way, should in process be peaceable lord and owner in manner of all Christendom; which the King's Grace can be contented the Emperor shall have, he concurring effectually with the King for recovery of his crown of France.

[The ambassadors are to tell Charles that Henry does not intend to claim all of Francis's kingdom. Charles will get Provence, Languedoc, and Burgundy and his ally Charles, duke of Bourbon, will recover his patrimony. If the Emperor is unwilling to let Henry have all of the remainder, he will take less. The ambassadors are to go down from the Angevin Empire without the crown to merely Normandy or Picardy and three or four towns. But they are to put] always the Emperor in mind that the more which shall come unto the King's Highness by this treaty, the more it shall be unto the said Emperor's profit: first, by reason that the French King shall be so much the more base and low; secondly, for the appearance and possibility depending upon my Lady

Princess as is aforesaid, whose deliverance unto the Emperor they shall in no wise condescend unto, but only in case of invasion and excluding of the French King, with his line and all other, save the King's Highness, from the crown of France.

15. Henry VIII to Anne Boleyn (*c.* 1528).

FROM *Lettres de Henri VIII à Anne Boleyn,* ed. G. A. Crapelet, Paris 1864, pp. 138–40.

Mine own sweetheart, this shall be to advertise you of the great elengeness [1] that I find here since your departing; for I ensure you methinketh the time longer since your departing now last than I was wont to do a whole fortnight. I think your kindness and my fervency of love causeth it; for otherwise I would not have thought it possible that for so little a while it should have grieved me. But now that I am coming toward you, methinketh my pains be half released, and also I am right well comforted in so much that my book maketh substantially for my matter; [2] in looking whereof I have spent above four hours this day, which caused me now to write the shorter letter to you at this time because of some pain in my head; wishing myself (specially an evening) in my sweetheart's arms, whose pretty dukkys [3] I trust shortly to kiss.

Written with the hand of him that was, is, and shall be yours by his will.

[1] i.e. loneliness.
[2] Probably a reference to a treatise in defence of the divorce that Henry was writing.
[3] i.e. breasts.

16. Henry VIII and Catherine of Aragon on the Divorce (1528).

FROM Edward Hall, *Chronicle*, ed. Henry Ellis, London 1809, pp. 754-6.

[Due to widespread talk that Henry 'would for his own pleasure have another wife' and had sent for Cardinal Campeggio to be divorced from Catherine, he called 'all his nobility, judges, and counsellors with divers other persons' to his great chamber at Bridewell on 8 November,] and there to them said as near as my wit could bear away, these words following.

Our trusty and wellbeloved subjects . . ., it is not unknown to you how that we, both by God's provision and true and lawful inheritance, have reigned over this realm of England almost the term of twenty years, during which time we have so ordered us . . . that no outward enemy hath oppressed you nor taken anything from us, nor we have invaded no realm but we have had victory and honour, so that we think that you nor none of your predecessors never lived more quietly, more wealthy, nor in more estimation under any our noble progenitors: But when we remember our mortality and that we must die, then we think that all our doings in our lifetime are clearly defaced and worthy of no memory if we leave you in trouble at the time of our death. For if our true heir be not known at the time of our death, see what mischief and trouble shall succeed to you and your children. The experience thereof some of you have seen after the death of our noble grandfather King Edward IV and some have heard what mischief and manslaughter continued in this realm between the houses of York and Lancaster, by the which dissension this realm was like to have been clearly destroyed. And although it hath pleased Almighty God to send us a fair daughter of a noble woman and me begotten to our great comfort and joy, yet it hath been told us by divers great clerks that neither she is our lawful daughter nor her mother our lawful wife, but that we live together abominably and detestably in open adultery, insomuch that when our embassy was last in France and motion was made that the duke of Orleans should marry our said daughter, one of the chief councellors to the French king said, It were well done to know whether she be the King of England's lawful daughter or not, for well known it is that he begat her on his brother's wife, which is directly against God's law and His precept. Think you . . . that these words do not touch my body and soul, think you that these doings do not daily and hourly trouble my conscience and vex my spirits. . . . For this only cause . . . I have asked counsel of the greatest clerks in Christendom, and for this cause I have sent for this legate as a man indifferent only to know the truth and to settle my conscience and for none other cause. . . . And as touching the Queen, if it be adjudged by the law of God that she is my lawful wife, there was never thing more pleasant nor more acceptable to me in my life both for the discharge and clearing of my conscience and also for the good qualities and conditions the which I know to be in her. For I assure you all, that beside her noble parentage of which she is descended . . . she is a woman of most gentleness, of most humility, and buxomness, yea, and of all good qualities appertaining to nobility, she is without comparison, as I this twenty years almost have had true experiment, so that if I were to marry again if the marriage might be good I would surely choose her above all other women. But if it be determined by judgment that our marriage was against God's law and clearly void, then I shall not only sorrow the departing from so good a lady and loving companion, but much more lament and bewail my unfortunate chance that I have so long lived in adultery to God's great displeasure, and have no true heir of my body to inherit this realm. These be the sores that vex my mind, these be the pangs that trouble my conscience, and for these griefs I seek a remedy. . . .

[A little later Campeggio and Wolsey went to Catherine] and declared to her how they were deputed judges indifferent between the King and her to hear and determine whether the marriage between them stood with God's law or not. . . . And when she had paused a while she answered: Alas my lords is it now a question whether I be the King's lawful wife or no? When I have been married to him almost twenty years and in the mean season never question was made before? Divers prelates yet being alive and lords also and privy councillors with the King at that time then adjudged our marriage lawful and honest, and now to say it is detestable and abominable I think it great marvel. . . . I think . . . that neither of our fathers were so uncircumspect, so unwise, and of so small imagination but they foresaw what might follow of our marriage, and in especial the King my father sent to the court of Rome, and there obtained a licence and dispensation that being the one brother's wife, and peradventure carnally known, might without scruple of conscience marry with the other brother lawfully, which licence under lead I have yet to shew, which things make me to say and surely believe that our marriage was both lawful, good, and godly. But of this trouble I only may thank you my cardinal of York, for because I have wondered at your high pride and vainglory, and abhor your voluptuous life and abominable lechery, and little regard your presumptuous power and tyranny; therefore of malice you have kindled this fire and set this matter abroach, and in especial for the great malice that you bear to my nephew the Emperor, whom I perfectly know you hate worse than a scorpion because he would not satisfy your ambition and make you Pope by force, and therefore you have said more than once that you would trouble him and his friends, and you have kept him true promise, for of all his wars and vexations he only may thank you, and as for me his poor aunt and kinswoman, what trouble you put me to by this new found doubt, God knoweth, to whom I commit my cause according to the truth. . . .

17. Henry VIII's First Succession Act (1534).

FROM 25. Henry VIII cap. 22; *Stat. Realm* iii. 471–4.

In their most humble wise shew unto your Majesty your most humble and obedient subjects, the Lords spiritual and temporal and the Commons in this present Parliament assembled, that since it is the natural inclination of every man gladly and willingly to provide for the surety of both his title and succession, although it touch his only private cause; we therefore, most rightful and dreadful sovereign lord, reckon ourselves much more bounden to beseech and instant your Highness, although we doubt not of your princely heart and wisdom, mixed with a natural affection to the same, to foresee and provide for the perfect surety of both you and your most lawful succession and heirs, upon which dependeth all our joy and wealth, in whom also is united and knit the only mere true inheritance and title of this realm without any contradiction: Wherefore we your said most humble and obedient subjects in this present Parliament assembled, calling to our remembrance the great divisions which in times past hath been in this realm by reason of several titles pretended to the imperial crown of the same, which sometimes and for the most part ensued by occasion of ambiguity and doubts then not so perfectly declared but that men might upon froward intents expound them to every man's sinister appetite and affection after their sense, contrary to the right legality of the succession and posterity of the lawful kings and emperors of this realm, whereof hath ensued great effusion and destruction of man's blood, as well of a great number of the nobles as of other the subjects and specially inheritors in the same; And the greatest occasion thereof hath been because no perfect and substantial provision by law hath been made within this realm of itself when doubts and questions have been moved and proponed of the certainty and legality of the succession and posterity of the crown; By reason whereof the bishop of Rome and See Apostolic contrary to the great and inviolable grants of jurisdictions given by God immediately to emperors, kings, and princes in succession to their heirs, hath presumed in times past to invest who should please them to inherit in other men's kingdoms and dominions, which thing we your most humble subjects both spiritual and temporal do most abhor and detest; And sometimes other foreign princes and potentates of sundry degrees, minding rather dissension and discord to continue in the realm to the utter desolation thereof than charity, equity, or unity, have many times supported wrong titles, whereby they might the more easily and facilely aspire to the superiority of the same; the continuance and sufferance whereof, deeply considered and pondered, were too dangerous and perilous to be suffered any longer within this realm and too much contrary to the unity, peace, and tranquillity of the same, being greatly reproachable and dishonourable to the whole realm.

In consideration whereof [we] . . . most humbly beseech your Highness, that it may please your Majesty that it may be enacted by your Highness with the assent of the Lords spiritual and temporal and the Commons in this present Parliament assembled that the marriage heretofore solemnized between your Highness and the Lady Catherine, being before lawful wife to Prince Arthur your elder brother, which by him was carnally known, as doth duly appear by sufficient proof in a lawful process had and made before Thomas, by the sufferance of God now archbishop of Canterbury and metropolitan primate of all this realm, shall be by authority of this present Parliament definitively, clearly, and absolutely declared, deemed, and adjudged to be against the laws of Almighty God, and also accepted, reputed, and taken of no value ne effect but utterly void and annulled. . . . And that the lawful matrimony had and solemnized between your Highness and your most dear and entirely beloved wife Queen Anne shall be established and taken for undoubtful, true, sincere, and perfect ever hereafter, according to the just judgment of the said Thomas, archbishop of Canterbury, metropolitan and primate of all this realm, whose grounds of judgment have been confirmed as well by the whole clergy of this realm in both the Convocations, and by both the Universities thereof, as by the Universities of Bologna, Padua, Paris, Orleans, Toulouse, Angers, and divers others. . . .

IV. And also be it enacted by authority aforesaid that all the issue had and procreate, or hereafter to be had and procreate, between your Highness and your said most dearly and entirely beloved wife Queen Anne, shall be your lawful children and be inheritable and inherit, according to the course of inheritance and laws of this realm, the imperial crown of the same, with all dignities, honours, pre-eminences, prerogatives, authorities, and jurisdictions to the same annexed or belonging . . .: [The succession is entailed in order of seniority first to the King's sons by Queen Anne and their heirs, second to the King's sons by future wives and their heirs, third to Princess Elizabeth and the King's other daughters by Queen Anne and their heirs, and fourth to the King's daughters by future wives and their heirs:] And for default of such issue then the said imperial crown and all other premises shall be in the right heirs of your Highness for ever.

[V. After 1 May it shall be high treason for anyone maliciously to do anything by writing, print, deed, or act to the peril of the King or to the prejudice of his marriage with Queen Anne, or of his heirs by this act.]

[VI. After 1 May it shall be misprision of treason [1] for anyone maliciously to commit by word only the offences mentioned in V.]

[IX. All subjects shall be sworn to the performance of this act on pain of misprision of treason.]

[1] i.e. association with treasonable activities without direct participation in them, not a capital offence.

18. Reginald Pole on Henry VIII's Divorce (1536).

FROM T. E. Bridgett, *The Life of St John Fisher*, 4th ed., London 1922, p. 148.

At your age of life, and with all your experience of the world, you were enslaved by your passion for a girl. But she would not give you your will unless you rejected your wife, whose place she longed to take. The modest woman would not be your mistress; no, but she would be your wife. She had learned, I think, if from nothing else, at least from the example of her own sister, how soon you got tired of your mistresses; and she resolved to surpass her sister in retaining you as her lover. . . .

Now what sort of person is it whom you have put in place of your divorced wife? Is she not the sister of her whom first you violated and for a long time after kept as your concubine? She certainly is. How is it, then, that you now tell us of the horror you have of illicit marriage? Are you ignorant of the law which certainly no less prohibits marriage with a sister of one with whom *you* have become one flesh, than with one with whom your brother was one flesh? If the one kind of marriage is detestable, so is the other. Were you ignorant of this law? Nay, you knew it better than others. How do I prove that? Because, at the very time you were rejecting your brother's widow, you were doing your very utmost to get leave from the Pope to marry the sister of your former concubine.

19. Henry VIII's Second Succession Act (1536).

FROM 28. Henry VIII cap. 7; *Stat. Realm* iii. 655–62.

[Recites and repeals 25. Henry VIII cap. 22 (first Succession Act) and 26. Henry VIII cap. 2 (act for an oath of succession).]

V. And over this, most gracious sovereign lord, forasmuch as it hath pleased your most royal Majesty, notwithstanding the great and intolerable perils and occasions which your Highness hath suffered and sustained, as well by occasion of your first unlawful marriage solemnized between your Highness and the Lady Catherine, late Princess Dowager, as by occasion of the said unlawful marriage between your Highness and the said late Queen Anne, at the most humble petition and intercession of us your nobles of this realm, for the ardent love and fervent affection which your Highness beareth to the conservation of the peace and unity of the same and for the good and quiet governance thereof, of your most excellent goodness to enter into marriage again, and have chosen and taken a right noble, virtuous, and excellent lady, Queen Jane, to your true and lawful wife, and have lawfully celebrated and solemnized marriage with her according to the laws of the Holy Church, who for her convenient years, excellent beauty, and pureness of flesh and blood is apt (God willing) to conceive issue by your Highness, which marriage is so pure and sincere, without spot, doubt, or impediment, that the issue procreated under the same, when it shall please Almighty God to send it, cannot be lawfully, truly, nor justly interrupted or disturbed of the right and title in the succession of your crown; it may therefore now please your most gracious Majesty, at the most humble petition and intercession of us your Nobles and Commons in this present Parliament assembled, as well for the clear extinguishment of all ambiguities and doubts as for a pure and perfect unity of us your most humble and obedient subjects and of all our posterities, that it may be enacted . . . that the said marriage heretofore had and solemnized between your Highness and the said Lady Catherine . . . shall be by authority of this present Parliament definitively, clearly, and absolutely declared, deemed, and adjudged to be utterly against the laws of Almighty God, and also accepted, reputed, and taken of no value ne effect, but utterly void and annihilate . . ., and that the issue born and procreated under the same unlawful marriage . . . shall be taken, deemed, and accepted illegitimate to all intents and purposes, and shall be utterly foreclosed, excluded, and barred to claim, challenge, or demand any inheritance as lawful heir to your Highness by lineal descent.

VI. And also . . . be it enacted . . . that the same marriage between your Highness and the said late Queen Anne shall be taken, reputed, deemed, and adjudged to be of no force, strength, virtue, nor effect; . . . and that all the issues and children born and procreated under the same marriage . . . shall be taken, reputed, and accepted illegitimate to all intents and purposes, and shall be utterly foreclosed, excluded, and barred to claim, challenge, or demand any inheritance as lawful heir or heirs to your Highness by lineal descent. . . .

[VIII. The order of succession is set as Henry's male heirs by Queen Jane, his male heirs 'by any other lawful wife', his female heirs by Queen Jane, and his female heirs by any future wife.]

IX. . . . [we] most humbly beseech your Highness that it may be enacted . . . by the assent of us the Lords . . . and the Commons in this your present Parliament assembled and by authority of the same, That your Highness shall have full and plenar [1] power and authority to give, dispose, appoint, assign, declare, and limit, by your letters patents under your great seal or else by your last will made in writing and signed with your most gracious hand, at your only pleasure from time to time hereafter, the imperial crown of this realm and all other premises thereunto belonging, to be, remain, succeed, and come after your decease, and for lack of lawful heirs of your body to be procreated and begotten as is afore limited by this act, to such person or persons in possession and remainder as shall please your Highness, and according to such estate and after such manner, form, fashion, order, and condition, as shall be expressed, declared, named, and limited in your said letters patents or by your said last will. . . .

[XII. It shall be high treason for anyone 'by words, writing, imprinting, or by any exterior act or deed' to do anything against the King's marriage with Queen Jane or the succession provided by this act, to 'accept or take, judge or believe' that either of the King's former marriages were lawful, to call Mary or Elizabeth legitimate, or to refuse to answer questions on oath relating to this act.]

[XIV. Upon the King's demise, issue male under 18 or female unmarried under 16 shall be, until they come of age, 'at and in the governance' of their mother and a council appointed by the King in his will, or of that council only, as the King's will shall direct.]

[XV–XVI. All subjects shall be sworn to the performance of this act. Those who refuse to take such an oath or who, when questioned about the act or anything contained therein, protest against declaring their 'thought and conscience' shall be declared guilty of high treason.]

---

[1] i.e. complete.

20. Robert Aske's Examination (11 April 1537).

FROM 'Aske's Examination', ed. Mary Bateson, *English Historical Review* v, 1890, 652–4.

Item, to the statute of the illegitimacy of my Lady Mary, the said Aske saith that he and all the wise men of those parts then much grudged she should so be made by the laws of this realm, seeing she on the mother's side was come of the greatest blood and peerage of Christendom, and the . . . plea hanging and appealed to the Church; and yet the said appeal not discussed . . . touching the marriage betwixt the King's Highness and the Lady Catherine. . . . And thought that the statute not to be good, for if hereafter the law of the Church should find or allow the said lady legitimate, yet by this statute she should be made illegitimate and not inheritable to the crown of this realm; wherein should be thought by all reasonable men, being strangers, that the said statute should have been made more for some displeasure towards her and her friends than for any just cause. And it was then thought that in reason rather she should be favoured . . . for the virtue and high peerage of her mother. . . . Also then it was thought that the divorce made by the bishop of Canterbury, hanging that appeal, was not lawful. . . . And also it was then thought the said Lady Mary ought to be favoured for her great virtues. . . . Also it was thought that the said Lady Mary ought to be favoured and that statute annulled . . . lest the Emperor . . . should think he had cause thereby to move war against this realm and stop the recourse of our merchandise into Flanders. . . .

Item, to the statute of the declaration of the crown of this realm by will, the said Aske saith that he and all wise men of those parts then grudged at the same and that for diverse causes. One was that before that statute, since the Conqueror, never king declared his will of the crown of this realm, nor never there was known in this realm no such law. . . . Also if the crown should pass by testament . . ., there would be great war risk if it were declared from the rightful heir apparent; and betwixt them and him to whom the same were given, who should be taken to be judges . . .? Wherefore it was thought necessary this statute to be annulled or qualified, so that either by statute the certainty might appear who were or should be heir apparent, or else to be as it were before, by the law of this realm; the same to go to the very next blood of the King as other realms doth. Also it is to be noted that . . . if the crown were given by the King's Highness to an alien, as we doubt not his grace will not so do, how should this alien by reason have it, for he in his person was not made able to take it, no more than if I would give lands to an alien, it is a void gift to the alien, because he is not born under the allegiance of this crown. . . . For as the voice of the most part of the people is, and I suppose the law is also, that no stranger can claim this crown by no descent of inheritance, unless he were born under the allegiance of this crown. Wherefore it were necessary to have this statute qualified. . . .

21. Sir George Throckmorton to Henry VIII (1537).

FROM PRO, State Papers 11125, fos. 254-5.

. . . But now, good and gracious lord, to open and declare unto you the
inward part of my heart and what was the original cause and ground of
all my prowd, lewd, and indiscreet handling of my self to you ward and
in all your affairs since the beginning of your Parliament anno vicesimo
primo [1] or thereabouts. It may like your Highness to be advertised that a
little before the beginning of your Parliament Friar Peto,[2] then being in
a tower in Lambeth over the gate, sent for me to come and speak with
him. . . . And he shewed me of two sermons that he and another friar
had made before your grace a little before at Greenwich and of a long
communication that was between your grace and him in the garden after
the sermon. And he shewed me that he did tell you that in his conscience ye
could never have other wife while the Princess Dowager did live without
ye could prove a carnal knowledge betwixt Prince Arthur and her,
which he said in his conscience could never be well proved, for he said
she should know best of any living creature and that she had received
the sacrament to the contrary, and she, being so virtuous a woman,
there ought to be more credence given to her than to all the other
persons, save the saying of Prince Arthur that he had been in the middle
of Spain, which he supposed was but a light word spoken of him. And
further said that he did shew your grace that ye could never marry
Queen Anne for that it was said ye had meddled with the mother and the
daughter.[3] And in conclusion he advised me if I were in the Parliament
House to stick to that matter as I would have my soul saved. And shortly
after the beginning of the Parliament and after I had reasoned to the Bill
of Appeals, Sir Thomas More, then being chancellor, sent . . . for me to
come speak with him in the Parliament Chamber, where, as I do
remember me, stood an altar, or a thing like unto an altar, whereupon he
did lean; and, as I do think, the same time the bishop of Bath was talking
with him. And then he said this to me, I am very glad to have the good
report that goeth of you and that you be so good a Catholic man as ye be.
And if ye do continue in the same way that you began and be not afraid
to say your conscience, ye shall deserve great reward of God and thanks
of the King's grace at length, and much worship to yourself – or words
much like to this. Whereupon I took so much pride of this that shortly
after I went to the bishop of Rochester with whom I was divers times

[1] i.e. 21. Henry VIII (1529).
[2] Friar William Peto, later Cardinal Peto.
[3] Earlier in this letter (fo. 253) Throckmorton recalled having told the king
that it was thought that he had meddled with both Anne's mother and Mary
Boleyn, to which Henry replied: 'Never with the mother'.

and had much communication as well of the Act of Appeals as that of Annates and of the Supremacy, and of the authority that our Lord gave to Peter above the other disciples. And at the last time I was with him he gave me a book of his own device to prove much of this matter, which book I delivered to my Lord privy seal [4] in his house in the Austin Friars. Also my lord of Rochester advised me to speak with Mr Wilson [5] and take his advice in this matter. And after all this I went to Syon to one Reynolds [6] of whom I was confessed, and shewed him my conscience in all these causes and other as they came to my mind at that time, who was of the same opinion that they were of, and advised me to stick to the same to the death, and if I did not I should be surely damned. And also if I did speak or do anything in the Parliament House contrary to my conscience for fear of any earthly power or punishment, I should stand in a very heavy case at the day of judgment. And further my speaking cannot prevail, which opinion was contrary both to the bishop of Rochester and Mr. Wilson, for their opinion was that if I did think in my conscience that my speaking could do no good, that then I might hold my peace and not offend. But he said I did not know what comfort I should be to many men in the House to see me seek in the right way, which should cause many more to do the same. Which sayings and counsels aforerehearsed entered so in my heart with the long customs of old times used that hath caused me to be so blinded as I have been. . . .

[4] Cromwell.
[5] Nicholas Wilson, like Peto, an active backer of Catherine.
[6] Father Richard Reynolds, a Bridgettine, martyred in 1535.

22. Henry VIII's Third Succession Act (1544).

FROM 35. Henry VIII cap. 1; *Stat. Realm* iii. 955–8.

[Recital of 28. Henry VIII cap. 7 (second Succession Act).

Henry intends to go to France to make war against Francis I and the succession is uncertain in the event of the death of Prince Edward. Henry can by the authority of the aforesaid act designate a further succession by letters patent or will,] yet to the intent that his Majesty's disposition and mind therein should be openly declared and manifestly known and notified, as well to the Lords spiritual and temporal as to all other his loving and obedient subjects of this realm, to the intent that their assent and consent might appear to concur with thus far as followeth of his Majesty's declaration in this behalf; His Majesty therefore thinketh convenient . . . that it be enacted . . . in this present Parliament . . . and by authority of the same . . . that in case it shall happen to the King's Majesty and . . . Prince Edward . . . to decease without heir of either of their bodies lawfully begotten . . ., That then the . . . imperial and all the other premises shall be to the Lady Mary the King's Highness's daughter and to the heir of the body of the same Lady Mary lawfully begotten, with such conditions as by his Highness shall be limited by his letters patents under his great seal, or by his Majesty's last will in writing signed with his gracious hand; and for default of such issue the said imperial crown and other the premises shall be to the Lady Elizabeth the King's second daughter and to the heirs of the body of the said Lady Elizabeth lawfully begotten, with such conditions as by his Highness shall be limited by his letters patents . . . or will . . ., anything in the said act made in the said 28th year of our said sovereign lord to the contrary of this act notwithstanding.

[II. On breach of Henry's conditions by Mary, the crown shall come to Elizabeth and her heirs.]

[III. On breach of Henry's conditions by Elizabeth, the crown shall revert to the person or persons designated by the King in his letters patent or will.]

[V. If no conditions be limited by letters patent or will, then the estate of Mary and Elizabeth in the crown shall be absolute.]

VI. And forasmuch as it standeth in the only pleasure and will of Almighty God whether the King's Majesty shall have any heirs begotten and procreated between his Highness and his . . . most entirely beloved wife Queen Catherine [1] or by any other his lawful wife, or whether the said Prince Edward shall have issue of his body lawfully begotten, or

[1] Catherine Parr.

whether the Lady Mary and Lady Elizabeth or any of them shall have issue of any of their several bodies lawfully begotten, and if such heirs should fail (which God defend) and no provision made in the King's life who should rule and govern this realm for lack of such heirs as in this present act is afore mentioned, that then this realm after the King's transitory life and for lack of such heirs should be destitute of a lawful governor to order, rule, and govern the same; Be it therefore enacted by the authority of this present Parliament that the King's Highness shall have full power and authority to give, dispose, appoint, assign, declare, and limit, by his gracious letters patents under his great seal, or else by his Highness's last will made in writing and signed with his most gracious hand, at his only pleasure from time to time hereafter, the imperial crown of this realm and all other premises to be, remain, succeed, and come, after his decease and for lack of lawful heirs . . . to such person or persons in remainder or reversion as shall please his Highness, and according to such estate and after such manner and form, fashion, order, or condition as shall be expressed, declared, named, and limited in his Highness's letters patents or by his last will in writing signed with his most gracious hand as is aforesaid. . . .

X. And be it further enacted by authority aforesaid, that if any person or persons, of what estate, degree, dignity, or condition soever they be, at any time hereafter by words, writing, imprinting, or by any exterior act or deed, maliciously or willingly procure or do, or cause to be procured or done, directly or indirectly, and thing or things to or for the interruption, repeal, or annulment of this act, or of any thing therein contained, or of anything that shall be done by the King's Highness in the limitation and disposition of his Majesty's crown and other the premises by authority of the same, or to the peril, slander, or disinherison of any of the issues and heirs of the King's Majesty being limited by this act to inherit and to be inheritable to the crown of this realm in such form as is aforesaid, or to the interruption or disherison of any person or persons to whom the imperial crown of this realm and other the premises is assigned, limited, and appointed by this act, or shall be by the King's Majesty's letters patents . . . or by his last will . . . limited and disposed by authority of this act as is aforesaid, whereby any such issues or heirs of the King's Majesty or such other person or persons might be destroyed, disturbed, or interrupted in body or title of the inheritance of the crown of this realm as to them is limited in this act . . ., or as to them shall be limited and assigned by the King's Highness by virtue and authority of this act, that then every such person and persons . . . and their aiders, counsellors, maintainers, and abbettors . . . for every such offence afore declared shall be adjudged high traitors, and that every such offence afore specified shall be adjudged high treason. . . .

23. Henry VIII's Will (30 December 1546).

FROM *Foedera*, ed. Thomas Rymer, London 1726–35, xv. 112–14.

... We will by these presents that, immediately after our departure out of this present life, our said son Edward shall have and enjoy the said imperial crown and realm of England and Ireland, our title to France, with all dignities, honours, pre-eminences, prerogatives, authorities and jurisdictions, lands and possessions to the same annexed or belonging, to him and to the heirs of his body lawfully begotten; and for default of such issue of our said son Prince Edward's body lawfully begotten, we will the said imperial crown and other premises, after our two deceases, shall wholly remain and come to the heirs of our body lawfully begotten of the body of our entirely beloved wife Queen Catherine that now is, or of any other our lawful wife that we shall hereafter marry, and for lack of such issue and heirs, we will also that after our decease, and for default of heirs of the several bodies of us and of our said son Prince Edward lawfully begotten, the said imperial crown and all other the premises shall wholly remain and come to our said daughter Mary and the heirs of her body lawfully begotten, upon condition that our said daughter Mary, after our decease, shall not marry nor take any person to her husband without the assent and consent of the privy councillors and others appointed by us to our dearest son Prince Edward aforesaid to be of counsel, or of the most part of them, or the most part of such as shall then be alive, thereunto before the said marriage, had in writing sealed with their seals. All which condition we declare, limit, appoint, and will by these presents shall be knit and invested to the said estate of our said daughter Mary in the said imperial crown and other the premises.

And if it fortune our said daughter Mary to die without issue of her body lawfully begotten; we will that after our decease, and for default of the several bodies of us, and of our said son Prince Edward lawfully begotten, and of our daughter, Mary, the said imperial crown and other the premises shall wholly remain and come to our said daughter Elizabeth, and to the heirs of her body lawfully begotten, [on the same condition as stated above for Mary].

And if it shall fortune our said daughter Elizabeth to die without issue of her body lawfully begotten, we will that after our decease, and for default of issue of the several bodies of us, and of our said son Prince Edward, and of our said daughters Mary and Elizabeth, the said imperial crown and other the premises after our decease and for default of the issue of the several bodies of us, and of our said son Prince Edward, and of our said daughters Mary and Elizabeth lawfully begotten, shall wholly remain and come to the heirs of the body of the Lady Frances our niece, eldest daughter to our late sister the French Queen lawfully begotten; and for default of such issue of the body of the said Lady Frances, we will that the said imperial crown and other the premises after our decease, and for default of the issue of the several bodies of us, and of our son Prince Edward, and of our daughters Mary and Elizabeth, and of the Lady Frances lawfully begotten, shall wholly remain and come to the heirs of the body of the Lady Eleanor our niece, second daughter to our said late sister the French Queen lawfully begotten.

And if it happen the said Lady Eleanor to die without issue of her body lawfully begotten, we will that after our decease, and for default of the several bodies of us, and of our son Prince Edward, and of our daughters Mary and Elizabeth, and of the said Lady Frances, and of the said Lady Eleanor, lawfully begotten, the said imperial crown and other the premises shall wholly remain and come to the next rightful heirs.

[If Mary marries without the specified consent, the succession shall revert to Elizabeth and her lawful heirs 'as though . . . Mary were then dead' without lawful issue.]

[If Elizabeth marries without the specified consent, the succession shall come to the lawful heirs of Frances 'as though . . . Elizabeth were then dead' without lawful issue:] the remainders over for lack of issue of the said Lady Frances lawfully begotten, to be and continue to such persons like remainders and estates as is before limited and declared. . . .

24. Protector Somerset's 'Epistle of Exhortation' to the Scots (1548).

FROM *The Complaynt of Scotlande*, ed. J. A. H. Murray, Early English Text Society, London 1872–3, pp. 239–43.

. . . Who that hath read the histories of time past doth mark and note the great battles fought betwixt England and Scotland, the incursions, raids, and spoils which hath been done on both the parties . . ., and shall perceive . . . that of all nations in the world that nation only beside England speaketh the same language, and as you and we be annexed and joined in one island, so no people so like in manner, form, language, and all conditions as we are; shall not he think it a thing very unmeet, unnatural, and unchristian that there should be betwixt us so mortal war, who in respect of all other nations be, and should be, like as two brethren of one island of Great Britain? And . . . what would he think more meet than if it were possible one kingdom be made in rule, which is one in language, and not to be divided in rulers, which is all one in country? And for so much as two successions cannot concur and fall into one by no manner of other means than by marriage, whereby one blood, one lineage and parentage, is made of two, and an indefeasible right given of both to one without the destruction or abolishing of either. . . . [When Henry VIII offered such a marriage between our Edward and your Mary,] you refused it; you loved better dissension than unity, discord than agreement, war than peace, hatred than love and charity. [Some of you say that] we seek not equality, nor the marriage, but a conquest; we would not be friends but be lords. [This is not so. Our aim is] not to conquer but to have in amity, not to win by force but to conciliate by love, not to spoil and kill but to save and keep, not to dissever and divorce but to join in marriage from high to low both the realms, to make of one isle one realm in love, amity, concord, peace, and charity. Which if you refuse and drive us to conquer, who is guilty of the bloodshed? Who is the occasion of the war? Who maketh the battles, the burning of houses, and the devastation which shall follow? . . . we offer equality and amity, we overcome in war and offer peace, we win holds [1] and offer no conquest, we get in your land and offer England. What can be more offered and more proffered than intercourse of merchandises, interchange of marriages, the abolishing of all such our laws as prohibiteth the same or might be impediment to the mutual amity? We have offered not only to leave the authority, name, title, right, or challenge of conquerors, but to receive that which is the shame of men overcome, to leave the name of the nation . . ., and to take the indifferent old name of Britons

_____
[1] i.e. strongholds.

again. . . . We intend not to disinherit your Queen but to make her heirs inheritors also to England. What greater honour can you seek unto your Queen than the marriage offered? What more meet marriage than this with the King's Highness of England? What more sure defence in the nonage of your Queen for the realm of Scotland than to have England patron and garrison? We seek not to take from you your laws nor customs, but we seek to redress your oppressions. . . . You will not keep her [Mary] sole and unmarried, the which were to you great dishonour. If you marry her within the realm, that cannot extinguish the title which we have to the crown of Scotland; and what dissension, envy, grudge, and malice that shall breed amongst you, it is easy to perceive. You will marry her out of the realm: our title remaineth, you be subjects to a foreign prince of other country, another language; and us ye have your enemies, even at your elbows, your succours far off from you. [We now occupy part of Scotland. If the foreign prince sends troops to Scotland, he shall oppress you and we shall fight him. If, due to war elsewhere, he removed his troops and your Queen from Scotland, you shall] be a prey to us and a true conquest. Then it shall be too late to say we will have a marriage and no conquest, we wish peace and amity, we are weary of battle and misery. . . .

25. Edward VI's Letters Patent for the Limitation of the Crown (21 June 1553).

FROM *The Chronicle of Queen Jane*, ed. J. G. Nichols, Camden Society, London 1850, pp. 91–9.

. . . [Edward's 'long and weary sickness' gives him cause to be concerned about the succession.] . . . notwithstanding that in the time of our . . . late father, that is to say, in the 35th year of his reign, there was then one statute made, entitled, An Act concerning the Establishment of the King's Majesty's Succession in the Imperial Crown of this Realm,[1] whereby it is enacted, that in case it should happen our said late father and us, then being his only son and heir apparent, to decease without heirs of our body lawfully begotten . . . that then the said imperial crown . . . should be in the Lady Mary, by the name of the Lady Mary our said late father's daughter, and to the heirs of the body of the said Lady Mary lawfully begotten, with such conditions as by our said father should be limited by his letters patents under his great seal or by his last will in writing signed with his hand; and for default of such issue the said imperial crown . . . should be to the Lady Elizabeth, by the name of the Lady Elizabeth our said father's second daughter, and to the heirs of the body of the said Lady Elizabeth lawfully begotten, with such conditions as by our said late father should be limited by his letters patents under his great seal or by his last will in writing signed with his hand. . . . And forasmuch as the said limitation of the imperial crown of this realm, being limited by authority of Parliament as is aforesaid to the said Lady Mary and Lady Elizabeth, being illegitimate and not lawfully begotten, forasmuch as the marriage had between our said late father and the Lady Catherine, mother to the said Lady Mary, was clearly and lawfully undone, and separation between them had by sentence of divorce according to the ecclesiastical laws; and likewise the marriage had between our said late father and the Lady Anne, mother to the said Lady Elizabeth, was also clearly and lawfully undone, and separation between them had by sentence of divorce according to the ecclesiastical laws; which said several divorcements have been severally ratified and confirmed by authority of diverse acts of Parliament remaining in their full force, strength, and effect. Whereby as well the said Lady Mary as also the said Lady Elizabeth to all intents and purposes are and be clearly disabled to ask, claim, or challenge the said imperial crown . . . as heir or heirs to us or to any other person or persons whosoever, as well for the cause before rehearsed, as also for that the said Lady Mary and Lady Elizabeth be unto us but of the half blood, and therefore by the

[1] Doc. 22.

ancient laws, statutes, and customs of this realm be not inheritable unto
us, although they were legitimate, as they be not indeed. And forasmuch also as it is to be thought, or at least much to be doubted, that if
the said Lady Mary or Lady Elizabeth should hereafter have and enjoy
the said imperial crown of this realm, and should then happen to marry
with any stranger born out of this realm, that then the same would
rather adhere and practise to have the laws and customs of his or their
own native country or countries to be practised or put in use within this
realm, than the laws, statutes, and customs here of long time used,
whereupon the title of inheritance of all and singular our loving subjects
do depend, which would then tend to the utter subversion of the
commonwealth of this our realm. . . . [Due to the above considerations
and others, Edward has often] weighed and considered . . . what ways
and means were most convenient to be had for the stay of our succession
in the said imperial crown, if it should please God to call us out of this
transitory life having no issue of our body lawfully begotten. And
calling to our remembrance that the Lady Jane, the Lady Catherine,
and the Lady Mary, daughters of our entirely beloved cousin the Lady
Frances, now wife to our loving cousin and faithful counsellor Henry,
duke of Suffolk, and the Lady Margaret, daughter of our late cousin the
Lady Eleanor deceased, sister of the said Lady Frances, and the late
wife of our well-beloved cousin Henry, earl of Cumberland, being very
nigh of our whole blood, of the part of our father's side, and being
natural-born here within the realm, and have been also very honourably
brought up and exercised in good and godly learning and other noble
virtues, so as there is great trust and hope to be had in them that they be
and shall be very well inclined to the advancement and setting forth of
our commonwealth: We therefore . . . [declare the order of succession,
in the event of our death without issue, to be (1) sons of Lady Frances,
if born in our lifetime, and their heirs male; (2) Lady Jane and her heirs
male; (3) Lady Catherine and her heirs male; (4) Lady Mary and her
heirs male; (5) sons of the fourth daughter of Lady Frances and their
heirs male; (6) sons of Lady Margaret and their heirs male; (7–11) sons
of daughters of those designated in 1–6 and their heirs male.] . . . we will
that this our declaration, order, assignment, limitation, and appointment be truly observed, performed, and kept in all things. And further
we will and charge all our nobles, Lords spiritual and temporal, and all
Commoners of . . . our . . . realms and the marches of the same, upon
their allegiance, that they and every of them do, perform, and execute
this our present declaration and limitation concerning the succession of
the crown . . .; and to see this our said declaration and limitation concerning the same established, ratified, and confirmed, as well by authority of Parliament as by all ways and means as they can, to the best of
their powers; and to repress, reform, repeal, and make void all acts of

Parliament and all other things that seem or be in any wise to the contrary, let, or disturbance of this our pleasure and appointment, as they will answer afore God, tender the commonwealth of . . . our realms, and avoid our indignation and displeasure. . . .

26. Mary I to Sir Edward Hastings (9 July 1553).

FROM John Strype, *Ecclesiastical Memorials*, London 1721, iii. App. p. 3.

Right trusty and right well-beloved cousin,[1] we greet you well. Advertising you that, to our great grief and heaviness of heart, we have received woeful news and advertisement that the King, our dearest brother and late sovereign lord, is departed to God's mercy upon Thursday last [2] at night. By means whereof the right of the crown of this realm of England, with the governance thereof and the title of France, justly come unto us by God's providence; as appears by such provisions as have been made by act of Parliament [3] and the testament and last will of our late dearest father, King Henry VIII, for our preferment in this behalf. Whereby you are now discharged of your duty of allegiance to our said brother the King, and unburdened and set at large to observe, execute, or obey any commandment heretofore or hereafter to be addressed unto you by letter or otherwise from or in the name, or by colour of the authority of the same King, our late brother; and only to us and our person are and owe to be true liegeman. . . .

[1] Hastings, via his Stafford mother, was a distant cousin of Mary.
[2] Edward VI died on 6 July.
[3] Henry VIII's third Succession Act (Doc. 22).

27. An Act Declaring Mary I Legitimate (1553).

FROM I. Mary st. 2 cap. 1; *Stat. Realm* iv. 201.

... Be it enacted by the authority of this present Parliament that all and every decree, sentence, and judgment of divorce and separation between the . . . King your father and the . . . Queen your mother and all the process commenced, followed, made, given, or promulgated by . . . Thomas Cranmer, then archbishop of Canterbury, or by any other person or persons whatsoever, whereby the . . . most just, pure, and lawful marriage between the said late King your father and the said late Queen your mother was or is pronounced or in any wise declared to be unlawful or unjust, or against the law of God, be and shall be from the beginning and from henceforth of no force, validity, or effect, but be utterly naught, void, frustrate, and annihilate, to all intents, constructions, and purposes, as if the same had never been given or pronounced.

And be it also enacted by the authority aforesaid that as well the . . . act of Parliament . . . made in the 25th year of the reign of the King your father [1] be repealed, and be void and of none effect, as also all and every such clauses, articles, branches, and matters contained and expressed in the . . . act of Parliament made in the . . . 28th year of the reign of the said late King your father,[2] or in any other act or acts of Parliament, as whereby your Highness is named or declared to be illegitimate, or the said marriage between the said King your father and the said Queen your mother is declared to be against the word of God or by any means unlawful, shall be and be repealed, and be void and of no force nor effect, to all intents, constructions, and purposes, as if the same sentence or acts of Parliament had never be had ne made; and that the said marriage had and solemnized between your said most noble father, King Henry, and your said most noble mother, Queen Catherine, shall be definitively, clearly, and absolutely declared, deemed, and adjudged to be and stand with God's law and His most holy word, and to be accepted, reputed, and taken of good effect and validity to all intents and purposes.

[1] Doc. 17.
[2] Doc. 19.

28. Simon Renard to Charles V (28 November 1553).

FROM *Span. Cal.* xi. pp. 393–5.

[Have conferred with Mary I and Lord William Paget. The Queen wanted to consider the question of the succession in case she were to die without issue. She thought the question might be dealt with in the treaty to be made for her marriage with Philip of Spain.] The rival claimants would be the Queen of Scotland, the affianced bride of the Dauphin, who had a real right by descent; the Lady Frances, wife of the duke of Suffolk, who would also have a claim if the Queen of Scotland were excluded as having been born abroad, as being a Scotswoman and married to the Dauphin of France; and my Lady Elizabeth, who claimed the crown because of the disposition of the late King Henry, authorized by an act of Parliament that had never been repealed. . . . As for the Lady Elizabeth, the Queen would scruple to allow her to succeed because of her heretical opinions, illegitimacy, and characteristics in which she resembled her mother; and as her mother had caused great trouble in the kingdom, the Queen feared that Elizabeth might do the same, and particularly that she would imitate her mother in being a French partisan. The Queen thought that if God were to call her without giving her heirs of her body, the Lady Margaret . . ., wife of the earl of Lennox . . . would be the person best suited to succeed. . . . Paget thought that if the succession were settled by the treaty the people and nobility might easily be brought to accept the idea of the marriage with his Highness, because it would allay the fears entertained by the English that his Highness, if the Queen were to die without heirs, might try to make himself king of England. . . . But it seemed to him that, as Parliament had accepted the Lady Elizabeth as proper to succeed, it would be difficult to deprive her of the right she claimed without causing trouble; whereas . . . if she were wedded to Courtenay . . ., the succession could be settled, Courtenay pleased, and Elizabeth turned away from the intrigues and evil disposition that had perhaps been encouraged by the French and heretics. It would be very hard, in Paget's view, to take her claim from her without having the act of Parliament repealed, which would be very difficult of accomplishment, although the Queen's arguments were compelling and Elizabeth was notoriously illegitimate. [The match with Courtenay, 'who seemed to be a Catholic', would keep Elizabeth 'in the religion she now professed'. Keeping Elizabeth in the succession would prevent her from becoming a French partisan, since] she could not be one without wishing to lose the crown, because it was impossible to make the heart of the kingdom French except by the utmost violence.

. . . [Paget] told me that if the Queen desired to induce Parliament to repeal the act regulating the succession, Parliament would, in his opinion, refuse, so the Queen would struggle in vain to have another heir appointed.

The Queen [told Renard] that it would burden her conscience too heavily to allow Elizabeth to succeed, for she [remained a heretic despite appearances] and it would be a disgrace to the kingdom to allow a bastard to succeed. . . .

29. An Act concerning the Regal Power (1554).

FROM I. Mary st. 3 cap. 1; *Stat. Realm* iv. 222.

Forasmuch as the imperial crown of this realm, with all dignities, honours, prerogatives, authorities, jurisdictions, and pre-eminences thereunto annexed, united, and belonging . . ., is most lawfully, justly, and rightfully descended and come unto the Queen's Highness that now is . . ., and invested in her most royal person, according unto the laws of this realm; and by force and virtue of the same all regal power, dignity, honour, authority, prerogative, pre-eminence, and jurisdictions doth appertain, and of right ought to appertain and belong unto her Highness . . . in as full, large, and ample manner as it hath done heretofore to any other her most noble progenitors, kings of this realm: nevertheless the most ancient statutes of this realm being made by kings then reigning, do not only attribute and refer all prerogative, pre-eminence, power and jurisdiction royal unto the name of king, but also do give, assign, and appoint the correction and punishment of all offenders against the regality and dignity of the crown and the laws of this realm unto the king; by occasion whereof the malicious and ignorant persons may be hereafter induced and persuaded unto this error and folly, to think that her Highness could not nor should have, enjoy, and use such like royal authority, power, pre-eminence, prerogative, and jurisdiction, nor do nor execute and use all things concerning the said statutes, and take the benefit and privilege of the same, nor correct and punish offenders against her most royal person and the regality and dignity of the crown of this realm and the dominions thereof, as the kings of this realm her most noble progenitors have heretofore done, enjoyed, used, and exercised: For the avoiding and clear extinguishment of which said error or doubt, and for a plain declaration of the laws of this realm in that behalf; be it declared and enacted by the authority of this present Parliament, that the law of this realm is and ever hath been and ought to be understood, that the kingly or regal office of the realm, and all dignities, prerogative, royal power, pre-eminences, privileges, authorities, and jurisdictions thereunto annexed, united, or belonging, being invested either in male or female, are and be and ought to be taken in the one as in the other; so that what or whensoever statute or law doth limit and appoint that the king of this realm may or shall have, execute, and do anything as king, or doth give any profit or commodity to the king, or doth limit or appoint any pains or punishment for the correction of offenders or transgressors against the regality and dignity of the king or of the crown, the same the Queen . . . may by the same authority and power likewise have, exercise, execute, punish, correct, and do to all intents, constructions, and purposes without doubt, ambiguity, scruple,

or question: Any custom, use, or scruple, or any other thing whatsoever
to be made to the contrary notwithstanding.

30. An Act of Recognition of the Queen's Highness' Title to the Imperial Crown of this Realm (1559).

FROM I. Elizabeth I cap. 3; *Stat. Realm* iv. 358-9.

. . . there is nothing that we your said subjects . . . can, may, or ought towards your Highness more firmly, entirely, and assuredly in the purity of our hearts think or with our mouths declare and confess to be true than that your Majesty . . . is and in very deed and of most mere right ought to be by the laws of God and the laws and statutes of this realm our most rightful and lawful sovereign liege lady and Queen; and that your Highness is rightly, lineally, and lawfully descended and come of the blood royal of this realm of England in and to whose princely person and the heirs of your body lawfully to be begotten after you without all doubt and ambiguity, scruple or question the imperial and royal estate, place, crown, and dignity of this realm with all honours, styles, titles, dignities, regalities, jurisdictions, and pre-eminences to the same now belonging and appertaining are and shall be most fully, rightfully, really, and entirely invested and incorporated, united and annexed as rightfully and lawfully to all intents, constructions, and purposes as the same were in the said late King Henry VIII or in the late King Edward VI, your Highness' brother, or in the late Queen Mary, your Highness' sister, at any time since the act of Parliament made in the 35th year of your said most noble father, King Henry VIII, entitled, An Act concerning the establishment of the King's Majesty's Succession in the Imperial Crown of this Realm.[1] For which causes we your said most loving, faithful, and obedient subjects representing the three estates of your realm of England . . . do but most humbly beseech your Highness that by the authority of this present Parliament it may be enacted, established, and declared that we do recognize, acknowledge, and confess the same your estate, right, title, and succession as is aforesaid to be in and to your Highness and the heirs of your body to be begotten. . . .

And that it may be enacted by the authority aforesaid that as well this our declaration, confession, and recognition as also the limitation and declaration of the succession of the imperial crown of this realm mentioned and contained in the said act made in the said five and thirty year of the reign of your said most noble father shall stand, be, and remain the law of this realm for ever. . . .

[1] Doc. 22.

31. Maitland of Lethington's Account of His Negotiation with Elizabeth I (*c.* September 1561).

FROM Martin Philippson, *Histoire du règne de Marie Stuart*, Paris 1891–2, iii. 445–50.

[During the first audience Elizabeth spoke on Mary Queen of Scots' claim.] You put me in remembrance that she is of the blood of England, my cousin, and next kinswoman, so that nature must bind me to love her duly, all which I . . . confess to be true. And as my proceedings have made sufficient declaration to the world . . ., I never meant evil toward her. . . . In time of most offence and when she by bearing my arms and acclaiming the title of my crown had given me just cause to be most angry with her, yet could I never find in my heart to hate her, imputing rather the fault to others than to herself. As for the title of my crown, for my time I think she will not attain it, nor make impediment to my issue if any shall come of my body: for so long as I live there shall be no other queen in England but I, and failing thereof she can not allege that ever I did anything which may hurt the right she may pretend. What it is I have not . . . considered, for the succession of the crown . . . is a matter I will not meddle in. . . . If her right be good she may be sure I will never hurt her, and I here protest to you in the presence of God I for my part know none better nor that myself would prefer to her, or that, to be plain with you, that case occurring that might debar her from it. You know them all,[1] alas, what power or force has any of them poor souls!

[At the next audience Elizabeth spoke on Maitland's request that she have Mary named her heir presumptive.] There be many necessary considerations to draw me back from granting your request. I have always abhorred to draw in question the title of the crown, so many disputes have been already touching it in the mouths of men. . . . So long as I live, I shall be queen of England; when I am dead, they shall succeed that has most right. If the Queen your sovereign be that person, I shall never hurt her. If another have better right, it is not reasonable to require me to do a manifest injury. If there be any law against her, as I protest to you I know none for I am not curious to inquire of that purpose, but if any be, I am sworn when I was married to the realm [2] not to alter the laws of it. Secondly, you think that this devise of yours should make friendship betwixt us, and I fear that rather it should produce the contrary effect. Think you that I could love my own winding-sheet? Princes cannot like their own children, those that should succeed unto them. . . . How then shall I, think you, like my cousin being declared my heir apparent . . .? But the third consideration is

---

[1] i.e. the other claimants.
[2] i.e. crowned.

most weighty of all. I know the inconstancy of the people of England, how they ever mislike the present government and have their eyes fixed upon that person that is next to succeed. . . . I have good experience of myself in my sister's time, how desirous men were that I should be in place and earnest to set me up. And if I would have consented I know what enterprise would have been attempted to bring it to pass. . . . [Some of those who expected much of me when I came to the throne may now be disappointed.] No prince's revenues be so great that they are able to satisfy the insatiable cupidity of men. And if we, either for not giving to men at their discretion or yet for any other cause, should miscontent any our subjects, it is to be feared that if they knew a certain successor of our crown they would have recourse thither; and what danger it would be, she being a puissant princess and so near our neighbour, you may judge. So that in assuring her of the succession we might put our present state in doubt. . . . [Maitland's promise of Mary's guarantee that Englishmen would have no recourse to her failed to move Elizabeth.] It is hard to bind princes by any security where hope is offered of a kingdom. And for her, if it were certainly known in the world who should succeed her, she would never think herself in sufficient surety.

[Maitland's conclusion was that in Elizabeth's] own judgment she likes better of the Queen of Scotland's title next herself than of all others, and failing of her own issue could best be content that she should succeed and that none of all others who had any interest were meet for the crown or yet worthy of it, and that the third consideration was the only stay why she had no will to assure her title and succession by order of Parliament.

32. A Clause to have been inserted in an Act meant for the Succession, but not Passed (March, 1563).

FROM PRO, State Papers xii/28, fo. 70.[1]

. . . Be it enacted by authority of this present Parliament that if the Queen's Majesty our sovereign lady should decease . . . without issue of her body or before the time that any person shall be declared by authority of Parliament to be the lawful heir or successor to her Majesty of the imperial crown of this realm, that then and from henceforth all such persons which shall be known to be of the privy council to her Majesty shall remain and continue councillors with like interest, authority, place, and degree as at the time of her Majesty's death . . . they or any of them did hold or exercise, and that such other person or persons spiritual or temporal whomsoever her Majesty by her last will signed with her hand and sealed with the great seal of England shall appoint or name to be sworn to be of the same privy council shall also after his or their oath taken be accepted and reputed of the same privy council. All which councillors shall also continue as councillors of state only until the day that by proclamation to be made by authority of Parliament it shall be declared to whom of right the imperial crown of this realm of England ought to belong. . . .

[1] This document is in the hand of Sir William Cecil. I am indebted to Dr D. J. Guth for providing a xerox copy.

33. Mary Queen of Scots' Claim to the English Succession Attacked on National and Religious Grounds (7 December 1565).

FROM BM, Harleian MS. 4627, No. 2, pp. 3–4, 26–7.

. . . [If Mary should come to the crown,] what should become of us and our country in effect but as bound and subject unto a foreign nation? Those should be put in trust, those should be the councillors, those the secretaries, those the great officers, those in favour and credit, those all in all, if not in name at least in deed. Those shall be rulers and governors here and we in our country become and made as strangers. . . . And with what mind can we suffer these things of the Scot? [They are] a people by custom and almost nature our enemies, thirsty of our blood, poor and miserable by their country and envious of our welfare. . . . What laws, what proclamations and other devices may daily be invented, practised, and set forth to open the way that the Scots may trade and communicate the commodities of our country? And not to be communicators with reason, but as tyrannous commanders . . . without reason or good policy for this state and contrary to the old fame and dignity of the same. . . .

. . . Corrupt religion, blinded with the hate of the truth of the gospel, and those that doth profess the same hath induced so many to affect the Queen of Scots in this case of succession, without all consideration of any lawful title. . . . So that they might once turn unto their accustomed idolatry and wonted cruelty to wash their hands in the blood of the faithful of which good likelihoods. And other dispositions here too many to touch – these late beginnings of the Queen of Scots to trouble the good people in Scotland and else the practices abroad, as well to Rome as other places [1] – for respects well enough known and discovered giveth daily and hourly abundant increase and apparent testimony. This branch, therefore, is to be seen unto, and that we go about therein to set some better order for such matters. Not that I wish . . . that any honest or quiet man, though yet not fully persuaded as he might or may be, to be more vexed or troubled, or that the malicious and open talkers and doers in their presumptuous and papistical practices and blind and most obstinate ignorances, or yet the dissimulated [2] or hypocritical Protestants in many their misbehaviours, should be thus lastly suffered. But that there might be for the honour of the truth, ease to the weak, and surety of the prince, and else of the whole realm, a better order in them both and a better deciphering of the behaviours of each. . . .

[1] In the fall of 1565, as a result of a futile rebellion of a few Protestant lords, Mary abandoned her previous policy of concessions to the reformers and sought aid from Rome and Spain.　　　　[2] i.e. dissembled.

34. The 'Common Cry of Englishmen' to Elizabeth I and Her Parliament (October, 1566).

FROM BM, Egerton MS. 2836, fos. 36, 38, 43, 64–6.

... We speak not ... of any private matter but of that which greatly toucheth us all, and you with us all, we say, high and low. ...

... if you O Queen do die ... void of issue and wanting a known successor, as the case now standeth, what good can continue? what evil shall not come? ...

... it is not your marriage, most noble Queen, which can help this mischief, for a certain ruin cannot be stayed by an uncertain means. It is uncertain whether you shall marry; it is uncertain whether you shall have issue in your marriage; it is uncertain whether your issue shall live to succeed you. ... But this is most certain, that unless the succession after you be, and that in time, appointed and ordered, England runneth to most certain ruin and destruction. And this is what we most humbly beg for England's sake, without verily it may be doubted whether England will long be England: that is, that you with your High Court of Parliament do both appoint your next successors and also set the succession and the inheritance in safe and sure order. ...

And if the Queen, either of timorousness to attempt a matter of so great weight or of any other singular respect, should seem not willing to hear and help, as we desire presently; then we turn our cry to you our Lords and Commons assembled now in Parliament. Though the delay made upon your last most godly request in this behalf [1] did daunt and grieve the hearts of you and of thousands which loved you for your good attempt, yet assay again. The matter is worth the labour, and it is meet, and only meet, for your travail. ... You know whether your last answer received was a delay or a promise. If it was no refusal, was it a promise? It is time to claim the performance. ... Was it a delay, peradventure but to try whether you did heartily affect the thing desired? Show forth again that affection which the cause requireth. But what if it was a refusal then? ... look not for it to happen again. If it should hap, yet considering the peril that hangeth thereon, as you do know what your authority is, so bestow your wisdom and power to put your country out of such peril. Princes ... sometimes let slip that which would be done. Sometimes they profit not. Sometimes they neglect it. Sometimes they go astray. Then do not only wise councillors stand instead, but chiefly such great assemblies of such persons so authorized and therewith privileged as Parliament men are. That is the place of free speaking. Speak there and let your action agree with your title. You be in place to

[1] In 1563.

consider as things arise and to provide remedy. Regard this matter duly. Deal for it with the Queen dutifully. . . . Good princes, because they have their authority not without their parliaments and states, are counted not to rule without them, but with them. Yea, ofttimes to be ruled by them. . . .

35. Elizabeth I's Second Treasons Act (1571).

FROM 13. Elizabeth I cap. 1; *Stat. Realm* iv. 527.

II. And be it . . . enacted . . . that all and every person and persons, of what degree, condition, place, nation, or estate soever they be, which shall, after the end of thirty days next after the last day of this present session of this Parliament, at any time in the life of our sovereign lady, Queen Elizabeth, in any wise claim, pretend, utter, declare, affirm, or publish themselves or any of them, or any other than our said sovereign lady Elizabeth . . ., to have right or title to have or enjoy the crown of England during or in the life of our said sovereign lady; or shall usurp the same crown or the royal style, title, or dignity of the crown of the realm of England during or in the life of our said sovereign lady, or shall hold and affirm that our said sovereign lady hath not right to hold and enjoy the said crown and realm, style, title, or dignity, or shall not, after any demand on our said sovereign lady's part to be made, effectually acknowledge our said sovereign lady to be in right true and lawful Queen of this realm, they and every of them so offending shall be utterly disabled during their natural lives only, to have or enjoy the crown or realm of England, or the style, title, or dignity thereof, at any time in succession, inheritance, or otherwise after the decease of our said sovereign lady as if such person were naturally dead. . . .

IV. And be it . . . enacted that if any person shall in any wise hold and affirm or maintain that the common laws of this realm not altered by Parliament ought not to direct the right of the crown of England, or that our said sovereign lady Elizabeth, the Queen's Majesty that now is, with and by the authority of the Parliament of England, is not able to make laws and statutes of sufficient force and validity to limit and bind the crown of this realm and the descent, limitation, inheritance, and government thereof, or that this present statute, or any part thereof, or any other statute to be made by the authority of the Parliament of England with the royal assent of our said sovereign lady the Queen for limiting of the crown, or any statute for recognizing the right of the said crown and realm to be justly and lawfully in the most royal person of our said sovereign lady the Queen, is not, are or shall not, or ought not to be for ever of good and sufficient force and validity to bind, limit, restrain, and govern all persons, their rights and titles, that in any wise may or might claim any interest or possibility in or to the crown of England in possession, remainder, inheritance, succession, or otherwise howsoever, and all other persons whatsoever, every such person so holding, affirming, or maintaining during the life of the Queen's Majesty shall be judged a high traitor and suffer and forfeit as in cases of high treason is accustomed; and every person so holding, affirming, or maintaining after the decease of our said sovereign lady shall forfeit all his goods and chattels.

Index

Bo   be   r before